A Theory of Feelings

A Theory of Feelings

Second Edition

AGNES HELLER

LEXINGTON BOOKS

A division of
ROWMAN & LITTLEFIELD PUBLISHERS, INC.
Lanham • Boulder • New York • Toronto • Plymouth, UK

LEXINGTON BOOKS

A division of Rowman & Littlefield Publishers, Inc.
A wholly owned subsidary of The Rowman & Littlefield Publishing Group, Inc.
4501 Forbes Boulevard, Suite 200
Lanham, MD 20706

Estover Road
Plymouth PL6 7PY
United Kingdom

British Library Cataloguing in Publication Information Available

Library of Congress Cataloging-in-Publication Data

Heller, Agnes.
 [Érzelmek elmélete. English]
 A theory of feelings / Agnes Heller.— 2nd ed.
     p. cm.
 Translation of Az érzelmek elmélete.
 Includes bibliographical references and index.
 ISBN-13: 978-0-7391-2966-1 (cloth : alk. paper)
 ISBN-10: 0-7391-2966-X (cloth : alk. paper)
 ISBN-13: 978-0-7391-2967-8 (pbk. : alk. paper)
 ISBN-10: 0-7391-2967-8 (pbk. : alk. paper)
 ISBN-13: 978-0-7391-3505-1 (electronic)
 ISBN-10: 0-7391-3505-8 (electronic)
 1. Emotions. I. Title.
 BF561.H4413 2009
 128'.37—dc22   2008047875

Printed in the United States of America

A Theory of Feelings
Table of Contents

Acknowledgments

The English translation of *A Theory of Feelings* was first published by Van Gorcum in 1979. It was translated by Mario D. Fenyö. Fenyö's translation is reproduced here with several slight modifications, the more important of which I mention in the new Introduction to this second edition. Carlos Padron was of help organizing the text for publication, for which I am thankful. I am grateful to Katie Terezakis for her care on behalf of the work.

Introduction to the Second Edition

Feelings, emotions and sentiments have been like the stepchildren of metaphysical philosophy. Moreover, they have played the role of the "other": the role of the confused, of the chaotic, of the impure. They have been treated as children in need of the constant guidance of Reason, or treated as the main obstacles to knowledge and morality. The degrading of feelings and emotions to a low status is not just a byproduct of metaphysics; it belongs to metaphysics' essential constitution. The model was set by Plato and has been followed ever since. In addressing one or the other special topic, some metaphysicians departed from this model, as did Aristotle in his *Rhetoric* and *Poetics*. Nonetheless, those works were framed outside the central metaphysical inquiry.

Metaphysics has cherished two connected ambitions. First, metaphysics aims to establish without doubt the primacy of the eternal as against the changing; of the necessary as against the contingent; of the form as against matter; of the spirit as against the body; of the universal as against the particular or the individual. Second, metaphysicians aim to make their vision of the world "click."

To that end, metaphysicians construe practical and speculative philosophies in a way meant to make them in fact click. Reason, in its different guises or costumes, warrants true knowledge. Reason, again in different guises, warrants virtue, goodness and justice. And in order to warrant truth and goodness, reason must be "pure" or as pure as possible. In the optimal case, to be "pure" is to be entirely without "matter"; in less optimal cases, purity means being dominated by logos, form, ratio, spirit, understanding, and so forth. What makes knowledge impure, contaminated? Sense perception, sensation, perception and experience. Even imagination is deceptive, and, like perception, is different according to the subject who happens to be imagining. Since Truth is one, absolute and unconditional, no one can arrive at Truth by starting from sensual experience or by letting sensual experience so much as mingle with rational thinking.

In order to warrant goodness, virtue and justice, practical reason likewise needs to be "pure" or as pure as possible. In this case, purity is also optimally without "matter," which is to say without feelings, emotions and sentiments. We can become virtuous, good or just if our feelings are taken under the control of reason or spirit in one of its guises. Reason, here, does not mean "cognition," since, as I try to illustrate in this book, emotion and cognition are always integrated. Rather, here I refer to the so-called "right reason," the Reason that is "right" in that it does not "follow" emotions; it is not guided and indeed is not

1

even influenced by desires and pleasures, which, on the contrary, answer to Reason.

Despite how jarring it may sound to us today, this metaphysical manner of understanding feelings remained dominant, despite certain exceptions, until the 19th century. One cannot deny, however, that within this general form given to the philosophical imagination, there *were* important exceptions and countercurrents. I will refer to only a few of them.

I mentioned that in his *Poetics* and especially in his *Rhetoric*, Aristotle paid attention to the feelings and emotions in their own right. Yet his aim there was not to establish the correct way to arrive at true knowledge or true virtue. In those works, he is not even interested in presenting the general structure of the soul. Yet in his *Metaphysics* as well as in *De Anima*, Aristotle was no less radical than Plato: the immortality of the supreme aspect of *nous* was warranted by its "pure" spirituality. The more purely spiritual and sublime, and the more absolute, so much the more warranty of Truth for the human capacity of thinking.

Christian philosophy followed in the footsteps of the ancients, including those of Plotinus and the Stoics, who influenced a special reading of the Bible. Christian thinkers also radicalized the ancients' metaphysical conceptions. Those who followed the path of desires, pleasures, emotions, and any feelings not unconditionally controlled by spirituality, were to be regarded not just as inferior men, but as sinners.

One might believe that from Descartes onwards the understanding and especially the evaluation of our emotional life has changed drastically. And in one respect this has happened. Yet in another important way, it has not. Descartes' *The Passions of the Soul* is a remarkable piece of writing. In the second part of the book, where he treats emotions proper, Descartes comes to the conclusion that we have in effect no bad passions at all; we only use our passions in the wrong way. In fact, the sole passion he considers to be evil in principle is extremely cognitive: it is fanaticism. Descartes even experiments with the idea that not all emotions can be subjected to reason, and sometimes and in some cases they do not need to be so subjected. Descartes scholars, however, point out that this book was written on the sidelines; that it is marginal and can hardly be integrated into the system of Cartesian philosophy. I love the book, but I agree with the critics' conclusion.

The third book of Spinoza's *Ethics* contains the most innovative philosophy of feelings and emotions since Aristotle. Among other initiatives, Spinoza formulates a conception of the "countervailing passions," which according to Hirschmann's in *Passions and the Interests* (1977) became one of the leading ideas of the 18th century. On this view, no emotion can be controlled by reason, but only by a stronger countervailing emotion. The third book of Spinoza's *Ethics* thus begins the war for the liberation of emotional life, as against the tyranny of Reason. This war of liberation, if consistently carried through, ends with the collapse of the metaphysical system altogether. Spinoza's ambition, however, was to design an infallible metaphysical system. This is why he had to succumb to tradition. In Book Five, we learn that emotions will be subjected to judgments of "adequate knowledge," and that the unity of Goodness and Truth will be reestablished through in the intellectual love of God.

In his critical philosophy, Kant not only confirms but even radicalizes the metaphysical tradition in regards to feelings and emotions. Pure reason, pure understanding and pure judgment—our a priori faculties warrant certainty and therefore secure true knowledge, morality and even taste. Still, especially in his pragmatic anthropology, Kant makes important contributions to the theory of feelings and emotions. First and foremost, Kant draws some important conclusions from his strict distinction between the faculty of desire on the one hand and the faculty of pleasure and displeasure on the other. I will talk about this in detail in the chapters that follow.

In Kant's times, a new wind began to blow within the British and French Enlightenment. Feelings, emotions, and sentiments stopped playing the role of the inconvenient stepchildren of philosophy. They were no longer regarded as the main obstacles of knowledge and morals. Indeed, for precisely the same reasons that they were previously treated with suspicion, feelings began provoking interest and even respect, in accordance with the particular character or function of the given feeling. Diderot and Rousseau, Condillac and Sade each scrutinize different feelings, such as lust and sentimental love, sensual impressions and the feeling of guilt. The modern novel joins their concert, addressing themes such as "sense and sensibility" and "pride and prejudice."

Every philosophy is unique and addresses its themes on different grounds. Nevertheless, I would like to mark the set of major turning points for questions about feelings and emotions in modern philosophy. By using the term "turning point," I do not have in mind a shift in innovation alone, but an upsurge of influence, especially in the wide sphere we might call the "permanent present," within which not only philosophers strictly speaking but also many other people come to accept the ideas of thinkers who they may not even be able to name.

The turning points I want to mark, then, may be best seen in Hume, Freud, Nietzsche, and Wittgenstein. My claim calls for justification. So why Hume, why not Shaftesbury or Hutcheson? Or Adam Smith? For that matter, why not Rousseau or Sade or Hegel? Why not Kierkegaard or Husserl or Heidegger?

I admit that this is my own choice, but it is not a random choice. All metaphysicians, as I mentioned, are wittingly or unwittingly system-builders. They want to tell "the truth" about the whole; about true and untrue forms of knowledge concerning the universe, God (or gods), and morality. And all their theories and ruminations must be fit together consistently, if in no other way then at least through the personality of the philosopher. Each of the philosophers I've mentioned so far was an original thinker. Not one of them was satisfied with interpreting the philosophies of others, only to add a little this and that; they each started something new in their manner of turning to the "thing itself," yet without resorting to metaphysical system-building.

I do not deny that there are others I have not mentioned who would also fit this bill, or who may be best interpreted as fitting it. Hegel, for one. Yet since the crowning of Hegel's system is Absolute Spirit, he remains, if only respect to the metaphysical intention at issue here, in limbo. To speak of other "missing" persons: Husserl and Heidegger were not interested in emotions for their own sake at all. Kierkegaard wrote some wonderful pages on anxiety and on passion, but he too remained uninterested in them for their own sake.

I hope that the reader will agree that all the members of my "quartet"— Hume, Nietzsche, Freud, Wittgenstein—fit the bill clearly and completely. They did not attempt to build metaphysical systems and they were passionately interested in feelings, emotions and sentiments, even if not exclusively for their own sake. Still, my choice needs to be justified.

So first and foremost, I must justify my assumption that all metaphysical thinkers who allocate a low, even ignoble place to emotions, drives and feelings, in comparison to eternal reason, are actually *addressing the same things, states, or events* as modern thinkers from Hume to Wittgenstein, who were passionately interested in passions for their own sake, when they discuss emotions or passions? Are the referents really the same?

Surely, a referent in such an involved examination is not ever or not often perfectly identical to another use of the same term. Curiosity, for example, is one of the elementary drives in Descartes, but not in Kant. *Ressentiment* as a feeling is first designated by Nietzsche, who differentiated it from rancor on the one hand, and envy on the other, and both rancor and envy are passions that Aristotle already examined in detail. Scheler's "sympathy" is not Hume's sympathy. The feeling of "alienation" did not technically exist before it was registered in the 19th century. Depression was once called melancholy, but the terms depression and melancholy do not cover exactly the same field of experience. Contact feelings are described by the ancients mostly in social terms (such as friend and foe), by early moderns as love and hate, or in physical terms (such as attraction and repulsion), and also sometimes in terms of chemistry (elective affinities). Later modern thinkers, with some exceptions (e.g., Carl Schmitt) tend to shun all bipolar expressions. Finally, emotional expressions rarely have exact equivalents between languages and cannot be transparently translated. These emotional expressions describe or rather encompass different emotional shades, and a different shade is not just a shade, it is also a slightly different emotion.

Having said that and thus thrown my whole project into question, it may sound astonishing if I add that within one cultural heritage, the referents of theories of feelings and emotions are actually surprisingly identical or almost the same. One does not need to read philosophy to come to this conclusion; it suffices to go to the theater and watch a performance. While there may be some modification in the reception of the fate of one or the other character (e.g., *The Merchant of Venice* has been played as a comedy), all in all, the same play elicited feelings from 16th century audiences that are indistinguishable from the feelings it elicits today. When we see a character act or suffer in a concrete situation, we feel sad or elated or curious or outraged, just as our great-grandparents did. That every concrete feeling differs from every other concrete feeling is also true about the selfsame age and selfsame environment and even the selfsame person. And this is also something upon which every theory of emotion has so far agreed.

But why the "quartet"?

The most frequently quoted sentence from Hume's philosophy of emotions is this one: "reason is, and ought to be, the slave of passions." The question is not *whether* reason follows the passions, but *what kind of passions* are those that reason follows or ought to follow. In other words, the whole project of traditional classification and hierarchy has already withered away. Feelings and emotions, here, are social relations. They are involvements with ourselves and/or with others. The old solution about refraining from such involvements is not just impotent (Spinoza knew this), it must remain impotent because it is also ludicrous and hypocritical.

Let me repeat: in Hume's philosophy it is not merely the answers that are different, but the questions themselves are. There is no mental hierarchy; there are no specific faculties. The relations between feelings and involvements are either symmetrical or asymmetrical, either reciprocal or non-reciprocal. Instead of scrutinizing isolated feelings, their rationality or non-rationality, Hume suggests to treat them as syndromes.

I named Nietzsche the second member of the quartet. I do not deem it necessary to justify my choice this time. Nietzsche continues an enduring yet suppressed genre of presenting philosophy: with epigrams, essays, story-telling, and dialogue. Nietzsche loved Montaigne, Lichtenberg and Emerson; he did not like La Rochefoucauld, yet he stepped into the boots of all of them. And they were all moralists.

Moralists are not moral philosophers, they are just moralists. They are critics of human character, of human folly, of social hypocrisy and foremost of moral hypocrisy. Nothing is "sacred" for a moralist except what he or she deems to be sacred. A moralist might be a skeptic, an ironist and a provocateur. Moralists provoke prejudices, be they the prejudices of a class, of individuals, of institutions or of philosophy. Moralists like laughter. Nietzsche, who calls himself an anti-moralist moralist, certainly loves laughter. Thus we seek in vain for a "theory of emotion" in Nietzsche, yet his biting epigrams, dissecting one or another emotion or sentiment, are positively engraved in the thinking of the 20th century.

I named Freud as the third member of the quartet. That Freud changed our whole understanding of the human psyche does not need to be documented. It was not the discovery of the unconscious that made Freud a great innovator, but his interpretation of the dynamic of the psyche, with the process of repression at its center. Due to Freud's novel way of posing questions, human emotional life came to appear, and still appears, in an entirely new light. Before Freud, emotional life was addressed from the vantage point of its direct expressions. Since Freud, it is scrutinized from the vantage point of its own non-expression, or its hidden indirect expressions, as in dreams, neuroses, and fantasies. Freud works on the tradition, just as Nietzsche does; both work on a tradition they acquire and reverse, as is perfectly shown in the bipolar or three-part typography that offers a hierarchical division of the psyche.

Wittgenstein, the last member of the quartet, was the greatest inspiration for this book. At the time of its writing, his two volumes of *Psychological Philosophy* were not yet published or widely available. Yet it was obvious on the basis of the *Zettel* and *The Blue Book* that something extraordinary had happened. What had happened?

If one looks at the genre only, Wittgenstein reminds us of Nietzsche. He writes epigrams, which he calls remarks. There may be two or three remarks at a time that are related, followed by others that are unrelated. This in itself is not astonishing, for Wittgenstein, after all, wrote these remarks to himself. It is also true that Nietzsche wrote some thousands of remarks to himself. But they are entirely different kinds of remarks. Nietzsche writes, even if only to himself, as the omniscient narrator of a novel, whereas Wittgenstein addresses us, the non-existent readers, all of us. "Let us suppose..." he invites, "imagine that...", and we, indeed, suppose and imagine together with him. This is no maneuver on Wittgenstein's part; it is not a test of rhetoric. For in these notes, Wittgenstein does not interpret, explain or build theories; he does not ask the question "why" but rather asks "what." "What happens ..." he queries, and then he describes. And he poses his questions for us as much as for himself: *Can you imagine?* he wonders, or more concretely, *What is so frightful about fear?*; *What is pain?*; *What is doubt?*; *What is belief?*; *What is rage?* Then he describes; he describes language games as we play them. And we all play them; this is how we can follow his invitation and embark together on this theoretical voyage.

It is obvious that in the first part of this book I was inspired by Wittgenstein. Whether discussing drives, affects, emotions, or emotional dispositions, I first described the phenomenon in question and frequently also through language games. Yet inspiration is not identical with influence. The first part of the book is systematic in a way, but it is different from a typical systematic approach. I do not start with the feeling pairs of pleasure-displeasure, or any allegedly good-bad feelings, not even love-hate, or attraction-repulsion. Although in the early seventies, at the time I wrote this book, the metaphysical fallacy of binary oppositions had not yet become the target of criticism and ridicule, I rejected this approach for the same reason that motivated the critique on the horizon. I wanted to avoid binary oppositions, and I did so, with the exception of orientative feelings. I found that I had to return to them in the discussion of categories of value orientation, but again here I talked only about orientation.

Even so, I needed to design at least a quasi-systematic approach. My project was thus to outline a new "anthropology," not in the American sense of the term, but in its European meaning. That is, anthropology as a philosophy that addresses the fourth Kantian question, "What is man?" I termed this book "theory" and not "philosophy" in order to announce the non-metaphysical approach of my quasi-system.

This work is, indeed, a systematic approach undertaken from the "anthropological" perspective. But before I presented different kinds of feelings I had to clarify the referent "feeling" and justify the general use of the term. Only afterwards could I discuss the different kinds of feelings, that is, begin the "anthropological" inquiry. I then believed it fitting, and I still do, to start with the empirically universal feelings, the drives and affects, which are the two instinct remnants that indeed appear in this order, for the "triggers" of the latter are socially specific. I continued with the discussion of typically cognitive—that is language dependent—social, historical, and individually specific emotions. The procedure of presentation explains why Hume plays little part in my phenomenology of feelings. He begins his theory of emotion with pride and humility, which is to say with certain already cognitive, thus language-dependent, social, historical and concrete feelings, respectively in their relation to self and others.

In my project, however, problems of how we learn to feel certain things or to evaluate feelings and emotions could follow only after distinguishing the different types of feelings. With this project, Hume's opening gambit is taken up almost at the end of the first part, yet even here without falling into binary oppositions such as love-hate. Instead of relying on binary oppositions, I distinguish two personality types. This is also consistent with the project of wanting to terminate the first part of the work at the point I do, in order to prepare the continuation of the second part. Whereas I once thought of this continuation a contribution to a sociology of feelings, I realized that it is more accurate to see it as a "contribution to the social philosophy of feelings."

A Theory of Feelings, as I said, originally was intended to be one contribution to a philosophical anthropology. The writing of the first part of the anthropological series, titled *On Instincts*, preceded the writing of this book. *On Instincts* is a mainly polemical work, far less systematic than this one, which was meant to be its follow up volume. The polemic in *On Instincts* takes aim at theories of human instincts, such as those advocated by the then-popular school of Konrad Lorenz on the one hand, and behaviorism on the other hand.

Let me briefly summarize the message of the book. There are very few human instincts, and even those—instincts such as sucking, swallowing, and sexual acts—are not fail-safe. If we pay too much attention to them, they cannot be performed normally. All other so-called "instincts" are abstractions or instinct remnants. One does not inherit abstractions such as the "instinct of self-preservation," the "maternal instinct" or the "aggressive instinct." On the contrary, the regularity, orientation, and repetition as much as guaranteed in non-human animals by instincts are secured among humans by social regulations. Thus social regulation has occupied the place of instinct regulation. Instinct remnants result from instinct demolition. Yet drives and especially affects are innate and they inhere in all emotions and sentiments. In humans then, activity is to be replaced by action. Consumption—the goal of the activity, even of the problem-solving activity of higher animal species—is not the purpose and even less the result of human action. Objectivation is the end of human action. The "other side" of objectivation is subjectivation, the constitution of the thinking, speaking "I."

The book *On Instincts* is in fact and in essence an introduction to *A Theory of Feelings*. The latter begins where the former ends. The two volumes were published together in five languages in the seventies, including English. My reason for now republishing the latter without the former is both theoretical and pragmatic. A polemical book is interesting while the concrete issues under discussion are still on the agenda. Although I still believe in my position, I do not think that my adversaries have remained important. One does not conduct polemics against ghosts, for if one does, one also becomes a ghost. Although neuropsychology and brain physiology have developed tremendously since the publication of *A Theory of Feelings* and I refer to sources prior to this development, the theoretical discoveries of those sciences are not pertinent to the philosophical position of this book, so reference to developments now appear mostly in notes.

In my original conception, at least two additional books were supposed to follow and extend *A Theory of Feelings*: first a theory of needs and then a theory of history. I soon came to the conclusion that a theory of needs would be redundant, at least for me, if not altogether. In my earlier book *The Theory of Need in Marx* I in fact proposed my own theory of needs already; and in a later, polemical essay ("Can 'True' and 'False' Needs be Posited?"), I elaborated and corrected it.

By dropping the volume on needs, I abandoned the whole "anthropology" project. Very soon afterward I did write *A Theory of History*, not as a sequel to the anthropology project, but as the first swallow of an entirely different series of books. I never again tried to answer the question "What is man?" for I came to the conclusion that either the question is unanswerable or all of philosophy is the answer to just this question. And whether the first or the second does not matter, for they amount to the same.

Thus, from the project of philosophical anthropology, only the present volume remains, at least in my view. Yet I still think that it stands on its own feet. I find its approach and its conclusions as relevant now as I did thirty years ago; time did not harm it. If I wrote a theory of feelings today I might, perhaps, rely more on Freud, but even of that I am not certain.

As for the second part of the book, it does not need a new introduction or an apology.

***

A note on the translation is in order. I changed very little of Fenyö's 1979 translation, but I did replace the term *Ego* with *Self*. As well, since there are no genders in the Hungarian language, Fenyö stuck to the old habit of translating everything in the male gender, such as "he" or "mankind." For this edition, I did not correct the former but did modify the latter. Finally, the Hungarian word "polgar" (as in "burgher" or the German *Burger*) is translated as "bourgeois," as in the "bourgeois world epoch." This might be misunderstood in English, namely as "capitalist." The possible confusion has been clarified in the addendum to the preface to the second part of the book. Where necessary, I replaced the word bourgeois by "modern."

New York, September 2006

Part I.
The Phenomenology of Feelings

Chapter I.
What Does It Mean to Feel?

A. I am Involved in Something

Is it possible or, better said, does it make sense to define and analyze what we call "feeling" in all its generality? After all, we are never confronted with "the feeling" either in our every-day existence, or in the activities and objectivations that rise above our every-day life. We are confronted with a variety of feelings, the concrete functions of which do not seem to have anything in common. The feeling of being found out, of enjoying the sunshine, of hunger, of contempt for something or somebody, all these feelings play such different roles in my life that it renders at least doubtful whether I am methodologically entitled to begin my anthropological analysis from "feeling in general." I will mention the hypothesis I intend to formulate here regarding the general anthropological function of feeling—in other words, the starting point of the analysis itself—to justify the choice of such a starting point. To feel means to be involved in something.

I am perfectly aware that this statement may seem to be a tautology. If to feel is to become involved in something, then what does it mean to be involved in something? But since I intend to furnish an explanation of this phrase further on, let us accept this apparent tautology as the starting point of my hypothesis. I feel—I am involved in something. This "something" can be anything: another human being, a concept, myself, a process, a problem, a situation, another feeling—another involvement. That I should be involved in something does not in the least signify that "something" is a concretely determined object. For instance, there can be desire or fear "without object" (anxiety). But the "something" in which I am involved, undetermined though it may be, is, at any rate, present. If I experience anxiety, I am involved, in a negative manner, in being-in-the-world. Involvement may be positive or negative, active or reactive, direct and indirect.

I want to solve a mathematical problem; in such a case I become actively involved. The involvement becomes positive and direct: the problem excites me, interests me and, at a certain stage, the feeling "oh, I see ..." enters into it. The involvement becomes positive and indirect: if I solve the

11

problem I win the competition, I will receive a prize, I will have attained recognition. The involvement becomes negative and direct: the whole thing bores me, it does not interest me; it gets me confused; I have the feeling "it is never going to work anyway." The involvement becomes negative and indirect: I am afraid I may get scolded if I do not solve the problem. I will get fired from my job, etc. In most cases a combination of factors is at work: I am excited by the problem, it does interest me, but "it does not work," I acquire the feeling of "it will never work this way," etc.

I read the papers: in this case I am reactively involved. Only that which means something to me in the papers elicits a reaction. I am directly involved if what I read relates to me, that is to my ideas, my goals, the circumstances of my life (this may be positive or negative). I am indirectly involved if the involvement does not relate to the informational content, but to the process of acquisition of information (I want to find a place for this bit of information in my environment, or I want to brag about how well-informed I am tonight, in company). I turn the page to the death notices; I take a look at who died, at what caused the person's death. I only glance at some of the items (I do not become involved). My glance stops at other items (I reread them). "I knew this man, what a pity!" Or, "well, well, even the bastards don't get to live forever!" Or, "He was exactly as old as I am" (*memento mori*). Or again, "he had the same disease as I do." In all these cases I become involved, because I have related the information to myself. In other words I feel pity; I rejoice at someone's misfortune, I feel fear, or at least anxiety.

The "breadth" of reactive involvement is in reciprocal relation with the degree of "familiarity" borne by the information. The broader the integrations, and the more general the concepts with which I identify, the broader the circle of my involvement; I get shaken up not only by the death of my neighbor, but I become capable of mourning even the death of a hero in a distant country.

Involvement is not an "accompanying phenomenon." It is not a matter of acting, thinking, speaking, procuring information, reacting, and all this being "accompanied" by involvement therein; rather it is a matter of involvement itself being the inherent constructive factor in acting, thinking, etc., involvement that is included in all of the above, whether actively or reactively. As Wittgenstein wrote: "Concern with what we say ... is something experienced, we attribute it to ourselves. It is not an accompaniment of what we say."[1]

The lower limit of involvement is "0": I am indifferent, the thing or event has no meaning for me, that is, "I do not feel." This limit, as we shall see, can never be attained completely. The upper limit of involvement is double: it is determined by the organism, and by the social circumstances. There is always an organic limit, but the "outer extreme" of this limit varies from individual to individual (hence it is biologically idiosyncratic). Likewise, there is always a social limit, but the "outer extreme" of this limit varies according to the society and the stratum (socially idiosyncratic). If the intensity of involvement disturbs the homeostasis of the organism, then the maximum has been exceeded: in an extreme case I suppose one may even die of rage, of happiness, or of pain. Yet the same happiness may cause the death of one person while another may survive (for this person the outer extreme had not been reached). An involvement of great intensity is also limited to a considerable degree in duration: energies subside, become exhausted (but there are no two individuals who become exhausted at exactly the same point). At the same time, there is no society that does not attempt to regulate the intensity of the expression of feeling and, in the case of certain kinds of feeling, even their content. This regulation usually takes the form of customs and rites. The feelings are regulated by social customs and rites in such a way that the upper limit of their socially prescribed and accepted intensity, as well as their content, do not reach the limit exceeding the one tolerated by the biological homeostasis. For instance, the regulation of mourning (how intense and of what duration should it be at the death of what person, and under what circumstances) varies considerably according to the culture. But to exceed the upper limit set by society, in this context as well, is considered "hubris." Thus if someone, in the process of mourning his parents, refuses to eat, or to drink, then this can be considered a deviation from the "limit of maximum pain" prescribed by society.

The lower limit of involvement (theoretically) is 0. Involvement may tend to point 0 infinitely, but will never reach it. Involvement is minimal (virtually 0) in the case of those repeated actions, including repetitive thinking, in which the innumerably repeated and spontaneously reflexive or practical actions (those executed without paying attention) have the character of means. As Tomkins states so accurately: "In the case of predominantly habitude action it is the rule rather than the exception that affect plays the minimal role."[2]

What does "repetition as a means" signify? I get dressed, that is I tie my shoes, I put on my clothes, I have done it a thousand times already. While I perform this act I do not think about it, I think of other things: things into which I am involved (my assignments, a date, etc.) The degree of my involvement is independent of the type of action. For the little boy who is learning to tie his shoes this means unusual concentration of attention: for him the tying of the shoelaces is an end in itself, and if properly executed, it signifies success. He becomes as excited about it as later on during the solution of a mathematical problem. It is precisely the repetitive nature of certain types of activity (which are means) that may alter them, that deprives them of involvement. If, however, the repeated act encounters obstacles (let us say, the shoelaces snap) the means becomes an end, and involvement enters into the game: we become impatient, irritated, etc.

Roger, Voronyin, and Sokolov's experiments with the EEG-rhythm lend support to this everyday experience. In the case of emotion, of concentration (as is well known in the specialized literature) the alpha rhythm becomes beta and gamma rhythms (greater frequency, narrower amplitude). According to the conclusions reached by the scientists, in case of several repetitions of the same act frequency becomes ever smaller, amplitude ever larger: the alpha rhythm, "sign" of a state void of emotional and attitudinal content, is reestablished. Examinations conducted with a galvanometer have produced the same results.

Our observation regarding the emotion-free nature of repetition should be narrowed down even further. First of all: repetition does not decrease involvement if the whole process, of which it constitutes an organic part, is, an end per se for the individual. The discus-thrower practices every part of the movement which later becomes spontaneous and repetitive; but these practiced movements, even if a thousand times repeated, become inseparable from the act of throwing the discus, from the entire process. If throwing the discus is a pleasure in itself for him or if he intends to win in discus-throwing events (direct or indirect positive involvement), then this involvement cannot be abstracted, in actuality, from a single one of the practiced and spontaneous partial element of motion. In these cases the intensity of involvement, as opposed to involvement in repetitive acts of a purely instrumental nature, can increase in direct relation with repetition; the less attention, the less concentration is required, the more enjoyable it becomes.

Furthermore: repetition does not decrease involvement if repetition looses its function—that is, when it does not become instrumental for any purpose. To be more precise, involvement diminishes for a while, then is replaced by an increasingly strong negative involvement, by boredom. Let us say, the schoolchildren begin to study new materials. They are excited, they are filled with curiosity towards the new body of knowledge ("do I know it?"; "do I understand it?"—"I know it already"; "I understand it already"). The material is repeated, knowledge becomes natural, tension relaxes. The material is repeated again and again. The reaction of the children is: "we go crazy with boredom." (Whereas in the case of brushing teeth no one says, no matter how often the act is repeated, "I am crazy with boredom.") The EEG experiments mentioned above also confirm this experience. If, after reestablishing the alpha rhythm, the task is repeated many more times, it will once again be replaced by the beta and gamma rhythms, The subjects of the experiment have grown bored with the task. Involvement approximates 0 not only in the case of repetitions of an instrumental nature in practice, we may consider involvement as 0 when we receive information which has no significance to us. Such information "passes by the ears," or else we immediately reject and forget it: thus, if someone should mention in our company that a person completely unknown to us purchased a dog yesterday, we are inclined to ask, "so what?" If, however, I should like to purchase a dog myself, then this bit of information acquires immediate value for me: someone has had the same desire as I, and has realized it. My involvement is no longer 0.

Involvement, quite independently from the object in which involved, can be: momentary or continued, affecting only part of the personality or its whole, intensive or extensive, deep or superficial, conserving or expanding, oriented towards the past, the present, or the future. Of course, these are aspects; in practice, every involvement includes a combination of several such aspects. Let us take a look at the following reports of feeling: "his distrust has hurt a little, but I will have forgotten it by tomorrow"; "it would hurt, if he were distrustful of me"; "his distrust hurt me very much, but I have overcome it"; "it hurt me all my life that he was distrustful of me: it humiliated me." It is evident that even such simple expressions display a complicated combination of various aspects of involvement. Thus the last expression is deep, affects the whole personality, is continuous, and indicates intense involvement. The third expression is intensive, deep, oriented towards the past, with momentary involvement. The first expression is superficial, oriented towards the past and the present, it is momentary, but does not involve the whole personality. The second is oriented towards the future, and indicates expanding involvement. But a similar kind of analysis of involvement can be applied to statements that have no character of emotional report. For instance, "I would like to write a little"; "yesterday I would have liked to write a poem, but today I no longer feel that urge"; "I would like to write better and better poetry"; "I would like to write about everything I see and experience"; "I will express my whole personality in my poetry," etc. Feeling means to be involved in something. This involvement, as I have mentioned, is an inherent structural part of acting and thinking rather than their mere "accompaniment." I can be involved in something specific, or simply involved in something. That is, involvement itself can be at the center of my consciousness, or the object in which I am involved can be. Depending on what is at the center of my consciousness, the feeling (involvement) can be "figure" or "background" (*Figur-Hindergrund*). "Vordergrund-Hinter-grundsvorgang ist ein Grundpänomen aller Leistungen des Organismus."[3]

In the case of fear, this feeling is unequivocally the figure (and so it stands at the center of consciousness) rather than its object. On the other hand, it is involvement again that becomes figure if, when listening to a melody, I am moved to the point of breaking into tears, or when I turn my head in lust towards the rays of the sun in the spring or if, in my rage, I smash the first object that comes within my reach. And what is more important and more general than this: in interpersonal relations (assuming that such a relation is not repetitive or purely functional) involvement also necessarily plays the role of figure, that is, it inevitably comes into the center of consciousness from time to time. So it happens in love, in friendship, in glee over the misery of others, in envy, in sympathy, in contempt, etc.

Here, however, we must point to yet another qualification. The role of figure when it comes to involvement in human relations does not mean in the least that during every moment of its presence, continually, it has to remain in the focus of consciousness. Love may not remain continually in the focus of consciousness, no more than can glee over the misery of others. These feelings become background, not only from the point of view of the totality of actions—which is obvious, for no one would argue that love is a figure feeling when the man in love is drafting a design in the office or crouching in the trenches—but it may also become background if we are confronted with the object of our involvement (should we study together with that person, or should we be discussing a program in common). I merely mean to say, by this, that in interpersonal relations only those emotive dispositions can be considered involvement in the other human being (in a positive or negative sense) which, from time to time, inevitably come into the focus of consciousness: that is, become figure feelings.

Furthermore, involvement becomes figure in all those cases when acting, thinking, relating to someone or something is blocked. Hunger is not in the focus of consciousness if we may go to the kitchen at any time and slice ourselves some bread; but it does get there if there is nothing to eat, or if we want to enter the door of our apartment, but our key which has worked perfectly well until now will not turn in the lock, if the solution of the problem "does not work," or if it rains continually during our vacation. Or, to speak of more serious occurrences: if our friend cheats us, or if the one we love dies. The existential uniqueness of the death of the beloved person—as opposed to all other cases—consists in the fact that it is no longer possible to find a detour by relegating the feeling into the "background." Where no detour is provided there can no longer be a task; relegating into the background can only take place with heterogeneous objects.

Involvement usually remains in the background of consciousness—whereas in the foreground stands the object of involvement—in the case of solution of problems. Problem solving can be cognitive or manipulative, from our point of view it makes no difference (I am looking for a street on the map, I chop wood, I make a grammatical analysis of a sentence). This, however, applies only to the process of solving problems, but does not necessarily apply to the inevitable stages in grasping and perceiving the problem. Plato already knew that the point of departure in recognizing something novel is the taumadzein, wondering. This wondering, the "what's this?" the "how is it possible?" kind of feeling, gives the impulse for the solution of the problem. At the same time, feeling can play the role of figure once I have found the solution. This is the situation both in the case of so-called intuition—I feel that the solution lies here, but it remains to be demonstrated, or I have to carry it out (this is the feeling Köhler calls the "aha-experience")—and in the case of finding the complete solution (the historical or legendary example of such an event is the "eureka!" of Archimedes).

In the process of solving the problem, the greater degree of concentration is required, the more the involvement relating to the problem retreats into the background of consciousness, and not only that involvement, but the most heterogeneous feelings as well (and at the same time, the most heterogeneous thoughts). This is what Lukács has called "homogenization." I have seen innumerable observations to the effect that pilots in charge of bombers during the Second World War have not even noticed the seriousness of the wounds suffered during the pitch of battle; their wounds only began to hurt once they returned to their base after the completion of their task.

Human life is identical with thinking life. The life of a brain-dead person is no more life in the human sense, even if her heart beats and she can be kept alive by being force-fed. We can distinguish between conscious thinking and unconscious thinking, yet we are constantly thinking or return to thinking. Thinking is one of the most heterogeneous human activities. As Wittgenstein writes: "Thinking is a widely ramified concept. A concept that comprises many manifestations of life. The phenomena of thinking are widely scattered" (*Zettel*, 110) or: "Thinking is an imaginary auxiliary activity, the invisible stream which carries and connects all of these kinds of actions" ("Remarks on the Philosophy of Psychology," II.228). All kinds of thinking are involvements whether we are just thinking about something or at something or whether we ruminate about meanings, whether we exclaim "eureka!" or ruminate about a problem, we are involved, we are feeling. Whether the feeling is in the background or is the "figure" phenomenon, depends on so many conditions that it would be foolish even trying to enumerate them.

In general, involvement remains in the background during perception. Again I have to point to certain qualifications. If the stimulus is sufficiently intense, then feeling immediately comes into the focus of consciousness (loud noise, sudden strong light—these stimuli generally provoke a fear response). This also occurs in the case of not particularly strong stimuli, if the perception has some unusual significance to us, to our self, to our personality. Hence if, for instance, we return home, and we discover that someone has moved the furniture around in our apartment: in such a case the feeling of "something is not in order," or "something is wrong" immediately enters into the focus of our consciousness. We become negatively involved in what we have perceived.

Yet involvement is present in the case of every perception, even if only as background, with greater or lesser intensity. Intensity is strong if we perceive something that is new to us. As Merleau-Ponty writes: "Physical stimuli ... play the role of occasions rather than of cause; their action depends on their vital significance rather than on the material properties of the stimuli."[4] Of course, Merleau-Ponty did not mean to deny the presence of physical stimuli by this statement, or their indispensability, from the point of view of perception. He only meant to say that these are not sufficient in themselves for perception; involvement in the stimulus must also be present in all cases (again we must add, to a greater or lesser extent).

The selection of what is significant for us is partly born with us; it is based in part on biological "patterns."

Finally, involvement generally gets into the background in the case of deliberate acts, especially in the process of selecting the means. I have already referred to this type of relegation in connection with the problem of the so-called "detour." If something "does not work" then involvement gets into the focus of consciousness. The process may even be interrupted at this point, or else it may continue: we search for the detour. How can the goal be reached after all, how can we solve the problem after all? We choose new means, which only becomes possible if feeling is once again relegated into the background. This case, however, is only one of the subcases of the problems. Relegating involvement to the background (or possibly: the conscious relegation to the background) is characteristic of every process of selecting the means. Think of the miser, who is very much involved in acquisition of money. In order to achieve his life purpose, the accumulation of money, he has to reflect: what investment would prove the most purposeful? The one that would bring him quick profits, but less? The one that would bring him profits only later, but more? Is the risk accompanying the investment not too considerable? etc. Greed, as background, is always present, otherwise our miser would not be meditating on the means towards this end. But he must suspend it (he has to relegate it to the background of his consciousness) precisely in order to better achieve his objective.

The figure or background quality of involvement is no more than two tendencies. In the majority of cases, especially in human relations, it would be preferable to speak of "rather figure characteristic" or "rather background characteristic." Yet in those processes, cases, etc., in which involvement plays the role of background, its ever-presence is an indispensable predisposition of the figure itself. In general, there is no normal problem solving, selection of means, perception, or thinking, without involvement in the background. "The emotions may be in the background, but they belong to the behavior, as in general the condition in the background belongs to normal 'Figure' formation."[5]

All I have said so far makes it clear that I consider the behaviorist approach to the description of the essence of feelings, as well as of their function, to be unacceptable. In the following I will confront two fairly widely accepted behaviorist theses with my own conception. These theses are: a) one may consider as feeling only that which manifests itself directly in action (in behavior); in other words, the only criterion for the presence of feeling would be the behavior expressing that feeling. b) In the case of an adequate "response" there can be no question of feeling at all.

a. That "it is by no means self-evident that our drives are transformed into action,"[6] is part of our constitution. Man is capable of keeping his feelings "to himself," to respond to certain stimuli with inner events without allowing these feelings to manifest themselves in action. This is particularly true with regard to interpersonal relations, especially when the feelings and the norms accepted by the particular person are in conflict with one another. Aristotle said that the brave man is not characterized by the fact that he is not afraid; the brave man behaves as if he were not afraid. The consequence of the attempt of the behaviorists to identify feeling with behavior would be that whoever is afraid will run away, whereas whoever does not run away is not afraid. Of course, if we raise the question, what is the proof that there are also feelings that do not show itself in behavior?, then we may answer, in the case of some feelings (for instance, affects), that we do have such proof. I cannot refer to sources other than mere introspection. If in the case of fear introspection proves to be a reliable source, then why should we doubt its relevance in the case of awareness of a higher order of feelings as well? It is true, the more a feeling is cognitive, situational and, at the same time idiosyncratic, the less unconditionally reliable a source would introspection be, and the more we may err in evaluating the nature of our feelings. This does not mean, however, that from the point of view of the presence or absence of emotions behavior would be the sole source of knowledge primarily because the higher order the feeling, the more we are inclined to keep it "to ourselves." Therefore an approximate, but never total, knowledge of these feelings can only be acquired through introspection and behavior taken together in the case of our own feelings; whereas in the case of a knowledge of others feelings, it would be behavior along with an account of the feelings of others.

"Keeping our feelings to ourselves" may also mean that the behavior stemming from the feeling is extremely delayed. In Ibsen's play *Nora*, not only spectators, but even the protagonist finds out that Rank is in love only when he pronounces the words "thank you for the light." I can become offended even when this feeling does not express itself in my behavior, if my involvement comes into conflict with another involvement: "I am ashamed to feel offended." I have to accept as authentic and sensible the following statement pronounced after the event: "I was offended, but I did not show it, because I was ashamed to feel offended."

Furthermore: I can become involved in the past, moreover I can become involved in such a manner that nothing results from it that affects my behavior or my actions in the present or in the future. For example, I become involved in the past when I evoke nostalgically the image of my late, beloved father. Of course, I could work out this feeling in behavior or action also (for instance, I could visit his grave often), but such a behavior consequence can in no way be taken as a criterion for the presence of feeling.

If, however, we go beyond the not at all negligible circle of interpersonal relations, the identification of behavior with feeling does not become convincing even with regard to the process of problem solving. I can accept as authentic someone's statement, according to which a certain problem excites and interests him, even if he does not proceed to its solution. It is, of course, possible to contend that in this case the problem did not "really" excite or interest him; this, however, would no longer constitute a statement of a psychological order, but rather a judgment. If the interested party says: "the problem excited me very much, but I did not have time to deal with its solution," then this statement can be understood to mean, and justifiably so, that he relegated a real feeling to the background.

b. The assertion that, in the case of an adequate reaction feeling does not occur, is undoubtedly erroneous as a general statement. It would not even be true in the instance already cited, when we do not encounter obstacles in the solution of a problem. Feeling is nevertheless present in the back-ground of consciousness.

Yet the assertion that the adequate reaction is not an organic part of the process, but an "end product," is most certainly wrong. Who has not derived a pleasure of triumph and satisfaction when answering an unexpected question in an appropriate, pert manner? Or when we answer a kiss with a kiss, should this be considered an inadequate response, should it be considered feelingless? And such is the case not only with complex feelings characteristic of interpersonal relations and related to cognitive processes, but also in the case of the most elemental drives and affects. If the person grasping for air immediately—and adequately!—opens the window, does that mean he had not felt anything? If the man falling overboard from his boat on a rough sea swims out—adequately!—to shore, does that mean he has had no fear? Or perhaps, later on, does he not experience relief? (It is even possible, in such cases, that fear grabs the person only after the escape, *post festum*; and that is when he begins to tremble, to sweat, etc.) I do not mean to deny hereby that there are cases in which intensive feeling (primarily affects) comes about if we do not find the adequate reaction, as in the case of impotent rage, or numbing fear. These cases, however, are the exception rather than the rule.

The two individual points of view I have criticized have in common the denial of the individual process of subjectivization (that is, its denial as significant and pertaining to our "inner life"). Subjectivization is nothing but the formation of the individual's own world in the organically connected process of acquiring the object and realizing our own self. If feeling would manifest itself only in behavior then there could be no subjectivization, the individual could not have its own world. If feeling appears only in the case of inadequate responses, then the construction of the subject's own world from the point of view of action and, in general, from the point of view of human life, would become dysfunctional. I am aware that the definition of feeling as involvement can only become valid if I prove that objectification and subjectivization are two inseparable, interdependent, and tangential directions in the development of the individual. This is what I intend to do below.

But let us turn back for a moment, in connection with this issue, to the theory of figure and background. I have averred that, if in the process of "being involved in something" the accent is on involvement, then feeling is in the center of consciousness; if the accent is on the "something" in which we are involved, then feeling becomes a background phenomenon which, nevertheless, remains indispensable in "normal" figure structure. It is questionable, however, from the point of view of the Self whether the identification of subject and object may come about. Can there be "events" in human consciousness in which figure and background become one, that is, in which there no longer is a background?

I believe that there are such events, for instance in the complete surrender to the object of our involvement, when we immediately subjectivize the object and become absorbed by it with our whole personality. In such instances involvement is both deep and intensive. This was what Plato had in mind when he wrote of happiness as the direct contemplation of ideas in the great moments of love, and in the contemplation of beauty. Speaking of contemporary thinkers, this is what Lukács called the *catharsis*, and Maslow the *peak experience*. Indeed, this is the character of every "great moment" in which two lovers unite surrendering temporarily the separate existence of I and the You—a surrender which, however, cannot be continued for long. Such is inspiration in the act of creativity, catharsis in the evocative experience such is religious ecstasy. Maslow is right: life that does not include such "peak experiences," life in which involvement has never become one with its object, cannot be complete. But he is equally right when he writes that it is not possible to remain long in a state of "peak experience." Generally, it is not the moments of peak experience that are characteristic of the course of life. To feel means to be involved in something and, in general, that is just the way we feel. Feeling is either figure or background or, to be more precise: tends to be either one or the other.

B. Human Being as a Whole

My initial statement, according to which to feel is to be involved in something, may appear to be a tautology as long as I do not answer the question, what it means to be involved. I intend to show, in what follows, that my initial statement is not a tautology.

Human beings as such are characterized by a basic antinomy. We are born with an organism into which are fed, by the genetic code, only the conditions for the "human species existence." At the same time this organism is an independent system—in each case an idiosyncratic system—which turns towards the world as such and which can "build in" everything only by departing from the self, by never transcending the self. Yet everything that makes man de facto man, that is all those items of information that constitute our species existence, are still external to the organism at the moment of our birth: they can be found in those interpersonal relations into which we are born. This species essence which remains, at the moment of our birth, completely external to ourselves (such as interpersonal relations in general, language, thinking, objects and their use, modes of action, objectivations), I will call from now "species character proper."[7]

The animal being has no such antinomy. The animal specimen receives ready made all the information pertaining to its species in its biological code at the moment of birth. It can widen these and apply them by learning, but basically it is led by biologically provided instincts. A horse reared in a human environment will remain a horse (a member of its species). An adult human being reared among horses (a hypothesis absurd in itself!) would not be a human being, would not be a member of its species.

We receive our "dumb species essence" with the whole organism as an organic entity. In what follows I have selected the brain to illuminate the aforementioned antinomy, because it is the directive center of the organism, and not because I consider the brain as the sole repository of the "dumb species essence." Should we, by an experiment in thought, transplant a human brain into the body of an elephant, then the experiment in thought can only conclude with the result that the elephant will not be transformed thereby into a human.

Let us consider, for the sake of analogy, the brain as a computer, well aware that this can be no more than analogy. Man is born with a computer (the brain) programmed for ideational operations (symbolical operations) and for projections[8]—with the capacity of memory storage and that of carrying out simultaneous operations. This "machine" can accomplish many things from the most primitive to the most complex operations "being fed into it." (How many, we cannot know in advance and probably will never fully know.) These tasks, however, have not been fed into the brain at the time of our birth. The tasks are fed into the brain by the world, by "being-in-the-world," by subsistence and orientation in it, by the existing system of symbols—such as language, forms of manipulation, objectifications in general—in other words by the species character proper.

The conception according to which even the "machine" (brain) representing "dumb species essence" is not quite completed at the moment of birth and that, moreover, the brain itself will become completed during its interaction with the world in the appropriation of "species character proper," is a conception more or less accepted in neurophysiology. Delgado proves wittily that this process cannot be circumscribed by the concept of "maturation." The constitution of the brain of the child born two months prematurely, when it reaches the age of two months, corresponds more or less to the constitution of the brain of a two months old infant born after a gestation of nine months. (If the fact could be explained by "maturity," then the constitution of the brain of the prematurely born should correspond, at the age of two months, to that of the just born infant after nine months' gestation.) Even Steven Rose, who is quite sparing with ideological explanations, observes: after birth "the neurons become noticeably larger, their cytoplasm and ribosomal content—a sign of active protein synthesis—increasing."[9]

So let us formulate the antinomy.

a. Our organism is "dumb species essence." At the same time it is an individual system, a unique organic whole. We can turn to the world only if we depart from the self, only with the "equipment" of the organism, and never transcending it.

b. Our species character proper is external to us at the moment of our birth. Consciousness is always socially conditioned, and can only be appropriated as such.

Our whole human existence is the solution of this antinomy, the bridging of this hiatus (to use the words of Gehlen). At the same time the contradiction can never be completely resolved. We are finite beings, finite in space and, more importantly, in time. We are also finite in our capacity to store information. Yet to live with this contradiction is permanent.

The human being begins to appropriate the tasks of the world departing from his own organism at the moment of birth. It is the world that provides the tasks to be appropriated. Everything that I appropriate ("build" into the self) becomes the Self, and in the future it is more and more the projection of the Self which leads the way in the further appropriation of the world. This relation includes the process of appropriation, as well as objectification, and the expression of the self. Better said, appropriation, objectification, and expression of the self are various aspects of the same process. Appropriation, objectivation, and expression of the Self alike are acting, thinking, and feeling. As Goldstein wrote: "Der physische Mensch setzt sich nicht zusammen aus seinem Denken, Sprechen, Wollen, Fühlen ... sondern er ist ein denkender, sprechender, fühlender, optische etc. Erlebnisse habender Mensch."[10] Dewey expressed the same idea with regard to thinking and feeling: "The distinction of cold intellectuality and warm emotionality is simply a functional distinction within this one whole action."[11]

I not only accept, I even emphasize that acting, thinking, and feeling characterize all manifestations of human life, that they can be separated only functionally; still, I would place greater weight on this functional aspect. For it is not enough to note that there is no thinking without feeling, no feeling without conceptualization and no action without either, but I also have to take their functional differences into serious account as long as I want to raise the question: what does it mean to feel? If we should not take this functional difference seriously, then the question: "what does it mean to feel?" would be synonymous with the question: what does it mean to think, what does it mean to act? Better said, all these questions would coalesce into a single question: what does it mean to "relate"? But it is not about this that I asked. I asked, what does it mean to feel, I asked about the specific function of feeling, I asked about what differentiates feeling from other human capacities within an integrated human system of relations.

Only in the case of the newborn infant may we speak of undifferentiated relations. The differentiation of acting, thinking, and feeling comes
about with the development of the Self (especially after the acquisition of
language). The person who cannot differentiate what it is that he does,
what it is that he thinks, that he feels, that he perceives, is an imbecile.
Even primitive statements such as the following would not make sense
without this differentiation: "it is raining outside, and the rain took away
my lust for life," or "I slapped him in the face, yet I remained ice-cold inside," or "evaluating my possibilities, I became even sadder." At the same
time, and this is the other side of the process, reintegration takes place simultaneously with differentiation. To mention the most important thing
from our point of view: feelings cannot become differentiated without conceptualization (cognition). Therefore, the development of the Self proceeds
along with the differentiation, and with the continuous reintegration of the
functions.

Let us abstract, for the time being, from the process of reintegration,
and let us concentrate on what is the function of being involved in perceiving, thinking, and acting? What does it mean to be involved? The Self selects from among the tasks provided by the world. The process of selection
is aimed at sustaining the homeostasis of the organism. This homeostasis is
not merely biological (as long as it is merely that, here really cannot be a
Self in the proper sense of the word), but social: it is always within a given
social environment that we must sustain and reproduce ourselves. The homeostasis is the preservation and extension of the Self system, and this extension is always carried out while insuring the continuity of the Self. The
Self selects that which insures its preservation (as a social organism) and
extension. These factors are not only selected; they are selected in a manner appropriate to the task. The Self which is incapable of performing this
selection would also be incapable of life.

All this does not in the least mean that the regulative function of the
Self is synonymous with the process of selection itself. On one hand, the
selection is only one element, although always present, of the regulative
function. The Self's relation to the world is intentional: the Self not only
selects but actively creates its own world. When I act, perceive, think, then
I not only "select" that which is decisive, fundamental to me, that which
threatens the preservation, extension, and continuity of my Self; but I also
realize myself, I render my own world coherent and I put my own stamp on
everything I do, perceive, or think. And vice-versa: not all selection is the
direct appendage of the regulative function of the Self. The "points of Self
view" of selection are often provided primarily by the task itself, as in the
case of cognitive selection. Even in such an instance, however, feeling is
present as background.

We know that there is no private language, there are no private concepts, there are no private objectifications; but what it is I express, and
what I refrain from expressing, what I reflect upon and what I do not reflect

upon from amongst the tasks assigned to me by the world—that is the projection of the Self, that which Husserl called "intentionality."

Involvement is nothing but the regulative function of the social organism (the subject, the Self) in its relation to the world. This is what "guides" in the preservation of the coherence and continuity of the subjective world, in the extension of the social organism. Human feeling (and its generality) is therefore the consequence of the hiatus. This consequence, however, does not mean that the bridging of the hiatus would be exclusively the function of feeling. Not at all! For in the process of appropriation it is the elements and processes of acting and thinking that are functionally of primary importance. Learning to use tools, the acquisition of language, the knowledge and practice of customs—these are the primary tasks. Yet I can acquire these skills only starting from my Self; I can select them only starting from my Self; I can evaluate these only from the point of view of my Self. Our social organism can only come about, and can only be sustained in its own continuity by our Self not just accepting, by means of thinking and acting, the world, but at the same time continuously "evaluating" its meaning for the subject. Let us make this clear with a simple example. In order for the child to learn to speak it is necessary a) that there should be speech as part of his environment and that objectification (language) should be present; b) that he be born with the predisposition of the "dumb species character" (first of all, with a brain programmed for ideation); c) that he should feel the need to speak, that he should become involved in speech. The latter becomes obvious from the primary selection which the child carries out on the speech of adults. Every intelligent parent knows that the child selects that which is most important from the point of view of his own Self (unless he is taught to repeat words parrot-like).

Therefore, "to be involved" means to regulate the appropriation of the world from the "point of view" of the preservation and extension of the Self, starting out from the social organism. The subject evaluates the world for himself with the involvement. Until now, I have spoken of involvement merely as the regulative function of the social organism, from the point of view of the relation of the object to the subject. Man, however, as Marx pointed out, makes even himself the object of his consciousness. In other words, the object of the Self is not only outside of the Self, but the subject itself can and does become the object of the Self. The consciousness of the Self is one of its primary constitutive elements. (Thus there is no language which does not have a term for "I.") Without Self-consciousness there can be no human being. Furthermore, "involvement" itself is an abstraction. Every single involvement is a differentiated, specific feeling. The Self can become involved even in being involved in something (positively or negatively): let us recall the statement "I was ashamed to feel offended." It is not merely involvement that pertains to the continuity (the preservation, the extension) of the Self, but also the hierarchy of heterogeneous involvements. It is precisely part of the Self's regulative function that it should relegate certain feelings into the background when it encounters feelings of a higher order in the hierarchy. Intentionality then becomes oriented towards oneself; we become our own object. The subject, however, can never become an object for the Self in the same manner as the world outside the social organism. If Richard the Third apostrophizes himself "Alack! I love myself. ... Oh! no: alas! I rather hate myself," and Catullus tells his beloved *odi et amo* these concepts expressing feelings in similar terms have different meanings and, of course, different functions. The words of Richard mean: I cannot identify with myself, I cannot be "on good terms" with myself, because what I had done was odious—in other words, he confronts an involvement in a valid value (a moral feeling) with his own personality evaluated in a morally negative manner. Hence the involvements are heterogeneous and hierarchical. Whereas the "odi et amo" of Catullus does not formulate hierarchical feelings at different levels but says rather: I love you, because you love me, because you give me happiness; I hate you, because you do not love me, because you cause me pain. Could someone say to himself, I hate myself because I do not like myself? The remark, sensible with respect to another person: I hate you because you do not love me, becomes completely nonsensical when applied to the Self. When the individual makes himself the subject of his consciousness (from the point of view of our problematic, becomes involved with his other involvements), then this must happen with the regulation, the guidance of the Self. The Self, as its own object, remains uninterruptedly the Self. In opposite cases we are dealing with serious psychotic disturbances.

Acting, thinking, feeling and perceiving are, therefore, a unified process. During the development of the Self acting, feeling, perceiving, as well as thinking all become functionally differentiated and, in a parallel process, immediately reintegrated into each other. As there are no human feelings without conceptualization, or at least without relating to conceptualization, in the same way there can be no thinking (placing in parenthesis plain repetitive thinking) without feeling. As Wittgenstein said: "Emotions are expressed in thoughts. [...] A thought rouses emotions in me."[12]

If we accept all this, then what is the explanation of the rigid separation of feeling and thinking in everyday consciousness and, as we have seen, in science as well? I must begin by allowing that this rigid contrast always moves on the level of abstract generalization. If, for instance, I should oblige someone to tell me whether he would classify disappointment in the cognitive or in the emotive "sphere," surely he would hesitate and would not be able to provide a clear answer. The situation is no different in the case of scientific classification. Thus when Maslow, who asserts the unity of man on the level of generality, nevertheless undertakes a concrete "classification," the outcome of this can only be an easily transparent absurdity. For instance, he lists under the cognitive-affective class "satisfied curiosity, feeling of learning and of knowing more and more," whereas he lists under the cognitive class "mystic experience with illumination and insight."[13]

The rigid contrasting of feeling and thinking in everyday consciousness and in certain scientific theories stems from different roots:

1) From the fact that "background" feeling is not regarded as feeling at all, but is abstracted from feeling.

2) From the fact that only a few of the infinite multitude of concrete types of feeling are considered as such; in the first place those which I, in my next chapter, will call affects (fear, anger, rage, etc.).

The relationship of affects to thinking is indeed different from the relationship of feelings in general to thinking. It is true that when affect-feelings come into the center of consciousness, when they play the role of figure (but only then), they do block thinking (but not necessarily action). It is certainly true that in a fit of rage, or in panicky fear, we are incapable of rational thinking. But how are we able to suppress or control this affect (if and when we are able to suppress it)? Is it by thinking? Although this cannot be verified empirically, experience proves rather the contrary, and it is not even in accordance with logic. If the affect blocks thinking, how could this affect be suppressed by thinking? And when it is suppressed (as often happens) then this occurs once more through an involvement; generally by means of an involvement standing higher in the hierarchy than the given affect, in other words with a feeling which is largely conceptualized as all feelings of a higher order are wont to be—what more, the reintegration of cognition into the feeling is often intentional (this is whence comes the impression that it was thought that suppressed the affect!). Spinoza had already noticed this process and formulated it thus: "Nothing can suppress a passion except a contrary and stronger passion." A perennially valid example of this is the story of the biblical Moses. The basic passion of the life of Moses was God, an enhanced love for the concept of a unique God. (Schönberg puts this into poetic form: "Ich liebe meinen Gedanken und lebe für ihn.") Is this not feeling perhaps? When he brings down the stone tablets from Mount Zion and sees the idol of gold, in his rage he smashes the tablets (hence the affect comes into the "center of consciousness!"). Later however, he climbs the mountain once again to obtain new tablets. Was it because he had been thinking? No! It was because his love for the law and for God was his dominating passion, and because it became master over his rage.

3) The contrast between thinking and feeling is extended to character as well. Thus the man who does not accept the hierarchically dominating feelings of a given society is not considered a "sensitive man" even though, frequently, the reason why he does not share those preferred feelings is precisely because he does not believe they are authentic (as in the case of a number of G. B. Shaw's heroes, such as Mr. Trefusis). The man of reflection, the type of person who becomes most strongly involved in a task, in justice, in truth, is not considered a "sensitive man."

Still, does this confrontation make no sense at all? To begin with, all the differentiations described above make no sense in the scientific or philosophical approach, but they do make sense in everyday life, from the point of view of a strictly pragmatic approach. Furthermore, the values prescribed by society and/or selected by oneself alone—hence the preservation and extension of our moral being—often collide with our particular feelings. Most of the time (but by no means all the time!) this conflict becomes conscious as tension between "true," "knowledge," "truth" on one hand, and feelings on the other.[14] Such a conflict occurs, first of all, in our evaluations of others. In our evaluations we strive towards "objectivity," towards "justice," or at least we pretend that we do. "Although I hate X, I must concede that he behaved irreproachably in this instance." Or: "My father was right when he scolded me." Of course, in spite of the fact that this conflict may become conscious as one of knowledge versus feeling, I do not mean to imply that "knowledge" or "truth" are void of involvement (of feeling). On the contrary, we can only approach "impartiality" and "righteousness" if we are directly or indirectly involved in impartiality or righteousness. Directly involved if we love justice, if we experience impartiality as a personal value; indirectly involved if we know that we can obtain the respect of others (always important for the Self) only by our impartial evaluation, by righteousness.

Furthermore, this differentiation is sensible in all those cases in which feeling precedes its conceptualization, its conceptual "insertion" into the world of the Self—in the words of Ernst Bloch: in the case of the "not yet known." Thus the object of feeling itself can be not yet known. "I am sad, but what makes me so?" The feeling itself may be conceptually undeterminable: "What is this oppressing feeling that has seized hold of me? Am I blasé, do I have Weltschmerz? No, no, surely not. Am I merely depressed? No, not that either." And then I happen to read about the feeling of "alienation." "That's it! This is what I feel."

Finally, this differentiation makes sense in the case of collision between our so-called "desires" and our so-called "Will"—that is in all those cases when our will turns towards the feeling itself, pro or contra. What does it mean "to desire," what does it mean "to want?" Desire is not one feeling among others, it is not one affect among others (although it is often listed as such: "fear, anger, desire, etc."). The human being, as a being oriented towards the future, is essentially a "longing" being. What we call "longing" is nothing but involvement in the extension of the Self in general (insofar as the mere preservation of the Self may be blocked, there is also involvement in that preservation—e.g. the wishful fantasies of the starving person revolve around food and feeding). The longing can be without object—an involvement in the extension of the Self without knowing, without becoming conscious of what it is which it will be extended to, in relation to what. The desire which is conceptualized in any fashion (which Ernst Bloch has analyzed so beautifully) is connected with anticipatory thinking. This may be mere day-dreaming, wishful thinking (*Wunschdenken*) or even the selection of some goal, the means for reaching which not being yet at hand. A person may dream about winning the first prize at the lottery, that his love, who has abandoned him, will return, that the revolution will break out, that—when he grows up—he will become a pilot, etc. He may even desire into the past, if he should recall the extension of his Self in the past: "How I would like to be twenty years old again, when my life was still ahead of me!" Or: "I hark back to those days when we met; how we loved each other!" The expression "I no longer desire anything" is never completely true; we desire as long as we live. The statement "I wish I would die" is likewise never completely true. The person who really wishes to die and nothing more, is no longer wishing, but has given up his Self to commit suicide. Yet even that gesture is full of wishes, at least in the great majority of cases! The suicide may harbor a desire for revenge, a desire to be missed and mourned, or, in the case of a representative personality, that his fate be a warning to others. Still, one may say that desires do have a negative outer limit: the indifference—never complete—towards the sustenance and extension of our Self, that is when one "gives up" life. Desire also has a positive frontier: these are the great moments of fulfillment. In these cases the wish or desire tends towards 0, in a positive sense. The nearly desireless euphoria of happiness, however, is very limited in duration. If I say: "I am happy living this way; I desire nothing more," this statement does not cover the notion of being without desire, because I am still anticipating, even in this case. In wishful thinking I prolong my present state in the direction of the future; I desire the preservation of that which allows my Ego maximum extension. The following statement is also latently included in the preceding one: "I am afraid that it may not last."

Will itself is desire, too. Desire is the *genus proximum*, will is the *differentia specifica*. Kant, although he considered the will as a faculty independent of "desire in general," was quite aware of this identity when he defined will as "the faculty of desiring of a higher order (*oberes Begehrungsvermögen*)." We have seen that will belongs to desire. The question is whether what we have named *differentia specifica* of the will really makes it of a higher order with respect to the other forms of desire.

Will is nothing else but concentration in order to reach a goal in which we are positively involved, including the selection of the means necessary to reach it. Thus will, first of all, presupposes (contains) involvement in (desire for) the goal. But one may wish or desire a goal the realization of which does not depend on the person wishing or desiring. Will, however, posits the goal as depending from ourselves. Otherwise we would not be able to concentrate on its realization and select the means for it. If I say "I will the weather to be nice tomorrow" or "I wish the weather were nice tomorrow" the two statements are practically synonymous. The "I will" merely emphasizes, if it does anything at all, that I wish it very much. Such is always the case when the "I will" and the "I wish" may reasonably be substituted for one another. It does not make sense, however, to say: "I wish I would sew on this button that came off." It only makes sense to say:

"I will, to sew on this button that came off." The former sentence may make sense only if we are actually talking about desire in general (for instance, I do not have needle and thread, or I can barely see, therefore I lack the necessary means to sew on this button). In this case the relationship *genus proximum—differentia specifica*, semantically, is similar to the relationship between "moving" and "walking." Certainly, to walk is to move. But the expression: "my little son learned to walk yesterday" cannot be replaced by the following expression, "my little son learned to move yesterday." The latter expression warrants additional information, just as in the case of "I wish I would sew on the button"—for instance, the fact that the above-mentioned little boy may have become paralyzed as a consequence of some illness.

In the case of will we posit the goal as something that depends on us, while in the case of general desire this is not so, our relation to the realization (or even the non-realization) of the goal wanted is different from our relation to the realization or non-realization, respectively, of the goal desired. The feeling of responsibility comes into play in the case of the goal wanted, in direct proportion to the significance of the goal; we are not only involved in the objective, but also in the fact that we want to attain this objective. To this extent will always has a moral implication, positive or negative. Heine has formulated this aspect in the most pregnant way: "Du, stolzes Herz, du hast es ja gewollt—Du wolltest glücklich sein, unendlich glücklich oder unendlich elend,—Jetz bist du elend."[15] There is no question as to Kant's relative truth, that he recognized the moral "faculty" in the type of will he named "faculty of desiring of a higher order." Yet to this "faculty of desiring of a higher order" Kant attached one single feeling: the feeling of respect, and excluded all other feelings, even the reflexive feelings of pleasure and pain (*Lust und Unlust*).

Will is desire, feeling—hence involvement. Is it, however, possible to tie this desire or involvement to a single concrete feeling, and exclude all others? Is there really a conflict, not between "feeling" and "will," for we have already seen that there can be no such conflict, but between the multitude of concrete emotions and the emotion of will? Will, as desire directed towards an end, is always a desire directed towards something (a desire directed to an indeterminate object could never become will). We are, however, involved—often many times involved—in this something. Concrete, polyphonic emotions connect to the object of my will. In the case of more complex situations, and practically all significant situations are complex, the goal itself is not homogeneous. For instance: I perceive that my friend has suddenly changed his attitude towards me, as if he had grown cool. I like my friend, his friendship is important to me. "I want to find out what it's all about!" What does this mean? First of all, I want to know why he has grown cool towards me. At the same time, and inseparably from the former, I want to reestablish our former friendship (the goal is not homogeneous either). I am disturbed; I have bad premonitions "perhaps I have offended him?" I feel insecure, I seek reassurance. Love, the yearning for reassurance, involvement in the past or in the future ("I want to reestablish things"), fear (of losing him)—all these feelings, and yet others, are attached to my objective as polyphonic emotions.

"I want to find out what it's all about"—that is, I concentrate on attaining the objective. At this time, and for this reason, I select the means leading to the objective. To reach the objective (the reestablishment of trust, of friendship, my peace of mind, the feeling of confidence in myself and in others) I must relegate certain figure feelings from the foreground into the background of consciousness; thus irritation, jealousy, suspiciousness, feeling upset, feeling offended, the feeling of insecurity, etc. Simultaneously, I must bring other feelings into the focus of consciousness: love, the feeling of gratitude to my friend, etc.

Relegating certain feelings into the background and bringing other feelings into figure are processes that take place in case of all acts of will, though these processes do not always take place with the same intensity. Let us look at the simplest example: I want to sew on the button that fell off. I push into the background: I do not feel like doing it, I prefer to do something else, I bring into the foreground: I would be ashamed of myself if my son were to go to school with a button missing. Or let us look at the most subtle occurrence: the novelist allows his favorite protagonist to be "cruelly" humiliated, or even to perish. He relegates into the background: the feeling of pity (or self-pity, since he identifies with the hero). He brings into the foreground: his involvement in the truth and perfection of his work of art (or self-pity, since he identifies with the hero). He brings into the foreground: his involvement in the truth and perfection of his work of art.

Because of this moment, I am justified in calling the will, as Kant had done, a "desire of a higher order" (Although not the "capacity" of desiring" [*Begehrungsvermögen*], since we are not dealing with a separate "capacity," but with a psychic event that can never be separated from other events). As for desire in general, it does not mobilize our involvement (or involvements). If, however, the desire is voluntary, we indeed do mobilize our involvement precisely from the point of view of the objective. Desire in general and desire having a voluntary character are, of course, not two clearly separable entities; and mobilization may be less or more intensive. Of course, the description of will as "desire of a higher order" does not mean that the feelings relating to the object of our will are necessarily of a higher order than the feelings attached to the object of our desire that does not have a voluntary character. One may just as much desire to redeem humanity as to destroy another human being. In this connection, we may specify the following: if the goal (and the feelings attached to it) is predominantly positive in value, than the value of the voluntary desire is more positive than that of desire in general. If the goal (and the feelings attached to it) is predominantly negative, then the value of the voluntary desire is more negative than the value of desire in general. What can be more natural than this since, as I have said, voluntary desire also implies responsibility (we desire that the starving eat well, or we assist in securing food for them; we desire that the beloved woman become ours after all, or we rape her).

Wittgenstein offered the following theoretical proposition regarding how to differentiate between acts that were voluntary and others that were involuntary: let us consider voluntary that act for which we may appeal for someone to carry it out and involuntary that act for which we may not make such an appeal. A sensible order: do this or do that! An unreasonable order: make your heart beat! Thus Wittgenstein considers as voluntary anything in connection with which it is possible (in order to use our own definition) that the goal become our own goal; that we concentrate on this goal and the selection of the means which will lead us to it. Hence Wittgenstein did not really define voluntariness, but its possibility.

This approach, with the above mentioned restriction, is indeed fruitful. The approach becomes problematic, however, as soon as Wittgenstein applies the same differentiation to the separation of feeling and thinking. One can appeal to others to think. "Think such and such a thing through!" would be a sensible appeal. But: "have this or that feeling" would be, according to Wittgenstein, an unreasonable appeal. In conclusion—although Wittgenstein who writes in aphorisms does not draw this consequence here and, elsewhere, he even attempts conclusions that contradict this one— feeling is not voluntary and cannot become the goal (object) of the will.

This statement, however, would be erroneous not only within our conceptual framework (will itself is feeling: what does it mean to say that feeling may not be directed towards feeling?), but it is also erroneous within Wittgenstein's own conceptual framework.

For it is possible to make an appeal to feel. What more, most of the time we are doing just that, appealing to feel.

1. Let us first examine the biblical commandment: "Honor your father and mother!" This commandment is really not an appeal in the strict sense of the word, but a norm. It is not directed to you or to me, but to everyone (at least to all those who believe in one God). We might say, the norm does not command the feeling of respect, but a behavior expressing respect; this, however, is not the case (the "authors" of the Old Testament were not acquainted with behaviorism). That all norms are at the same time conductors of feeling as well does not mean that the norm itself is the cause of feeling, or of the change in feeling, but rather—in the social average—that the norm is an indication of it. Everyone can experience this on himself, even if only in a negative way. If someone acts according to a norm accepted by him, yet does not feel that way, then he is well aware that he did not satisfy the requirements of the norm. If I accept as a sacred prescription that I must "honor father and mother" then, while I may behave in a most respectful manner, as long as I do not feel that respect, I will feel guilt. Consequently I voluntarily "relegate into the background" those feelings which disturb

respect, because I want to honor my parents.

2. On the other hand: an appeal taken in the strictest sense of the word can also be directed at feelings. We do say "you should be ashamed of yourself!" We do say "have trust in me!" We do say "don't be afraid!" We do say, "calm down, take it easy!" In these cases we are dealing with appeals of different types. Let us analyze, first of all, two related appeals: "You should be ashamed of yourself!" (Let's say, because you reported somebody to the teacher) and "Don't be afraid!" (Let's say, of crossing the street). What do we mean in the case of such injunctions? We communicate a social experience (both appeals have to do with behavior), in the form of an appeal, regarding a social norm. Of course, it is true that the person addressed will not necessarily feel ashamed as a result of our saying "you should feel ashamed of yourself!" The fear of the person addressed will not necessarily disappear by our saying "don't be afraid!" But one thing is for certain: the person who has never been told that he should feel ashamed of himself will never feel ashamed in such cases, at least in the social average. The person who has never been told not to be afraid, but rather that lie should feel afraid will, in the social average, feel fear regarding a given object, in a particular situation. It is the injunction "fear God" which provokes the fear of God in every human being in whom this fear is present, although not everyone who has been enjoined to do so will actually fear God. The injunctions—especially the ones often repeated in childhood—leave such a deep trace in life, that they appear even when a person no longer considers that particular feeling rational. How many adults feel ashamed when discarding dry and inedible bread because on such occasions their parents used to tell them in childhood "you should be ashamed!" If the injunctions would not be capable to evolve feelings or to fix them, then the majority of concrete feelings would not have a chance to develop.

It is true that it is possible to answer injunctions such as "you should be ashamed of yourself!" or "be afraid of this!" or "don't be afraid of that!" in the following manner: "I am not ashamed of myself" or "I cannot be afraid" or "I don't want to be afraid." But this does not differentiate feeling from thinking. If we should appeal to someone: "think it over!" he can likewise answer "I cannot think it over" or "I don't want to think it over." But just as the injunction "think it over!" may be an indication that the person appealed to will actually think it over, in the same way any injunction regarding any feeling can be an indication that this feeling actually develop later on in the person.

The appeal to feel does not elicit feeling in the same way as a command directed towards a simple action, let us say "face right! face left!" will elicit the action itself. In the case of feelings the will is not only directed "outwards" but also "inwards"; it elicits a feeling or brings it into the foreground respectively, while it relegates into the background or eliminates another. A single injunction is usually not enough for all this, it is necessary to repeat the injunction; but it is not necessarily another person that has to repeat the injunction. If the person who appealed to me is a "significant other" in my eyes, then I may repeat the appeal to myself. This is what we call, among other things, internalization.

Those injunctions pertaining to feeling which do not convey norms or general experience belong to another family. If I say to someone: "trust me!" then this does not mean "you must trust in human beings!" and not even "you should have trust every time you meet someone like me" but may even mean the opposite "do not trust anyone, but me." If I tell a crying child "calm down!" it may be that I do not even know the cause of his distress; hence the injunction cannot be synonymous with the following: "you must calm down in all such or similar cases!" (while the injunction "you should be ashamed of yourself!" did mean "you should be ashamed of yourself in all such or similar cases!"). I do not mean, however, that the injunctions belonging to this family will not influence feeling in a given situation (do not elicit them; do not relegate them into the background). The injunction may become effective—and very often is effective—in such cases, because it is the presence of the other person, his "commiseration" or "participation" in my misery, in my aspirations, or in my happiness which lends a guarantee to the injunction. The "participation" of the other person is an indication whether I should relegate certain of my feelings into the background or bring them into the foreground, whether I should evolve them or eliminate them.

3. It is easy to conceive that the selection of means plays quite as important a role in will directed at evolving or modifying my own feelings as in all instances of voluntary acting. "Don't think about what bothers you, and then it won't bother you any more!" "I think about something else." "Is it better now?" "Yes, it is better." As the example shows: among the means of the will aimed at feelings, thinking or "thinking about it" plays a particular role. (Of course, I can reply to the above appeal in the following manner: "I cannot help thinking about it"—just as much as I can reply "I cannot think this over"). Among the conscious means aimed at the formation of feeling we find "concentration of time" (for instance, I go on a trip), the formation of involvement in somebody or something else, etc. What is most important, however: the "means" of formation of feeling are often socially "provided"—first of all through social rites. They can be provided in the rites of mourning, in Christian confession, in psychoanalysis or also in certain forms of entertainment. The forms of entertainment, the means for becoming happy, are received mostly "ready-made," even though we may select between various forms, at least nowadays, in modern times. I will return, further on, to the issue of how certain forms of entertainment perform a questionable (ethically problematic) role among the means for formation of feeling. There can be no doubt, however, that entertainment is such a means.

4. The appeal to think or to act, in all the more complex cases is, by the

same token, an appeal to feel. "Learn your lesson!" also means "you must have enough feeling of responsibility to learn your lesson!" If I tell someone "Now do it on your own!" I appeal to that person: "Feel that you can do it on your own!" At the same time it also means: I suspend—I relegate into the background—the feeling of insecurity, the fear of failure (the hand must not tremble!), and I bring into the foreground the feeling of "I must show what I know," I project the experience of success.

It is possible that I want to feel this or that: which does not mean, of course, that I inevitably feel what I want to feel, or that I don't feel that which I don't want to feel. But I need only prove the former.

C. Feeling and Homeostasis

I have said that it is the Self which selects from among the tasks provided by the world and that this selection is aimed at the preservation of homeostasis. This statement warrants a more detailed explanation.

Since Cannon we have become aware of the "wisdom of the body," we know of the fact and the secrets of biological homeostasis. We have also learnt, since that time, that we feel the danger of the upsetting of the biological homeostasis well before its actual occurrence, through the so-called drives such as thirst, hunger, and furthermore physical pain. These feelings are the "signs" of the danger of the homeostasis losing its equilibrium, equally present in the higher order of animals and in man. Since I will return later on to an analysis of drives, I only wish to state the following for the present: in man even the appearance of the drive feeling is, within limits, socially codetermined. For instance, within the same biological state we may feel hungry or not hungry, depending on the rhythm of meals in the society in which we were raised. In regard of the fact that the possibility and importance of social codeterminations varies greatly according to the drive (let us "list" some of these in order: sexual desire, hunger, thirst, need for air), no proof is required.

The regulation of the psycho/social homeostasis includes, of course, the regulation of the biological homeostasis, but there is no society, no matter how primitive, in which the former is not much broader, much more variegated than the latter. It is not that we must merely maintain ourselves, we must maintain ourselves in a given social context, we must acquire the attitudes towards work, the aptitudes for the manipulation of objects, the system of customs and norms, the language, etc. To remain with an elementary example, that of eating: our feelings regarding feeding do not limit themselves by far to the hunger-drive. It is feeling that regulates even the matter of what is tasty and what is less tasty, what manner of preparation is the tastiest, whether we prefer something raw or cooked, what it is towards which we feel disgust (including disgust towards things which are not harmful to our health!), whether we take our meals alone or in company, furthermore what and when do we take alone or in company, what tools we eat with, what rituals are connected with absorption of food, etc. (Let us just remind ourselves of the creatures that are taboo, the complicated system of prescriptions and prohibitions regulating our table-manners, and all those collective images that pertain.) These purely social feelings relating to feeding may nevertheless be so strong that they even impede the satisfaction of the drive. Eskimos, for instance, would rather die than hunt seals at certain seasons. Disgust can also be stronger than hunger. Of course, such cases are rather exceptional. In general, as I have said, the regulation of the psycho-social homeostasis includes the regulation of the biological homeostasis as well.

The two basic categories of psycho/social homeostasis are preservation and extension: feelings regulate, on one hand, the preservation of the subject (within a given social context), and they also regulate the expansion of the subject (the Self), on the other. The proportion of the two functions of preservation and extension varies according to social structure. In stagnant societies preservation and maintenance are prevalent, whereas in dynamic ones it is extension that dominates. The function playing the dominating role, and the degree of domination, determine to a large extent what types of feelings will develop and, furthermore, to what degree do these feelings differentiate. Thus the fear of strangers played a much greater role in static and closed communities than it does today, in the era of general worldwide communication. On the other hand, the "thirst for knowledge" is considerably stronger and more widespread today. Both of these existed before, and exist now, only in different proportions. Another example: the feeling of shame and guilt, as Darwin already knew, do not differ in primitive community cultures; whereas nowadays these are two very different feelings.

Whether preservation (maintenance), or extension dominates, both of these are always present. Without extension the Self cannot come into being: thus in every society it plays a basic role in the process of growing up (whether this process takes 12 or 24 years is another matter). In societies that are open and oriented towards the future this extension does not at all come to an end with adulthood, but rather becomes permanent, although on a different level. Even in simple societies this process does not cease completely: on one hand, because even in these societies the acquisition of life experiences means that the Self is expanding and, on the other hand, because social tasks vary according to age. Yet, even in the most "expansive" societies, such as our present one, "preservation" plays a decisive role. As we know, the Self could not have continuity without such preservation (for instance, new knowledge can only be related to previously acquired knowledge). It is feeling that "leads" in the formation of the proportions between new and old. True enough, the more open a society, the more our feelings lead idiosyncratically in these. There are people longing for adventure, and others who prefer the security of home; but there is no person longing for adventure who never "repeats" in his adventure, or who does not feel some longing for a *lieu fixe*—a house, a home, a "reliable" man. And there is no person preferring a home (security), who does not also feel some impulse towards the new, towards change, towards trying out his strength on something relatively "unknown." (If it were otherwise then we would be dealing obviously with a pathological case.) Feeling always "gives a signal" in situations that are purely of preservation, or purely of extension; and this signaling is always negative. If we should understand not a word of a certain book, we become not only curious, but are seized by the feeling of *Unbehagen*. The same thing happens if we should find ourselves in a totally unknown environment in which we encounter absolutely no base (we are afraid of the absolutely unknown)—for feeling prompts us to seek bases, to link up with "preservation." But the same kind of negative feeling may seize us in the case of repetition of something already known, of something completely familiar. I remind the reader of repetitive action or thinking with a non-instrumental character. In such a case we are seized by torturing boredom: we want to extend our Self. Where the repetitive activity (and thinking) forms the major part, there appears, as a social characteristic, the "thirst for experiences." Witness the accident in the street (finally an experience!). This kind of "thirst for experiences" has often played a rather negative role in history; people living the monotony of everyday life with its repetitive activities felt the outbreak of World War I as an exciting experience and potential for the "Great Adventure."

So far I have spoken of the homeostatic function of feeling in relation to preservation and extension, the old and the new; but this homeostatic regulation is just as important from the point of view of the "more!" and the "enough!" We are lifting a heavy object. We feel that we need yet a little effort and we will be able to place it there, where we wish; a little "more!" and it's done. The good military commander feels: one more attack and victory will be won. The feeling of "enough!" also leads us from the simplest regulation to the most complex. "I am sated, I cannot any more"; "I am tired"; "I feel sleepy"; in order to do my work properly, I first need to sleep." "Let's stop!" we say, if we feel that there is too much tension in a relationship or too much irritation, disappointment, sadness, that all this is not in proportion with the value the relationship has for us—or for the other person. But the feeling of "it is enough!" not only signifies the unbearability of an activity, but also its opposite, the unbearability of the lack of activity: "I can no longer stand doing nothing!" in the case of motionless lying in bed, the feeling of "it is enough!" breaks out with an elementary force. If this immobility does not have an instrumental character (for instance, in case of severe illness), then within a short time it upsets the homeostasis and leads to psychic disturbances.

The third homeostatic function of feeling is the regulation of tension in general, usually described under the categories "tension" and "tension reduction." It is easy to conceive that this function is completely different from the ones mentioned above. Preservation as well as extension can be either tension or tension reduction; also, the "more!" and the "it is enough!" (For instance the feeling of "it is enough!" can arise in the case of sexual desire, as well as in its satisfaction.)

Many criticisms have been directed at the theory of tension reduction, particularly coming from persons with whose work I happen to sympathize (for instance, Maslow). Undoubtedly, these criticisms have legitimate elements; these legitimate elements, however, have only rationally questioned a peculiar (and rather narrow) interpretation of tension-reduction. Tension reduction (in its narrow and for me likewise unacceptable interpretation) means that every feeling has a tension-character initially and the tension is terminated by a "consummatory" action biologically connected with the specific feeling: hence the tension is dissolved by the satisfaction of a biological drive. Thus the reduction of hunger-tension would be eating till sated, the reduction of anger-tension would be a fit of anger, the reduction of fear-tension would be fleeing, the reduction of sexual tension would be copulation. If the theory of tension-reduction is interpreted in this naturalistic sense, then Maslow's counterargument, according to which there is no reduction in love or in creativity, would be justified; the need is infinite, therefore insatiable.

But I do not interpret the concept of tension-reduction as one of the functions regulating feelings homeostatically, in the sense so rightly criticized by the third trend in American psychology. What is it that can be sensibly placed under the categories of "tension" and "reduction?" In order to preserve the homeostasis of the social organism a state of tension is a must; the need for this state of tension is not at all limited to the satisfaction of the needs, hence affects and drives, of the socially codetermined organism. The need for this state of tension becomes a general condition for our action and thinking, not to mention our interpersonal relations, our communications. Yet one cannot live in a state of constant tension; furthermore, tension directed at one activity, relation, or thought must at the same time dissolve, terminate, or force into the background the tension directed at the other action. Every specific state of tension must describe a "curve" until the tension becomes relaxed in order to be replaced—albeit only relatively speaking—by a state of lack of tension, or make room for the development of tension directed towards a different object (which in turn must dissolve). This "curve" of tension, without which the psycho/social homeostasis would become impossible (partly because the energy reserves of the organism would dry up and partly because activities or relations will not function simultaneously): this is what I place under the categories of tension and tension reduction.

Thus not only fear and fleeing, anger and fit of anger, desire and copulation can be placed under the categories of tension and tension reduction, but the following are also curves of tension—tension reduction: fear and self-discipline, anger and self-control, desire and disregard of desire. In these latter cases the state of tension likewise diminishes, and may disappear altogether. Furthermore, the feeling of reduction appears as well: for instance, the pleasure of having stood one's ground, the pleasure of having exercised self-control, or the pleasure of having avoided an unpleasant situation (compensation). Setting these examples aside, we may say that the attainment of any objective (together with the pleasure derived from it) results in reduction of tension. Thus: I passed my exams, I was able to collect the harvest before the rain set in, etc. The realization of desires also results in reduction of tension (together with the feeling of relief, of pleasure). Thus: my son has returned from the war, or, finally Christmas is here! etc.

Of course, all attainment of objectives or realization of desires (the dissolution of the state of excitement) brings about a renewed state of excitement or, at least, may bring it about. I passed my exam—next week I shall begin to prepare for the following examination. My son has returned from the war—where will he find a job? We cannot find a theory of tension reduction with such a narrowly homogenizing character that it can prevent the abovementioned phenomena from arising. I am hungry—I eat till sated—I become hungry again; after a while reduction is once again replaced by tension. But the essence of my theory of tension reduction, taken in a broad sense, is precisely that, with due regard to the generality of social homeostasis, the objective or object of the new tension may differ from the object and objective of the previous and reduced tension; or, if the object remains identical, then the tension and its reduction does not take place on the same level: the activity is not merely sustaining, but extending as well. The schoolboy in the second grade feels tension when he undertakes the solution of an assignment in multiplication; if he is successful the tension relaxes. The schoolboy in fifth grade feels the same tension while solving an equation; and although he has to carry out multiplication in the process, that operation does not fill him with tension, and the successful solution of the multiplication does not mean the relaxation of tension. Tension relaxes when he has successfully solved the equation. In this case the object was identical (i.e. a mathematical assignment), but the activity was "extending."

The tension curve has a fundamental significance in the case of those feelings which I will refer to, from here on, as actual emotions (situational-cognitive feelings) and, within this "family," as emotive dispositions or character-feeling. If we hate someone (I have a rather intense feeling in mind), this does not at all mean that we are "hating" every moment of our life, whatever we may be doing, thinking, or whoever else we may be dealing with, etc. Constant hating would signify a tension that would make impossible all other activities including those that have nothing to do with the hated person. "To hate someone," does not mean constant hating but rather that, should the object of our hatred be mentioned in our presence, should we meet with that person on some occasion, or whenever we make a sensible thought association leading to that person, then—but only then!—the state of excitement, the intense tension which signifies that we are negatively (directly, and intensely) involved in the person in question, does appear. It is possible that our hatred, in a rather intense case, is present in the background of our consciousness, as background-feeling, when involved in heterogeneous activity. If we are envious, the intense feeling of envy grips us when we hear of success achieved by someone who resembles us, or when we compare in thought our own situation, property, or achievements with those of others; but we cannot do this and do not do this constantly, simply because we are usually otherwise occupied. Unreduced feelings, as we know, upset the homeostasis: the mind of Lady Macbeth was unbalanced by a permanent bad conscience. The curve of tension-reduction is, in all cases, the self-regulation of feeling. Whether a concrete involvement achieves its end (object) or turns away from it, or turns towards it and away from it functions homeostatically: "it takes care" of the preservation and extension realized by means of heterogeneous activity-types of the social organism.

Beyond the aforementioned general regulation I must say a few words about the homeostatic function of feeling (involvement) in knowledge. 1. Involvement selects in all instances of perception. If we should disregard, for the time being, the biologically provided selection patterns, then we select (perceive) that in which we are positively or negatively, directly or indirectly involved, etc. If we were to select exclusively under the leadership of biological patterns, then what Gehlen calls *Reizüberflutung* would occur: the flood of stimuli selected purely biologically would render us incapable of living. Without involvement our consciousness would become "reflecting." But reflecting consciousness is non-human consciousness, non-functional consciousness. Reflecting consciousness—as we shall see further on—would become "satiated" with incredible speed, and the reflecting brain, if such a thing can at all be imagined, would be an idiot's brain.

2. An act of intelligence (cognitive thinking, problem-solving) cannot exist empirically, is theoretically impossible to imagine without involvement. Learning and feeling proceed in parallel fashion already in the animal world. In those cases where we encounter, even if only scattered, acts of intelligence in the animal world, we also find feelings. (Think of the Aha-experience of Köhler's apes!) The circumstance that acts of intelligence are fundamental in the case of man means that the regulation of feelings appears in a developed form.

At the beginning it is the world that provides the tasks for man. The more developed the Self, the more it gives tasks to the world (and, at the same time, to itself), and quite often, new tasks. Feeling as the regulator of our self-sustaining makes all problems solvable for us, all those problems that are a condition of our continued existence. But feeling, as the regulator of the "extension" of our Self, can also parry problems (those that are not among the conditions for the sustenance of our existence); furthermore, it can ask about the world, and does it every time and everywhere it is involved. The inquiry, or formulation of a question (towards others or towards myself) always stems from some feeling; it may be wondering, curiosity, or simply the feeling of "being intrigued by something" but in its highest form it is the thirst for knowledge: involvement in recognition itself, in the extension of the already-known for my own sake and for others. If we were not always involved in more than what is strictly necessary for the preservation of our life, then the child would not take his toy apart in order to see what is inside, then Abraham would not have discovered "his only true God," and Copernicus would not have ferreted out the secrets of the solar system.

The Self builds up "its own world" under the leadership of the objectifications of general social consciousness. Its own world may be narrow or broad (for a while during the process of growing up it widens rapidly, and later it may broaden more slowly, but at times also more quickly), but it is always a complete world. Yet this world also has many "blank spots": interconnections about which I know that I am not aware of them I know that I do not understand them, that I cannot build them into my own world. When I spoke of the regulative role of the feelings in ensuring the sustenance of the continuity of the Self, I also wanted to say: man is involved in that his own world should not fall apart. Therefore, the Self always presents and seeks the problems from "the point of view" of the blank spots—and here too there is intentionality. Naturally, the filling of the blank spots brings about further blank spots, and at the same time always modifies the structure of the relatively formed "own world." Let us say: a five year old child who sees a picture about the Second World War for the first time classifies the fascists among the "bad people." This fits into his "own world"; the so-called "bad people" already have a place in it. When he is six he reads a book in which a fascist, let us suppose, is very fond of his son. The child who reads the book falls prey to a "bad feeling": somehow "his world" does not "jibe." He has to "reduce" the bad feeling. This may happen in one of two ways. He may say, "the book is stupid," and the bad feeling disappears or fades into the background, and his "own world" remains unchanged. Or he may turn to his father and ask "how can this be?" "Why? Why?" (those whys that are so commonly and so wrongly put down by adults stem precisely from the feeling to extend his own world). The child receives an explanation that does not shatter the old world, but expands it, and he begins to make distinctions within the category of "bad people."

3. Last but not least, the homeostatic function of feeling is basic in the process of memory storage. There are various scientific hypotheses concerning the process of memory storage. It seems more than likely that short-term memory is an electronic process, whereas long-term memory is

a biochemical one; in the latter case storage takes place in the protein cells. The quantity of data that may be stored in long-term memory is quite large, but by no means infinite. John Griffith attempts to prove a relatively exact number of storable mental bits; according to the estimate of Steven Rose the quantity of data that may be stored in the brain is of the same order as the data contained in the *Encyclopedia Britannica.*

Now feeling not only selects that which is "important to us" in perception, but it also has a second system of selection. From among the perceptions stored in the short term memory it "rejects" that which is insignificant (that in which we are not involved) and transfers into long-term memory that in which we are involved. In the case of the lingual conceptual bits of information it is precisely this selective mechanism that plays a determining role; certain data are rapidly rejected (i.e. completely forgotten), others are stored. This is one of the most significant from amongst the homeostatic functions of feeling: to be able to forget is just as important as to remember. This function of selection may be spontaneous, but may also be more or less conscious. Such would be the case when, for instance, we let our eye "roam" over the page and then stop suddenly: this is important, we must make a note of it.

It is easy to see why this homeostatic function of feeling (rejecting-retaining) is so fundamental. I have said that the memory storage capacity of the brain is considerable, but not infinite. If it were not for the selection of that "which is essential for us" we would have to talk not only of *Reizüberflutung* but also of *Informationsüberflutung.* The memory storage place would simply become "satiated" incredibly fast with all kinds of data that are not needed from the point of view of the maintenance and extension of the Self. It seems probable, however, that this kind of memorization would also lead to the complete unbalance of the equilibrium of the organism. The child-prodigies of former times are well known: all of them have died young (almost in childhood).

Steven Rose has compared memory storage to a library, with stacks lined up in zigzag and with complicated storage labyrinths. The library, to build up the analogy further, contains non-conscious bits of information. There always is, however, a more or less extensive "reference section": that about which we know at a given moment. Sometimes the non-conscious becomes conscious by simply removing a book from the shelves and, by accident, finding another next to it (below it, above it). This is what we call "association." Making conscious the non-conscious, however (we look up the book and take it with us to the reference section in order to exchange it for something that has become superfluous), does not usually happen in this fashion. And this is where I wish to bring up the second, and no less important, function of involvement in connection with memory. The non-conscious gets rendered into conscious mostly by our becoming involved in it. If I face an assignment, if I wish to solve a problem or meet an old friend, then I "return" to the place where I had stored the memory and evoke it. This may seem a simple process (the memory "jumps in"), but it is sometimes very complex (in case of willful remembering). "I know," "I feel" that there is something in my library, but I cannot put my finger on it, or even on where I am to look for it. The very same mechanism operates here as in the case of will in general. I specify the goal: I want to recall, I concentrate upon it, I suspend all other activities and thoughts (we won't think of anything else!), and I select the means necessary for the operation; for instance, I consciously resort to association, "I go around the book" (when did I find out about it, under what circumstances, with whom was I at the time? And then, all of a sudden: that's it, I've got it!). Among the tools, another person may play a decisive role. What do you remember? Let's say: how does that poem begin? The other recites a short verse from it, I now recall the whole: I've got it![16]

All perception, thought, action, etc. is stored in our memory storage together with the specific involvement pertaining to it. We have pleasant and unpleasant, happy and sad, good and bad memories. If we evoke the concentration camp, if we recall an old face, the taste of grapes in our childhood, our former place of work, etc., we cannot do any of this without at the same time evoking all those feelings (whether they be positive or negative), which are associated with these memories. Naturally, the feelings stored in memory units may also be figure or background feelings.

The double role of involvement in the memory (in the selection process, or in the process of recollection) also explains the time-experience problem analyzed by Plessner. According to Plessner's appropriate observation what is new and significant seems short in the present, and long in the recollection. "The vacation has just begun, and it's already over!" we say, but if we recall our vacation, then we evoke so many moments, so many details, that this "brief" vacation becomes an entire world. On the other hand, repetition and activity that merely "maintains" seem very long in the present. During dull classes the last two minutes before the bell rings seem like infinity, we begin to believe that "they have forgotten" to ring the bell, we keep looking at the clock: "only half a minute has passed!" The more repetitive our work activity, the less does the work time "want" to come to an end. And in remembering? Dull classes, the work days passed in repetitive activities "shrivel up," scarcely anything remains from them except a "bad feeling" and "impression"—our recollections "run together." The relationship of the Self to the world—and along with it the Self's "own world"—changes. We become involved in things in which we were not involved earlier in life, and vice versa. This is the origin of the double characteristic of feeling in the evocation. We evoke the involvement that had been present during the event, but the person who evokes lives not in the past but in the present; he relates differently, or at least may relate differently, to the involvement evoked in the experience. At such times we say (feel): "How stupid I had been to cry so much, just because that impossible fellow did not love me!" or "It is absolutely amazing that I could really believe in that principle!" But it is also possible that the involvement contained in the recollection not only does not disappear or change, but becomes more powerful yet; in such cases the recollection receives a greater emotional weight during the evocation than at the time of its "storage." This too is a double relationship, even if we are not often conscious of it. (We recall the first meeting with our beloved, when we felt merely attraction towards that person: but in the recollection this feeling assumes the significance of "love at first sight." The poet recalls the first poem he had written in his childhood. The meaning of this experience: the calling, the finding of the form of self-expression becomes more intensive than it had been at the time of the "storage" of the experience. This same event is recalled by an engineer in the following manner: "I attempted to write verse in my childhood; I wrote bad poems, yet it caused me a lot of pleasure"—the Self of the present assumes a distance with regard to the experience of the past.)

The memory storage "library," I said, was unconscious (only the "reference section" is conscious). The unconscious, however, can be of two kinds (and this is one of Freud's great discoveries): it may be preconscious (*vorbewusst*) or unconscious in *sensu stricto* (*unbewusst*). The only point about which I deviate from the Freudian interpretation is that in my opinion, the pre-conscious plays a much more important role in memory storage than the unconscious, except for some of those who suffer from neurotic disturbances (and Freud started his analysis from them).

Freud's theory about *trauma*, both of *structural trauma* (like the Oedipal trauma) or the strictly *individual trauma* (like rape trauma), confirms whatever has been said about the strong relation between emotional involvement on the one hand, and memory storage on the other hand. A devastating traumatic episode of a person who finds himself entirely at mercy to an overwhelming and external power (like in an extermination camp), helpless, passive and in the state of fear for life, is the strongest emotional experience of victim-hood beyond the power of human understanding. It is precisely because of its devastating emotional and incomprehensible power, that such an experience will be repressed deep into the unconscious. This is why it cannot be erased from unconscious memory at all, this is why it appears only in neurotic trauma syndromes; this is why even relative healing depends on success in translating the unconscious memory into a conscious one which, as such, can be treated.

Yet, if we do not remember something, or if we don't want to remember something, if we "resist" the trace-back, this is no sufficient proof that one is dealing with an unconscious memory unit. It often happens that we do not remember conceptualized events of which we had grasped the meaning, because we are involved in not tracing them back. Such negative involvement is also a defence of the Self, but this defence is aimed at the preservation of a sham-continuity. Thus, while I scold others, I forget that I have committed the very thing for which I condemn them. If others should remind me of this, or should confront with the facts, I answer: "Not true, I have never done this, there must be a mistake!" and not because I want to lie, but because I really have forgotten. This type of "forgetting" becomes a moral problem. I will call inauthentic Self that Self which evokes the "beautiful" from its past but forgets the morally negative acts and thoughts. I repeat: the forgotten is not unconscious, but preconscious, and the individual is not suffering from neuroses, but morally incompetent. (The circumstance that moral incompetence may also cause neuroses is another matter.)

I had said: if we are involved in something then this guides us in memory storage; and we trace it back in accordance with our involvement. In the trace-back it is not only the involvement in a task, in a relationship, in a thought, etc., that may become our guide, but a specific feeling as well, a feeling we want to conceptualize, of which we want to grasp the meaning. We feel something. This feeling is not tied to some present involvement of ours. Does it derive from some memory perhaps? To find the feeling tied to the memory we seek the memory itself (its content, its meaning). Heine queried: "Ich weiss nicht, was soll es bedeuten, dass ich so traurig bin"—and his reply is "Ein Märchen aus uralten Zeiten, das kommt mir nicht aus dem Sinn."[17]

D. Motivation and Information, Expression and Communication

I find almost a consensus in psychological literature to the effect that feeling is not information, but motivation. Before we decide, however, to classify the phenomenon of "feeling" under the category of "motive," we must examine whether the category "motive" makes sense at all—from the psychological and anthropological points of view. What is the meaning of "motive?"

Kelley states correctly: "The construct of 'motive' has been traditionally used for two purposes: to account for the fact, that the person is active rather than inert, and also for the fact that he chooses to move in some direction rather than in others."[18] Let us pick, at random, certain definitions and explanations of motive. According to the theory of information (see Tomkins) feeling as motivation is nothing but the source of energy of the open self-regulating system. Newcomb defines it thus: "Der Prozess der Motivation ist . . . der Prozess der Selektion."[19] Maslow observes: "Most behavior is overdetermined or multi-motivated."[20] According to Ryle: if a man behaves selfishly in a given situation, then the motive of selfishness is the selfish character itself. According to Young, to ask about motive is to "search for the determinants (all the determinants) of human and animal activity."[21]

We can see at a glance that all these psychologists denote completely different things (events) by the concept of motive. The feeling-motive as source of energy simply excludes all the other definitions. If motive is a process of selection, then the explanation of "overmotivation" is just as irrelevant as the explanation of motive as energy. If motive is character, then to ask about all the determinants of an action is something completely different from asking about motive (inasmuch as motive is only one of its determinants). If motive were equal to the sum total of determinants, then its definition as selection, as energy, as character is all irrelevant, everyone of these would be too "narrow." Hence it is already obvious: the concept of motive is the joker in psychology—it can replace any card, and it is used to replace a different card by all concerned.

Assuming, but not allowing, that I accept the identification of feeling with motivation, which concept of motive would be operational from among the many contradictory ones? I could not accept Tomkin's theory; the "energy" simply operates the "machinery," but does not select. I find Newcomb's definition the most acceptable, but selection, in my opinion, is only one function of feeling, therefore it cannot be identical with it. In Maslow's definition motive is equated with the subjective determinants of a given action (and the number of these always exceeds that which is necessary for the action). But every subjective determinant—insofar as the term "determinant" has any meaning—contains feeling, it contains, however, not merely feeling. This concept, by the way, is the psychological version of an ancient philosophical problem, that of freedom versus determinism. (The "combat of motives" of Murray has a similar meaning.) Ryle describes this philosophical inquiry even more forcefully: in his concept motivation is equal to autonomy, with our actions being in accordance to our own nature. How can this be identified with "feeling?" Regarding Young's approach, I can bluntly say that it is the most non-sensical theory of motives. To ask about all the determinants may mean to ask about all specific determinants. Hence the idea of the state, Brussels sprouts, the rise of sugar in the blood, family, or vitamin D can all be motives (feeling). This approach may also mean: having brought the factors to a common denominator, to ask about the final—and abstract determinants. They are in the case of man (as the terminal point in the process of the regress of knowledge): on one hand the genetic code, on the other hand, environment. And what have we said by asserting that the genetic code and the environment are "motives"? Nothing. Let alone trying to identify these with the concept of "feeling!"

Therefore, wherever the definition of motive makes sense (and placing aside whether I am in agreement with it or not), issues of the type are "slid" behind the psychologico-anthropological approach that are heterogeneous, that are totally distinct. The question of "what motivates man," however, does not make sense. For man is never an inert being, his active character is part of his essence. To define the essence of man as "motive" would be a redundancy. If, on the other hand, we ask "what motivated him precisely in this or that" then—if we remain faithful to our psychological approach—we must really use the method of regression in order to answer: "and what motivated him in that it was just this or that that motivated him?" etc. And finally, we indeed reach, as Young had done, the genetic code and the environment. But this too is a redundancy. Kelley is justified in writing: "Within our system ... the term 'motivation' can appear only as a redundancy."[22]

Therefore the statement according to which feeling is a motive is unacceptable, since the concept "motive" is redundant and nonsensical in the psychological and anthropological sense. Yet the category of motive does make sense, and can become interpretable, but not in the psychological and anthropological respects. When we ask about motive then we always base our question on some point of view. The questioned entity may even be our own psyche, but the system of reference of the question is never psychological or anthropological.

1. We never ask: "What motivated this mother to raise her children?" We may ask: "What motivated her not to raise her children?" The point of view of our question is pragmatic, its system of reference is the prevailing system of habits. Thus we are asking about idiosyncratic factors regarding the departure from the mores. We are not asking about all the factors, only those which explain to us (make it possible to describe, to grasp) the action that constitutes a deviation from the mores, since we want to place the idiosyncratic action (behavior) in our own world.

2. In the case of irregular actions (in those deviating from the ruling pattern), our point of view is identical with our value-preferences, our system of reference is the system of valid values in general. If the action corresponds to our value-preferences, we do not ask about "motive," but about cause. If the action contradicts our value-preferences, then we ask about the motives. "He killed his wife, because she was unfaithful," they may say in Southern Italy. That she was unfaithful is not a motive, but a cause (this is how it would be explained). In a different environment, however, where the value-preferences are also different, where "unfaithfulness" is not a sufficient cause for someone to kill his wife, we would ask about the motive. "He killed his wife in a fit of jealousy"—the fit of jealousy being not a cause, but a motive. When it is a question not of irregular (deviating), but of habitual action, we do not even ask about the cause—thus, "what was the reason the mother raised her child?" makes as little sense as "What motivated the mother ..."

3. We ask about motive if the action of the person does not correspond to the image we have formed of his character. If a man known to be envious behaves accordingly, we would not be asking about the motive anymore. "He acts this way because he is envious" (cause-explanation). But if in some situation a man always known to be brave runs away unexpect-

edly, then we ask: "what happened to you?" "What took hold of you?"—in other words, we ask about the motive. Why? Because we want to understand his flight, and something is "missing" from our understanding, something that was not missing as long as the man known to be brave behaved bravely. The situation is the same in the case of non-action. What motivated someone not to act in a given situation? This question would make sense only if we had expected the action on the basis of our previous experience. It makes no sense to ask a man who is not inclined to grow angry: "Why didn't you smash the vase?"

4. Everything I have said so far also applies to the cases of introspection. When I return someone's greeting in the street, I do not ask myself what motivated me to do so, as long as I act according to my own values; nor do I question myself if I act according to the image I have formed of myself until now. But if I act, behave, think, or feel in a contrary way, then it all seems "irrational"; I search for the motive in order to better understand myself. "Why did I behave so stupidly?" "What struck me, that I became so angry?" etc.

5. From an ethical point of view, it always makes sense to ask about motive; and in these cases we speak of intention. We decide: is our contemplated act led by moral sense (*Gesinnung*) or by something else; that is, we decide whether the other person was led by moral or by some other intention in such and such an action. I may say: "X only raised her children that they may support her later on"; and although the action was customary, it still makes sense to ask about the motive (intention, sense) from a moral point of view.

6. It always makes sense to ask about motive from a juridical point of view. In such a case we are asking primarily about purposefulness. Somebody hit a man and the man died. Did that somebody want to kill him or not (was it first degree murder)?

7. We may also ascribe diverse motives to the same act—especially if we only know about the act, but not about the person, or very little about him. Our point of view is still evaluative, and actually we are not interested in the difference between the motives, but in their heterogeneity. Somebody stood up for a cause. We seek the "subjective factor." What was his motive? His love for the cause? Vanity? Lust for power? Or perhaps several of these? We do not seek for "motives in general," but for the heterogeneous and, at the same time, typical (possible) motives. For instance, we do not ask in the following manner: was it "friendliness?" Was it "directness?" Not even if the man about whose motives we ask is indeed friendly and direct; after all, these "subjective factors" are irrelevant from the point of view of our inquiries. This kind of seeking for motives has a basic significance from the point of view of knowledge of human character, and also from a pragmatic point of view, because thus it is possible to ascertain: can one trust him? Under what conditions can one trust him? What can I entrust him with? etc.

8. This same factor plays a decisive role in introspection. I ask myself: why did I do this or that? Insofar as I am certain that it was my values, my morals that have led me in my act, most of the time I do not ask the question; in such cases there is a cause for my behavior, not a motive. If I despise a man I judge to be despicable from every point of view according to my system of values, there is no seeking for motives: the cause of my contempt is the person, his—in my opinion—despicable self. But if I am unsure about my values or whether I have applied them correctly, then I undertake the process Bedford has called "detective work." Is this person really so despicable? Is it not because I envy him that I despise him so? Is it possible that I, who am not an envious kind of person, should feel envious? (Seeking the motives.) This "detective work" is very necessary because men—precisely for the sake of the preservation of the continuity of the Self for the sake of the maintenance of its pseudo-harmony—are inclined to rationalize, are inclined to elevate motives to the rank of cause. In spite of this, the "detective work" itself can become harmful from a homeostatic point of view: in such cases we are dealing with moral hysteria.

About all the cases enumerated it can be said: when I ask about motives I also ask about feelings (either as "figure" or as "background" ones). "Asking about" is also involvement (of the figure or of the background type). But we must stop here. It would make no sense to ask: what motivates me to ask about motives? This question would lead back into redundancy, everything I had lifted out of there. We are involved in the preservation and expansion of the Self; in the continuity of the Self, in knowledge of human character, in finding our way in the world, in arranging, understanding, ordering the facts of life, in ascribing meaning to actions. We are involved in our values, our habits, our objectifications. We are involved in the world and in our self: this is why we ask about motives, it is from this point of view that we ask about motives. But all this cannot be described by the category of "motive" in a reasonable way. Thus we have excluded from our analysis the identification of feeling and motive.

However, the thesis which we have rejected sounded as follows: feeling is not information but motivation. Let us now examine the first part of the statement: is it true that feeling is not information? What I intend to prove below is not at all that feeling equals information, but rather that feeling is also information.

Among the circumstances threatening the biological homeostasis of the Self, feeling signals precisely this threat. The feeling of hunger informs us that we need to eat, the feeling of tiredness that we need to rest. The feeling of physical pain, the feeling of "not feeling well" informs us that something is "out of order" in our system. It can easily be seen that without this informative function of feeling the Self would be unable to maintain its homeostasis.

In the case of the feelings which regulate the social preservation and extension of the Self, feeling always informs regarding the relationship of the Self to the object. If I am filled with pleasurable feelings when in the company of a certain person, then these feelings inform me that the person is important to me. It is again the specific nature of the feelings that enlighten us as to why he is important, and from what point of view is he important. If the feeling of pleasure is accompanied by the feeling of respect, of admiration, of erotic desire or if, perchance, all three of these should be present, we judge differently the importance-for-us of the person concerned. If we are excited or left cold by a problem, this feeling says something about its significance-for-us. Thus feeling does not inform us about the "nature" of the object, event, or person, but about the importance-for-us of that object, event or person. This information, however, is just as necessary from the point of view of the preservation and maintenance of the Self, as the information we gain directly about the "nature" of objects, events, people.

Let us examine, however, the problem of feeling-information from another aspect. What kinds of information may the feelings of one person provide for another person? "Being involved in something," that is, feeling, is not merely a subjective experience, but an expression as well. Feeling is expressed directly: in mimicry, in gestures, in phonics (e.g., ouch!), in inflexion, in types of reaction, in action (including abstention from action), in behavior in general. It is expressed indirectly through reports about feelings. We cannot sharply differentiate the direct from the indirect expression of feeling. If a mother, being delighted by her child, should smile spontaneously, this constitutes direct expression. If the child sits in the chair of the dentist, and she smiles at him reassuringly, this would constitute a rather indirect expression, and would mean approximately: I like you, I feel with you, don't be afraid! If the child, sitting in the same dentist's chair, cries out: ouch!—this would be direct expression. If he says: when you touch my upper tooth it hurts very much—this would be indirect expression. But when the man in love takes the hand of his beloved—who could then distinguish direct from indirect expression?

Not every type of feeling is equally prone to be expressive, especially not as far as direct expression is concerned. The different types of feeling are expressive in different ways, when it comes to mimicry, to inflexion, to action, etc. Thus drives can be least forcefully expressive in mimicry and in tone of voice, most forcefully in action. For instance, there is no "hungry tone of voice," but we need only see the way a starving man eats! In the case of cognitive feelings, the situation is just the reverse. If someone discusses a topic with conviction, this conviction is expressed first of all in the tone of the voice, furthermore in gestures and mimicry; and not in whether the person speaks rapidly or in measured tones, whether he stammers or not, whether he speaks while sitting or while walking! (Let us recall the Mynheer Peeperkorn portrayed by Thomas Mann.) In the case of instrumental action (manipulation), theoretically the feeling cannot even be expressed in action, because the object and the means "guide" the movements. But let us just glance at the face of a child engaged in solving some difficult technical problem! His eye is acutely "observant," his mouth is open—the child often licks his lips with his tongue—the facial muscles are taut: his face shows he is involved, and how intensely at that!

Direct expression of feeling is spontaneous; this, however, does not in the least mean that it is not learned, i.e., not learnable. Only the expression of affects is not acquired. As to why this is so, I shall explain later. Darwin has already analyzed (in his epoch-making work on animal and human expressions), that from the repression of certain expressions of feelings new expressions will arise. In other words if, in certain cultures, certain affects (i.e. their expression) are not allowed or at least not preferred, new feelings will be produced by relegating these affects into background, and the new feelings will be accompanied by new expressions of feeling. That is, the assimilation of rules, the process of learning, bring about a feeling and along with it the expression of feeling. I only want to add that it is not merely as a result of the repression of certain affects that new feelings and expressions are brought about. The differentiation of types of feeling, as we shall see, is related to the cognitive and situational differentiation (and this was why I had talked of reintegration earlier). Cognition and situational understanding—and of course, everything that is acquired—differentiates, together with the feelings, the expression of feeling. Otherwise the commonly known fact, that most expressions of feeling—again excepting the expression of affects!—differ according to societies, according to nations, what more, according to social class and strata, would not have occurred. This, however, is not in contradiction with the spontaneous nature of direct expression. Once we have acquired the feeling, we do not "separately" acquire the expression of it (only the actor practices expressions of feeling in front of a mirror), but rather it is expressed in our features without our awareness and our volition: it is expressed not only in our features, but also in our tone of voice, our gestures, etc. We even gesticulate during telephone conversations, without taking notice. But the extent of gesticulation, its intensity, and even the motions differ widely. (For instance, Italians are more inclined to gesticulate than Englishmen.)

The fact that expression is primarily spontaneous does not imply that it cannot be imitated. I add, however, that not all expression is equally imitable. Mimicry is most difficult to imitate. The imitation of mimicry (the expression of feeling without feeling) is usually not authentic, and what we are then dealing with is actually the grimace. True enough, there are people who have a "talent" for the imitation of mimicry; they will make good actors or clever hypocrites. The tone of voice is easier (yet not altogether easy) to imitate—but not the phonic! The gesture is easiest to imitate, although still not perfectly.

Of course, man may control the expressions of his feelings, and he does control them. Keeping one's feeling "to oneself" also means to control the expression of feeling. "Nakedness is uncomely, as well in mind as body," wrote Francis Bacon.[23] Control over the expressions of feeling does not signify that the face becomes expressionless, but rather that the given feeling is not expressed intensely or "clearly" in the face, it is not "written on the face." By so doing we do not conceal that we are feeling, we only conceal what it is we feel, and how intensely we feel it. There can be no face completely void of expression. If we say about a face that it is "expressionless," we mean that it expresses dullness, lack of sensitivity, stupidity.

We are least able to control the expression of our feelings in the case of so-called "emotional situations" (an intimate relationship, encountering an unfamiliar situation); furthermore, when our feelings are rather intensive. To quote Francis Bacon once again, good observer as he was: "A man's nature is best perceived in privateness, for there is no affection; in passion, for that putteth a man out of his precepts; and in a new case or experiment, for there custom leaveth him."[24]

Bacon stated the problem from the point of view of knowledge of character. And thus we return to our initial query: what kind of information does feeling communicate? As we have seen, all feeling is, more or less, directly or indirectly, expression. Yet all expression is at the same time information. The expression of feeling is always a signal which bears some significance. Not only must we learn the differentiation of expression of feeling; we must also learn their significance (as signs). We do not learn this on ourselves (in front of a mirror), but on the face, in the gestures, in the tone of voice, the reaction types, in the behavior of others. In order to be able to move in our social element we must acquire the "language" of feelings just as much as we acquire the language of concepts. What more: since the two languages presuppose one another, their acquisition also presupposes one another's. To provide a simple example: it is from the tone of voice that we know whether the request "come here" is an appeal or a command. As Wittgenstein wrote: we can say the same thing descriptively, exclamatorily, ironically, hintingly, familiarly, skeptically, or with conviction; the conceptual—lingual meaning is the same, but the meaning as a whole is not the same.

Expression of feeling is one of our principal sources of information regarding the other person. The eye is truly the mirror of the soul. I have said that expression of feeling varies according to society, to nation, to stratum. Because of this it is important to "learn over again" the new and different expressions of feeling when in a new and different environment. Unless we do this we cannot "move" in the new environment, we become lost, we become ridiculous. But the more developed the individuality, the more idiosyncratic moments we find in the expression of feeling. Not only must we learn the signs in general, but we must also learn the specific significance of the specific signs of individuals. He who learns to "read" the idiosyncratic signs quickly, he who solves the hieroglyphs of the unique individual and understands their significance, has a good knowledge of human character. (True enough: even in the understanding of the specific signs of the individual we are always guided, at least in the beginning, by the general meaning of the signs.)

The principal proof that expression of feeling has the value of information (a sign that has significance) is that we may use it to lie. The repression of the expression of feeling (especially if it is idiosyncratic!), furthermore its imitation (without feeling), is a lie just as much as any untrue statement. Further proof of the informative character of the expression of feeling is that we may make an error in its understanding: we may misunderstand an emotional sign much as we may misunderstand a thought.

Expression gives information not only about the other's character, his mood, and his relation to me, but also about his relation to the world in general. If two people should tell me: "the king has been beheaded," but one of them should say it happily, and the other tragically, then I know what is the opinion of the one and the other regarding monarchy, the use of violence, etc. If I should tell someone: the Picasso exhibit will open tomorrow, and he shrugs his shoulders, then I know he is not interested in the fine arts, and I am entitled at least to assume that he is indifferent towards arts in general. This one shrug of the shoulder elicits in me the feeling of "I know it already" just as if my partner in conversation had held a little lecture concerning the uselessness of fine arts.

Expression of feeling is information; but it is exclusively the expression of feeling that informs us as to the feelings of others. Signs of emotion have a significance; but our signs are explained by means of the guidance of general signs. All this can be formulated antinomically. The more developed the individuality, the more we experience it as an antinomy. Thus the antinomy is as follows:

1. We express our feelings and thus we communicate them.

2. Our feelings in their totality and in their concretion are uncommunicable. Wittgenstein formulated this antinomical experience as follows: a) "Consider tone of voice, inflexion, gestures, as essential parts of our experience, not as inessential accompaniments or mere means of communications."[25] b) "We are inclined to say that when we communicate a feeling to someone, something which we can never know happens at the other end. All that we can receive from him is again an expression."[26]

This antinomy formulates in specific terms the general antinomy we have met with earlier, while analyzing the *condition humaine*, with regard to human relations, to the possibility or impossibility of meeting between the I and the Other. Let us recall: with our own social organism we turn towards the world as an integrated system. This idiosyncratic system can "build in" the world of objects only starting from itself, never transcending the self. No matter how much the subject permeates the object, no matter how much it realizes its own self by assimilating the object through the process of selection, the subject remains always the subject, and the object remains the object. Our life is finite for the approximation of the infinite.

The Other is always object, too, it never is I; yet it is a subject-object to which we relate as to an acting subject; it is the "other Self." We know that the Other is just as much I as ourselves; we recognize ourselves in the Other—it is a mirror in which we contemplate ourselves. (Let us recall: we first "learn" the meaning of the expression of feeling, and only later do we apply them to ourselves.) There can be no alienation so thorough as which would afford to relate to the other person completely as to an object; nor can there be even a negative affect like that. (The sadist derives pleasure from treating the subject as an object—yet he remains conscious of his character as subject.)

Although we never consider the other subject as mere object (but always as subject-object), the antinomy mentioned above does not play a role in all interpersonal relations. In the purely pragmatic (or primarily pragmatic) personal relations—and our interpersonal relations are mostly of this nature—we do not experience any feeling of antinomy. Nobody is interested in what the streetcar conductor feels when he finds out that I have failed to purchase a fare, and if I feel shame, it is not because the controller is angry, but because I have trespassed against a norm, against rules of proper conduct, etc. If I go to an office to settle some business I am interested in whether the employee there finds me pleasant or not only if this may play a part in settling my problem. Insofar as I want the employee to understand my feelings I no longer have a functional relationship with him; the function merely creates a possibility for me to make myself understood by a "sensitive person." (In György Konrád's novel *The Case-Worker*, we can find the extensive formulation of both types of relationship—functional and non-functional—with the employee.)

The experience of the antinomy seizes us at the time we intend that the Other should understand our feelings in their concretion in all their complexity, what more: that he become involved in them. Moreover: that he become involved in them to the same degree as we are. The expectation of the Self, that the other should feel the same as I, and to the same degree as I, is always absurd and senseless. (Which does not mean that the expectation never arises.) Yet the British moral philosophers (Hutcheson and Smith to begin with) have already analyzed that this is not generally what people expect, but something totally different. The Self expects sympathy from the Other: a positive involvement in his own feelings. If my beloved returns my love, I do not expect my friend to feel the same as I, but rather that he sympathize with me—that he feel pleased that my love is returned. If I have a bad conscience, then I do not expect the Other to have a bad conscience as well, but rather that he should sympathize: that he should feel pained by my plight. Even in the case of homogeneous feelings it is absurd to expect complete identity in the feelings of two persons. The meaning of the phrase "do you love me the same way?" is "do you love me as strongly as I do?" Let us add that the oft-heard reply to this question: "Yes" makes actually no sense. (How can one know, that we love each other equally strongly?) The sensible reply would be, "I love you very much." In the case of homogeneous feelings (whether we are aware of it or not) it is never a matter of identity, but always of equivalence. If the feeling of the other is equivalent to mine then I should be satisfied.

I have already mentioned: how absurd and senseless it is to expect the Other to feel the same and to the same degree; yet this does not mean that the expectation never arises. If it does arise, then this too is a sign of something, this too has significance: the love of self. Only the person whose self-love exceeds his love to the Other in every regard can expect such a thing. Thus it is not an anthropological antinomy we are dealing with, but a negative human value. (This negative value may even increase to the point of hatred: the sick man can hate the healthy one, because the latter does not feel his physical suffering.)

From the antinomy of the human condition two real and inseparable problems derive, namely the ones formulated by Wittgenstein. One is: am I capable of communicating, of expressing what I feel adequately, am I capable of feeling "that's just it?" The other: can I interpret the "signs" of others in an adequate way? More precisely when I read the "signs" of the Other, do I understand their significance in an adequate manner? Can I actually know exactly what he feels? (Which is not the same thing as: do I feel exactly as he feels?)

Both questions, deemed realistic in the sense above, barely present themselves, or present themselves only peripherally in traditional societies. The greater the consensus about the signs of expression of feeling, the more "naturally" we may infer, mostly spontaneously, their significance from the signs. Thus, for instance, if a man should offer a lady a serenade, this is a sign that she is the "chosen of his heart"—this being the significance of the conventional sign. During the Renaissance—where a society guided by traditions was in the process of disintegration—one of the principal sources of comic and tragic conflicts was that people were beginning not to understand the significance of signs; these are interpreted traditionally, although their meaning is becoming individualized. The serenade offered by Don Juan is interpreted by the maid: "I am the chosen of his heart," although, in this case, the sign actually means: "I want you because you too are a woman" This is why the problem of knowledge of human character emerges with unheard—of intensity precisely in this age: suffice to mention the Shakespearean drama.

But the fact that there develops a modern individual and, along with it, the idiosyncratic meaning of expressions (of course, even here there can be no complete idiosyncrasy, and the idiosyncratic meaning only exceptionally collides with the general system of signs, and moves mostly within the boundaries of this system)—this fact does not necessarily provoke a painful experience of the antinomy. Those who behave according to the norms and customs of modern society are usually led by interest, and generally ascribe interest motives to the Other; to wit, they do not seek the specific "nature" of the feeling behind the sign, but the interest. Only with the denial of the interest motive does the need for the adequate communication of the concrete character of my feelings, does the need for the adequate interpretation of the Other's idiosyncratic signs actually arise. So it was in the case of Rousseau, Feuerbach, Kierkegaard, the young Lukács (first of all in the Esthetic of Heidelberg), and of Wittgenstein.

I have said: I deem the problem to be realistic. Yet I do not believe that the antinomy cannot be resolved, nor that it is necessarily tragic. True enough, the antinomy can never be resolved at one blow, but only consecutively. And it cannot be resolved completely: this would only become possible in an infinite progress, and we are finite beings. We can only express approximately what we feel; but we may try again and again, and we may approximate the feeling ever more closely. We never reach the state of "now I know it," "now I have expressed it accurately," if only because the personality itself is changing. Maybe tomorrow I will have to express something different from what I have expressed today, and tomorrow maybe the significance of the Other's signs will also be modified. This, however, is not tragic. Tragedy is something final. And if something can be continued we may not speak of tragedy.

Our need to express ourselves "completely," and to understand the Other "completely" is a positive value. That this need can never be "completely" satisfied, is not "our limitation." After all, we can never "completely" satisfy a single one of our qualitative (proper) human needs (thus the one directed at knowledge, at beauty, at free activity, etc.). The complete (total) satisfaction of our qualitative needs would terminate our being; would terminate our involvement in the extension of our Self. And is it "bad" to be human?

Thus feeling means to be involved in something. Feeling guides us in the preservation and extension of our Self. Our feelings are expressed: they give the main information as to what we actually are. A man without feeling cannot even be imagined. In one of his thought-experiments Wittgenstein supposed the existence of a culture in which there would be no expression of feeling (and thus no feeling). Such a culture could in no way be even analogous to ours:

> "For here life would run on differently. What interests us would not interest them. Here different concepts would no longer be unimaginable. In fact, this is the only way in which essentially different concepts are imaginable. We could not possibly make ourselves understood to them. Not even as we can do to a dog."[27]

Notes

1. This definition is close to Plessner's formulation: "Feeling is essentially the

relation of my self to something, "although not completely identical with it. See Plessner, Helmuth, *Lachen und Weiner* (Laughing and Crying) (Arnhem: Van Loghum Slaterns Uitgeversmaatschappij, 1941), 147. Wittgenstein, L. *Zettel.* G.E.M. Anscombe and G.H. von Wright, eds. Cambridge: Blackwell Publsihers,. 239.

2. Tomkins, Silvan. *Affect, Imagery, Consciousness* (New York: Springer, 1962), Vol. I., 122.

3. "Foreground and background is a basic phenomenon in all performances of the organism." Goldstein, Kurt. *Ausgewählte Schriften* (Selected Papers), (The Hague: Nijhoff, 1971), 142.

4. Merleau-Ponty, M. *The Structure of Behavior* (Boston: Beacon Press, 1963), 161.

5. Goldstein, 429.

6. Gehlen, Arnold. *Studien zur Anthropologie und Soziologie* (Studies in Anthropology and Sociology) (Luchterhand, 1964), 52.

7. In *Everyday Life*, I have differentiated within the concept of "species character proper" on one hand "the species objectivations being-in-themselves" (*an-sichseiende gattungsmässige Objektivationen*) from the "species objectivations being-for-themselves" (*für-sich-seiende gattungsmässige Objektivationen*). For the time being we do not need this differentiation.

8. I am loosely referring to the theory of Noam Chomsky here.

9. Rose, S. *The Conscious Brain* (London: Cox and Wyman Ltd., 1973), 153.

10. "Physical man is not a combination of thinking, speech, will, and feeling ... on the contrary, he is man thinking, speaking, feeling, having optical etc. experiences." Goldstein, 163.

11. As quoted in Arnold, Magda. *Emotion and Personality* (New York: Columbia University Press, 1960), 121.

12. Wittgenstein, 88f.

13. Maslow, Abraham H. *Motivation and Personality* (New York: Harper and Row, 1970), 96-97.

14. See my *Everyday Life* concerning the particularity or individuality of feelings. I will return further on to the analysis of the relationship between feelings and values.

15. "You, proud heart, you have chosen—you wanted to be happy, forever happy or forever miserable—and now you are miserable." (my translation)

16. We can easily see how appropriate Rose's library analogy is (in spite of being a model analogy), if we think about the successive nature of recollections. We recall a melody only from beginning to end, never in reverse!

17. "I know not what it means that I am so mournful. ... A legend from very old times, which does not leave my senses." (my translation)

18. Kelley George A. "Man's Construction of His Alternatives" *Assessment of Human Motives*, Gordon Lindsay, ed. (New York: Rinehart and Co., 1959), 50.

19. Newcomb Theodore M. *Sozialpsychologie* (Meisenheim: Anton Hain, 1959), 66.

20. Maslow, 55.

21. Young, P.T. *Motivation and Emotion* (New York: John Wiley and Sons, 1961), 24.

22. Kelley, 50.

23. Bacon, Francis. *Essays* (London: Macmillan, 1900), 13.

24. Bacon, 114.

25. Wittgenstein, L. "Preliminary Studies for the Philosophical Investigations" otherwise known as *The Blue and Brown Books* (New York: Harper and Row, 1965), 182.

26. Wittgenstein, 185. The 22 year-old György Lukács expressed this same experience in the following manner in a letter to his friend, Leo Popper: "On the other hand I know so well that I can know only that which happens from me to you, and not that which happens from you to me—that I am afraid."

27. L. Wittgenstein, *Zettel*, 69e–70e.

Chapter II.
The Classification of Feelings

Until now we have spoken of feelings "in general." People, however, have specific feelings. We must somehow systematize this heterogeneous variety of feelings; we must classify them into "types of feelings," and list individual feelings, insofar as possible, under the various "types."

I am aware of the difficulties and traps of classification. Each feeling (even the simplest one) is a syndrome composed of heterogeneous components. "Emotion words do not refer to things, in the sense that a table or even an atom is a thing, but rather to syndromes, in the sense that a disease is a syndrome."[1] When dealing with syndromes we emphasize one or several factors, necessarily neglecting others, for the purpose of ordering according to types. We must render the factor the basis of our classification which is essential from a certain point of view knowing full well that we are abstracting from the totality of the syndrome. In the classification of feelings the difficulties are even greater than in the typology of other syndromes. The types may be separated from one another only in theory, since they intertwine, fuse into one another, in every single, specific syndrome. Let us take a look at some of the traditional approaches to classification.

Linguistic analysis

Here the basis of classification is the colloquial, everyday language, the common language. I consider this kind of classification to be haphazard. There are few areas of human life (possibly not a single one), in which the word usage of the various vernaculars would be as divergent as precisely in the case of words denoting feelings. Where there is a colloquial distinction in one language, in another scientific terminology would be required to translate the distinction, while in one language there may be a concept for it, in another we may have to circumscribe it. Thus the distinction between the Hungarians words: *érzés* and *érzelem* does not exist in English or German (both are "feeling" or *Gefühl*). In German and Hungarian—unlike English—the feeling "I am afraid" is expressed with the word "*ich fürchte mich*," "*én félek*"—i.e., with verbal forms of the term fear. I have seen an analysis of the word "homesickness," which relates said feeling to illness—logically so, on the basis of the English term. But this same feeling is designated in German as *Heimweh* (thus relating it not to disease, but to pain), and in Hungarian as *honvágy* (relating it to desire). The connection that exists in German between *Leid* and *Leidenschaft*, and in Hungarian between *szenvedés* and *szenvedély*, does not exist in either French or English, although it did exist in the original Latin (*passio*). Only Hungarian differentiates between *szeretet* and *szerelem* (the nouns), but in the colloquial the distinction between "I love" and "I like" (in German, *ich liebe, ich habe gern*) does not exist.

The Differentiation between Simple and Compound Feelings

The basis of the differentiation has been laid by Wundt, but a section of those thinkers who in other respects are far removed from Wundt have also accepted his differentiation. This differentiation is rendered in English by the categories feeling and emotion. According to Wundt—simplifying him somewhat—feeling is a homogeneous affective element, whereas emotion is a combination of heterogeneous affective elements.

It is typical that those who have elaborated the above categories have applied the attributes "pleasant" or "unpleasant" exclusively to "simple feelings"; furthermore, they have endeavored to determine experimentally, in the case of simple feelings, the point at which the feeling is physically transformed from pleasant into unpleasant. A weak stimulus is pleasant, a strong stimulus unpleasant—so runs the argument. Naturally, in the case of most sensations there really does exist a physical boundary beyond which the stimulus elicits a negative feeling. (Which, of course, is not invariably "unpleasant"—deafening noise, or a sudden blinding light is "painful" rather than "unpleasant.") At the same time: no matter whether such a physical boundary exists or not, this boundary can be regarded as irrelevant from the point of view of the analysis of feelings. In a person's real life and real activities it is only in borderline situations that one is confronted with such stimulus because our senses usually manage to make the adjustment. What feeling is elicited in us de facto depends to a large extent on the context in which it emerges, and not on the stimulus itself. Loud rock music may sound very pleasant to someone who happens to listen to it, but unpleasant to someone who wants to have a conversation. The same may be said about "weak" stimuli. It is possible that under laboratory conditions caressing is always pleasant, but if someone is caressed by someone he abhors, then this same stimulus may become hateful or repulsive. The same may be said about the analysis of practically all the "simple feelings" mentioned by Beebe-Center.

More sophisticated than the purely laboratory distinction presented by Beebe-Center is the theory of Magda Arnold: she differentiates simple and compound feelings (feelings and emotions) by their relationship to the object. "Emotions are going out to some object while feelings merely indicate our reactions to a particular aspect of an object or a situation," she writes.[2] Yet the same Arnold classifies fear—in all its varieties—under emotions. But should we meet with a wolf in the forest, we would notice only one particular aspect of this circumstance, namely that it is dangerous for us; but if we were sitting in a lukewarm bath (this is one typical example of "feeling!") then we would no doubt enjoy not only the tepidity of the water—that is one aspect of the object— but rather the entire "situation."

The most questionable aspect of the differentiation feeling—emotion is the reductionism involved. Most of the advocates (but not all) of this differentiation consider complex feelings as merely a combination of simple ones. Thus Wundt argues as follows: "Wo sich dagegen eine zeitliche Folge von Gefühlen zu einem zusammenhangenden Verlaufe verbindet, der sich gegenüber den vorausgegangenen und den nachfolgenden Vorgängen als ein eigenartiges Ganzes aussondert, das im allgemeinen zugleich intensivere Wirkungen auf das Subjekt ausübt als ein einzelnes Gefühl, da nennen wir einen solchen Verlauf von Gefühlen einen Affekt."[3] (Wundt denotes as "affect" that which Beebe-Center and Arnold call emotion.) But this statement does not correspond to experiences. Successive feelings may be disunited from the before and from the after without there being a question of emotions (without there being anybody who would speak of one emotion). We wake up to a noise, we become frightened, we want to know what is causing the noise, we find a squealing cat, we are relieved, we sympathize with the animal, we laugh at ourselves for our fright, we go back to sleep. Let us suppose, however, that our example does not cover Wundt's conception, because we have here a combination of emotions (affects) rather than of simple feelings–in other words, what we have is a combination of combinations. Therefore let us look at the sequence step by step. The *Verlaufsform* began with fright; and indeed, Wundt considers "fright" an affect and not a "feeling." But in the case of fright where is the "series of feelings succeeding one another in time?" The fright is undoubtedly an unconditioned reflex, and yet a completely homogeneous feeling. Let us look further: "we want to know what caused the noise." This in itself is a combined feeling: anxiety (fear) and, simultaneously, deliberate overcoming anxiety, curiosity, etc. The only trouble is, the "combination" of these emotions in no way adds up to the feeling of "I want to know what caused the noise." If someone is sent out on an expedition, for instance, he may "combine" precisely the same "feelings" and still not feel the same; for the feeling cannot be separated from the situation and the cognition. The supposition that the combination of simple feelings "adds up to" the affect (or emotion), is analogous with the supposition that the superimposition of the colors of a painting will add tip to the painting itself.

Bedford and Ryle criticize this reductionism, but at the same time they insist on the fundamental character of "simple feelings." With them, simple feelings become differentiated from object sensations and become identical with "bodily sensations." According to these authors "bodily sensations" are "occurrences" (emotional occurrences); and the emotions proper are the cognitive—situational interpretations of these occurrences. What we de facto feel is always "aching" or "itching" or "qualm" or "pang" etc., but these same occurrences may be interpreted in a variety of ways according to the situation and the cognition. Thus aching, in the case of a game of cards lost, is vexation; if our beloved has a date with another man, it is jealousy. No doubt, this too is reductionism, although of a much higher order than with Wundt. It is reductionism because it disregards the fact that cognition is reintegrated into the feelings. That is to say, if we lose a game of cards, or our girlfriend has a date with someone else, then it is not a matter of feeling the same but interpreting it differently (using a different emotion concept to describe the situation), rather it is that we simply do not feel the same. True, I am not able to prove my assertion. I cannot justify it any other way than by referring to introspection and to the works of art. But Bedford and Ryle are just as incapable of proving their assertion—and introspection and the arts vote against them.[4]

It was Hume, in his *Treatise on Human Nature*, who formulated the most context and situation related theory of feelings. Contrary to his predecessors and successors alike, he has not started his inquiry with simple feelings, yet with relational and thereby concrete feelings, that is emotions. Although I had not followed Hume's procedure in this respect, his work corroborates my theory.

I consider Karl Leonhard's attempt at classification rather significant. His classification is as follows: sensual feelings, drives (drive—feelings, instinctual feelings, and associative feelings (the feelings that belong to this last category are always complex, whereas under the other three categories we find both simple and complex feelings). The point of view of the division: the anthropological function of feelings. I will adopt into my own classification the group called drives, and the one which Leonhard designated by the term "associative feelings." I will not adopt the category of "sensual feelings," not because this group makes no sense, but because my own anthropological ordering principle is not strictly functional. Nor will I adopt the category of "instinctual feelings," because I have theoretical objections against it. This "type" is Leonhard's weak point, for understanding it he collects completely heterogeneous feelings (for instance, the instinct of suckling with the pleasure of suckling, the instinct of possession with the pleasure of owning, the instinct of "felicitation" with the pleasure sharing happiness with others, the instinct of right with the feeling indignation, etc.). I will classify feelings from a philosophical point of view. I will progress, in my typology, from the feelings pertaining to bio-social reproduction to the feelings of purely social reproduction; from the feelings in which we have little liberty to those which insure or presuppose greater liberty and greater scope of activity; from less cognitive feelings to the cognitive ones; from those pertaining to the entire human race to those that are socially and individually idiosyncratic; from feelings that are value—indifferent by their essence to feelings that bear value (from the philosophical point of view it is indifferent whether the feelings are positive or negative). These feelings classed into a single type from this point of view constitute a family—to quote Wittgenstein—but there are no two feelings which can be placed under the same concept by all its particularities, by all its functions. Even the direction indicated above cannot and does not become unconditionally valid in every instance. But since all possible classification of feeling is conditional and imperfect, conscious of this I accept the risks involved in my typology.

My classification is as follows: drive feelings, affects, orientative feelings, emotions proper (cognitive situational feelings), character and personality feelings, emotional predispositions. This classification makes it necessary in many cases to bracket the homogenizing quality of emotion concepts. Thus, for instance, "fear" is a concept, but fear can also be an affect; fear can be an emotion, and fear can be a "character-feeling." If I am afraid of the bombings, fear is an affect; if "I fear that my party will be defeated in the elections," then fear becomes a cognitive-situational feeling (emotion); and, if fear is a general type of reaction—that is, I am a coward—then fear is a character or personality feeling.

The Drive Feelings

To speak of "pure" drives in the case of man would always be an abstraction. The drives not only become differentiated rather early during the process of growing up, but at the same time they became situation-specific and socially codetermined. The newborn is simply hungry. The infant and the small child become increasingly hungry for something: for that which their social environment offer them to quench their hunger.

This abstraction, however, does make sense. The social codeterminations built upon the drives do not abolish their character of drive feelings. No matter how much the drive may be combined with affects, with orientative feelings, or with emotions, their distinctive traits are maintained. Feelings built upon drives do have certain common characteristics which distinguish them for feelings that are not built upon drives. At the same time the drive itself can be abstracted from the social codeterminations built upon it; in so-called "borderline situations," the attempt to satisfy the drive may suspend all social codetermination—the shipwrecked on the verge of starvation frequently eat one another; they are no longer hungry for something, but rather for anything that is edible.

What are the approximately common traits of drives?

1. Drives are the signals of our organism; they signify that something is "out of order" in the organism, that the biological homeostasis is threatened. "The body employs a 'drive' only when it lacks the information necessary to maintain the body," writes Tomkins.[5]

2. These signals are addressed to the Self and not to others. This is probably why the drives are expressed neither in facial expression, nor in the modulation of voice, nor in gesture: they are feelings that have no communicative function. The meaning of the drive—as signal—is: "seek a solution!"

3. The drives are indispensable from the point of view of the biological preservation of the race. With the exception of the sexual drive they are also indispensable for the preservation of the individual organism. Hence there is no culture, and theoretically there can be no social prescription which would aim at the general repression of any of the drives. Even Christianity did not intend to repress the sexual drive; it merely designated the institutional framework (marriage, "the sacred institution"), within which—and within which alone—the satisfaction of the drive is permitted, what more, becomes an obligation. By the same token it intended to repress, to push into the background, the sexual affect.

4. The drives, or their intensity, are not diminished by habit. And they are not diminished in three ways. First, I do not get used to the presence of the drive: e.g., I cannot get used to feeling suffocated or being thirsty. (Whereas I can get used to melancholy or the feeling of mourning—not to mention getting used to positive feelings.) Second, I cannot get used to the drives not being satisfied: If I cannot take a rest, I will become increasingly tired. (But if a friend does not return my affection, then my friendship may die away just as it may increase.) Finally, I cannot get accustomed to the drive in relation to a single specific object. If I receive always the same dish, then the affect aimed at food (my appetite) may decrease, but not my drive; if I am hungry, I will eat it. In the concentration camps the same repulsive food was invariably desirable, because it diminished the torturing hunger.

5. The satisfaction of one drive may not replace the satisfaction of another; rather, one drive may not be repressed by another. In this case, there can be no projection, nor possibility of canalization. If I am tired, drinking water is of no use, my fatigue will not decrease. (But an erotic desire may be sublimated into love; anger may be canalized by the feeling and the gesture of pardon.) It is, of course, possible to repress drives temporarily, although different drives can be repressed to differing degrees; thus, if I drink a lot, the torturing feeling of hunger may be diminished for a while. Of course, such a thing is possible only within a very definite time space for sooner or later the biological homoeostasis will be upset. (On the other hand, the desire to humiliate someone may be once and for all and completely repressed by a feeling of solidarity or a feeling of duty.)

6. All drives are also the signals of a need; it is our need, therefore, to satisfy all drives.

7. How, under what circumstances, in what form, where, etc., do we satisfy the needs signaled by the drives—these factors are always socially determined: e.g. how and what should we eat or drink, how to rest and how to satisfy our sexual needs, our need for warmth or for coolness, where should we eliminate, etc. Even because of this our drives are socially codetermined—with the exception of borderline situations. The conditions and forms of the drive reduction are not simply prescribed by norms, but also by fixed systems of customs which often assume the form of rituals. Feeding is especially rich in such rituals: the common meals of the Spartans, the feasts of the Athenians or of the Middle Ages, the absorption of the body of Christ in the case of Christian

sacrifice or, even today, the family dinners on Thanksgiving Day, these have always been foci of the regulation of social existence (and have remained so to some extent to our day).

8. We know that the drives are the signals of the social organism, and that the drive reduction is a need. The need is always a social need; the need is not that we should eat, but that we eat this or that. The social need, however, is always related to some biological factor: the insurance of organic homoeostasis. Man produces for the insurance of the organic homoeostasis: every drive reduction is connected with production. In this regard, however, it is especially important that we may only speak here of a "family." The satisfaction of the hunger for food, the thirst for liquid, the "hunger" for heating has always played a fundamental role in all human production, moreover, every society produces in the first place for the satisfaction of drive needs of those types. Other drive feelings rather set the limits of production, so first of all fatigue. As well-known, it was the need for the appeasement of fatigue and the need for sleep in the extensive phase of capitalist industrialization that constituted an insurmountable barrier for the production of surplus value. According to certain more recent conceptions, such a limit will be set in human production by the hunger for air: beyond a certain limit pollution will make the hunger for air "unsatisfiable." In the case of other drives (for instance, the sexual drive) production does not play a greater role than with many feelings that are not drives. Although the "decoration" of the object of sexuality is as old as humanity itself, its significance in production is no greater than that of *aesthetic* production, shall we say, or of production for the sake of entertainment in general.

Affects, cognitive-situational feelings, and orientative feelings are built on drives; so it is with taste in dress and in food, preference as to lodging, or sexual affect (erotic feelings). This remains valid even though we may barely be conscious of it: for example, when we take a deep breath of fresh forest air. In practice, the drives cannot be separated from the heterogeneous feelings connected to them or built upon them. Gehlen writes: "... ist der Trieb des Hungers von dem Interesse, an dieser bestimmten Stelle nach Nahrung zu suchen, und von dem Bedürfnis, sich dahin zu begeben, im konkreten Erlebnis gar nich unterscheidbar, und daraus folgt, dass es eine objektive Grenze zwischen Antrieben und Interessen, Bedürfnissen und Gewohnheiten gar nicht gibt."[6] In a scientific approach, however, it is necessary to isolate, to abstract, in spite of the intertwining of various types of feelings. Thus, Tomkins is justified in reproaching Freud for not having distinguished between the sexual drive and the sexual affect. Freud ascribed the Oedipus complex to the repression of the sexual drive; whereas—where such a complex does exist—it is the consequence of the repression not of the drive, but of the affect. And this distinction is extremely important, inasmuch as it implies the entire complex of relations between the "natural" and the "social," and suggests widely divergent proposals regarding the interpretation of these relations.

The eight common characteristics listed for drives prove sufficiently that they belong to a single family, that their separation from other families is justified. All this, however, does not alter what I had emphasized many times, that every specific drive is a particular syndrome, and there are no two drives which would satisfy each of the criteria listed above to the same extent and in the same manner. For instance, in the case of the elimination drive the social codetermination relates almost exclusively to the circumstances surrounding the satisfaction; affects may build around it (as Freud has shown, in the case of anal eroticism), but not necessarily. On the other hand, in the case of the sexual drive or the hunger drive it is of decisive importance that some of their potential objects are excluded, others preferred (the incest taboo develops along with societality proper), which means that the drive functions only along with the affect. This conversion into an affect regulates even the manifestation of the feeling (for instance, the periodicity of the sexual drive that is characteristic of the animal world vanishes, and the feeling of hunger becomes relatively independent of the emptying of the stomach). In the case of hunger for air, however, we can hardly speak of feeling becoming independent of the state of the organism. In the case of the hunger drive we are able to intentionally regulate, and to a considerable extent, the timing of its satisfaction; in the case of thirst our scope of potentiality becomes more restricted, and even more so in the case of sleepiness.

Although not a member of the family of drives, the feeling of bodily pain is nevertheless closely related to them. If we were to start from a linguistic analysis, we would be obliged to place all "pains" into a single family. Yet the concept "pain" is very heterogeneous: it comprises feelings that are basically different as to their content as well as their function. There is but a single thing in common between having a pain in the stomach, and that "it is painful that I have committed that mistake": namely, both are "bad feelings." Under bad feeling, however, we may fit a number of other feelings that are not designated by the category "pain." (For example, the feeling "I am sad that I made a mistake" is closer to "it is painful that I have committed a mistake," than the latter is to stomach pain.)

Wittgenstein saw the difference in status between bodily pain and so-called "mental pain." According to him, bodily pain is a separate category of feelings: a transition between perception and emotion. I have said that bodily pain is a relative of the drives. What justifies such a grouping?

1. Bodily pain is also a signal for the organism, and once again the signal means that something is "out of order" in the organism. Intense bodily pain means that the homoeostasis is about to be upset.

2. The signals of bodily pain are also addressed primarily to the Self: "seek the solution!"

3. The feeling of bodily pain is also indispensable from the point of view of the preservation of the species and of the individual. Those individuals born without the capacity to feel pain can only be saved from death by close and constant medical supervision.

4. Pain is not diminished by habit. At the most we may be able to work out the means for making it bearable but, within the biological limits, this situation applies to the drives as well.

5. The feeling of pain can likewise not be stopped by a heterogeneous involvement. It cannot be sublimated or canalized. The heterogeneous involvement, or even a stress situation, may force pain into the background, but only temporarily. An orgasm will not stop the toothache, at the most we will not feel it for a few minutes.

6. We also produce for the cessation (or reduction) of pain. There is no primitive society which ignores medicine.

7. The feeling of pain (and the feelings of sickness, of illness which belong to the same family) likewise bring about everywhere the system of customs for its regulation (i.e., for the regulation of its reduction). A network of collective images (*Kollektivvorstellungen*), or magical and religious rituals are connected with the feeling of pain just as in the case of the hunger drive or the sexual drive (i.e., their reduction).

After this we may well ask: why do I not classify the feeling of pain in the same family with drives, why is it just a matter of "parentage?" And the question becomes all the more justified if we consider that there are "transitional" feelings among them: thus hunger for air (which I have listed among the drives) could also be classified among feelings of pain (or sickness). If we disregard this transitional feeling, however, then I can state clearly the differences which justify ascribing these feelings a merely "parental" relationship.

1. The feeling of pain (unlike drives) is expressive: it is expressed in phonics, in facial expression, in modulation of voice. Hence the "signals" of bodily pain are communicative. The signal not only means "seek the solution!" but also "help me!" The expressions of bodily pain are in part identical with those of mental pain (for instance, moaning). The partial identity of expressions may be the reason (or one of the reasons) why bodily as well as mental pain are referred to as "pain."

2. Bodily pain is not satisfied, but ceases. Satisfaction always means active enjoyment (such as feeling sated, drinking, the sexual act, resting, etc.), whereas the cessation of pain is simply the non-existence of feeling, hence a relief. This also applies to hunger for air: when the drowning man finally manages to reach shore, he does not enjoy, he feels relieved.

If we never felt the sexual drive, we are not familiar with orgasm either. But not knowing bodily pain does not deprive us of any form of enjoyment. The commonplace observation that there is no pleasure without pain is undoubtedly true in the case of mental pain, but not in that of bodily pain. Who would argue that a familiarity with headache or toothache is a condition of happiness?

The Affects

That I should call the family of feelings analyzed below "affects" is merely a matter of terminology. I might have called them emotions, and I might have called the feelings listed under "emotions" affects. I have chosen the designation arbitrarily, or rather I am adopting the designation of Tomkins. The name is therefore indifferent per se. What is basic, is that we are indeed dealing with a separate and very significant family of feelings.

In spite of the fact that I have accepted Tomkins' terminology in this instance, I am not convinced by his statement according to which "the drive signal must be amplified by the affect system before it has sufficient motivational power"[7]—nor am I convinced that this affective amplification takes place by means of the "activating system" of the *formatio reticularis*. If this were true then an affect would build upon every drive, and the signals of these drives could never become conscious without the affects. But not every drive constitutes the foundation for an affect (or at least not necessarily); nevertheless, the drives can carry out their function successfully. At the same time there exists a number of affects which are not built upon drives at all. The function of affects differs from the function of drives. (That some drives are indeed amplified by affects—for instance, hunger by appetite—is true, of course, but this does not constitute sufficient grounds for the aforementioned generalization.)

The theory of Gehlen and of Claessens regarding the origins and function of affects is much more convincing. According to this theory affects, much like drive-feelings, result from the "instinct demolition" (*Instinktabbau*), only in a different regard. Drives are the result of the demolition of animal instinct reactions to inner stimuli, whereas affects are the result of the demolition of instinct reactions to outer stimuli. While the drive feeling originates in the demolition of the series of instinct reactions: inner stimulus—appetitive behavior—consummatory actions, the source of the affect is the series: trigger stimulus-instinctual action (*auslösender Reiz-Instinkthandlung*) which, in the case of man, proceeds as follows: trigger stimulus—feeling impact—expression (auslösender *Reiz—Gefühlstoss—Ausdruck*)—the expressions "müssen nämlich aufgefasst werden als nicht praktische (in der Aussenwelt nichts verändernde) Abfuhrwege von Gefühlstossen ..."[8]

The basis of this conception has been laid by Darwin. According to him every expression of affect is the "remnant" of an instinctual act. The expression of rage, for instance, is the "remnant" of the seizure of the prey. Hence its characteristics: bared teeth, urge to strike, trembling, etc. Disgust is the expressive "remnant" of the instinctual vomiting reaction; the vomiting, the expectoration "appears" in the features without the actual occurrence of the instinctual reaction.

And indeed: in the case of every affect there is a "trigger stimulus," whereas it is not at all necessarily so in the case of drive feelings. My stomach may ache without any outer stimulus, but I can feel disgust only in the presence of an outer stimulus. I may feel hunger regardless of whether I see food, but appetite is elicited by the presence of food. I may have a hunger for activity without any possibility for activity (in fact, only at that time!), but I can be curious only if something provokes my curiosity.

I have said: affects are not built upon every drive. But in our emotional life the drives that play the most important role are those upon which affects and even emotions more complex than affects, are built. Thus with the sexual drive, hunger for activity and, although in smaller measure, hunger for food.

The affects play a decisive role (in the case of man) not primarily in biological, but in the psychological/social homoeostasis. Better said: there are affects the homeostatic function of which was most significant at the time of the formation of the human species; that is, during the development of the social homoeostasis—as rage, for instance. Today rage no longer has such function of social homoeostasis, and that is why every culture seeks to repress it, or at least to corral it in some respect.

What are the most characteristic common—family—traits of affects?

1. The concrete presence of the trigger stimulus (*auslösender Reiz*). When the trigger stimulus is not concretely present—for instance when we evoke it in our fantasies—the affect is not "pure," but is connected with cognitive-situational emotions; so it happens when I recall a shameful situation, or when I recall somebody who has provoked my rage. From this point of view, however, the status of the affects built upon drives, as for instance appetite or sexual desire, is relatively different. Precisely because of their drive foundation they can be evoked in fantasy without their assuming the character of emotions: thus when I look at an erotic picture, or think of my favorite food.

2. All affects are expressive: in facial expression, in phonics, in modulation of voice, in gesture. In the case of strong affects the whole body becomes expressive. This indicates that the affects, without exception, are communicative. The expression of affects are signals for the Other; and they are signals the significance of which can be interpreted without further clues.

3. Affects are part of sociality. All affects without exception pertain to the human species in general, and are not idiosyncratic either socially or individually. There is no culture which would not know the expression of fear (and fear itself), expression of shame (and shame), expression of rage (and rage), expression of disgust (and disgust), expression of curiosity (and curiosity), expression of gaiety and sadness (and the feeling of gaiety and sadness, laughing, crying), etc. Such was already Darwin's assumption, and this was why he sent questionnaires regarding expression to missionaries stationed around the world, who eventually verified his hypothesis. Since then this hypothesis has undoubtedly been confirmed.

I must add that the expression of affects may be modified (idiosyncratically) in spite of the universal character of affects (and of the expression of affects). These modifications, however, are the consequence of secondary emotions, of cognitive—situational emotions built upon affects. This was also known to Darwin. If we intentionally repress our rage, we no longer have a "pure" expression of rage—the expression changes. The social prescriptions pertaining to affects, furthermore individual decisions and preferences, may diminish the intensity of expression, and the habit or practice of repressing expression may go quite far. Today it is only on the face of small children that we may find "pure" expressions of affects.

It is easy to realize the universal human quality of affects. We recognize the expression of affects without hesitation on the faces of individuals of any nation or race even if we know nothing of their values, customs, or modes of thinking. Children's drawings—with mouths curbed upwards or downwards—are "evidence" to any person: the corners of the mouth turned upwards means "happy" the mouths turned downwards means "sad."

At the same time, we recognize without any hesitation the expression of affect, even if we have no notion of the situation. If we are shown a face full of fear, it is not necessary to see next to it the axe about to drop, or the beast snarling in front of it, in order to realize: this man is afraid. If we see a face full of disgust I need not see what repels that person: I know he is disgusted. Whereas it is not at all so in the case of non-affective (emotional) expressions. There is no photograph that would show that the person on it is in love. If a man and a woman smile at each other on a wedding picture we say: they are in love with each other. It is the situation (the cognition) that gives the clue to our understanding. If we take the child out of the arms of Mary, then we "take away from her face the motherly love," the tenderness. No use referring to portraits to prove the contrary: for portraits always express a complex of character feelings (respectively personality feelings): we never find an unambiguous expression of the portrayed person—and thus the expression can always be interpreted in different ways, through the filter of the cognitive-situational emotions of the recipient.

4. Expressions of affects are not acquired; and I may add, only expressions of affects are not acquired. Already Darwin spoke of a girl who was blind and deaf-mute, yet had the same expressions of fear, rage or gaiety, as anyone else. Hence the expressions of affects are spontaneous. There are moments which cannot be elicited intentionally, for instance paling or blushing. This is why we often feel that the expressions of affects "break upon us," as if they were compulsory actions. Of course, even these expressions can be "imitated," manipulated. (For instance, Richard III manipulates fits of rage.) But this kind of manipulation is seldom really successful, and the person must be an excellent actor if we do not see through him. Emotional expressions, precisely because of their idiosyncratic nature, can be manipulated much more easily and successfully.

5. The object of affects (that provokes the affect) is not specific except for affects built upon drives. We may be afraid, or feel rage, or be disgusted by the most diverse objects, events, people, etc. (On the other hand, we can only be hungry for food, we can only be thirsty for drink, etc.)

In the case of affects built upon drives the affect narrows down the object of the drive, within the specific nature of the object. My appetite is directed not at food in general, but at good, savory food; my sexual affect is directed at an individual that strikes one as particularly desirable (and not at the other sex in general).

6. Whereas in the case of drives we never seek tension, the tension in the affects may be sought after. What in antiquity has been called "a life directed at pleasures," was essentially a mode of life developed from the affective tensions built upon sexual and feeding drives (and the satisfaction of these drives). The so-called "life of danger" is built upon the search or provocation of the tension of the fear affect.

7. Unlike drives, affects are diminished, or at least may be diminished, by habit. Sexual affect directed at the same object diminishes with habit, unless it is paired with emotions of a higher order. The medical student who is disgusted at the first dissection gets accustomed to the sight of corpses later, and the affect dies away. (Similarly with fear, rage, curiosity, etc.)

8. It is possible to intentionally diminish the affect by turning away from its object.

9. The affect—as Gehlen has fittingly stated—is always connected with fantasy. The satisfaction of the affect is at the same time fantasy satisfaction.

10. One affect may repress another; and in this affects, unlike drive feelings, are similar to emotions. Rage or curiosity may repress fear, shame may repress the sexual affect, and vice-versa.

11. One of the objects of the affect may repress the other, affects can be sublimated and channeled.

Affects are regulated primarily not by a system of customs, but by norms (ethical norms). Thus Aristotle defined the brave person as: he who is afraid when he should, that from which he should, in the manner in which he should, in the place where he should. (It would make no sense to say that a person should feel thirsty when and where, etc., he should.) Sublimation and channeling become significant precisely because of the normative regulation (in other words, normative regulation becomes possible because affects can be sublimated and channeled); furthermore, we are speaking of feelings that can be decreased intentionally, or stopped through practice. If a person is afraid of something (at a time, in the manner, etc.) he is not supposed to be afraid of according to the accepted norms, then he can either repress his fear with the help of other affects or emotions, or he can sublimate and channel them; he comes up with a situation in which fear is permissible, and then he feels fear. Often the stimulus eliciting the affect does not even become conscious. The only conscious stimulus is the one we have found for the sake of the affect, and in relation to which we can sublimate or channel the affect. In the case of an affect directed at the forbidden sexual object (as we have been told by Freud) we indeed have to deal mostly with such a process of sublimation.

12. Affects are contagious. Certain theories posit all feelings as contagious; this, however, does not correspond to the facts. How could the drive of hunger become contagious in a situation where one man is starving and the other sated? Appetite, however, can become contagious. But emotions of a higher order are

likewise not contagious: neither contempt nor *aesthetic* enjoyment can be caught. Fear is undoubtedly contagious, and so is rage, curiosity, disgust and, though to a lesser extent, shame as well. The demagogues play upon the affects in order to provoke a contagion. Contagion is likewise "played up" in orgies (the sexual affect of another person is itself a stimulus which arouses mine; but the other person's love feeling is not).

Contagion is the most dangerous property of the affects. Affects *en masse* (homogeneous affects) may force into the background within a matter of seconds the norms regulating these affects, even in the case of persons in whom these norms were strong: thus with lynching, or in the case of panic. Of course, danger is the corollary of specific affects. The affects of disgust or of curiosity are no less contagious, but less dangerous than the affect of rage or of fear.

13. Affects are not inevitably needs, and in this they resemble emotions. Thus the pure affect of rage, or fear, is certainly not a need; hence all cultures attempt to repress them in part, or at least to channel them normatively. Moreover, we do not necessarily produce for the affects (we necessarily produce only for the affects that are built upon drives). It would be absurd to produce for disgust!

Until this point we have delimited affects "downwards," that is by contrasting them with drives. In the following I will delimit them "upwards," by contrasting them in some respects with the emotions to be discussed later.

The following factors definitely separate affects from cognitive-situational feelings (emotions): My own person cannot become the object of my affect; insofar as I am afraid of myself, or angry at myself, or feel ashamed in front of myself, or feel disgust towards myself, these are not affects, but cognitive emotions. In such cases the expressions characteristic of affects are lacking: I do not blush, I do not become pale, I do not lower my eyes, the expression of so-called "physical" disgust does not appear on my face.

The affect in itself does not express my personality. The person who flees in panic from a fire, because of contagion, is not necessarily a coward. If someone is scolded in public and then feels shame, we still know nothing about his moral makeup (it is possible that he does not even have a bad conscience, and next time he may repeat the action for which he had been scolded, if he can get away with it).

The affect is not "binding" in itself. Only the action which derives from it is "binding," if indeed there is an action. A person cannot be held responsible for becoming angry, he can only be held responsible if he reacts to it with an aggressive act or behavior. Emotions, however, contain the "binding" element in themselves, even if no act ensues. We are responsible for our emotions. In Balzac's short story "The Red Inn," both young heroes think of killing the rich traveler out of lust for money. One of them carries out his thought, the other does not. But the one who did not act may also have a bad conscience, because even the mere desire to commit murder for money is "binding."

The affects, characteristics of all humanity, were born with us to the same extent (to a greater or lesser extent—i.e., with a greater or lesser "tendency") as the drives. On the other hand, all the emotions are learnt; their only organic or physiological basis is to be found in the drive feelings or the affects.[9] Let us now analyze some affects: some that are built on drives, and some that are not built on drives.

The Sexual Affect

When speaking about drives, I said that we are dealing in abstractions. This is particularly true about the sexual drive. For with human beings, the sexual drive does not exist in a pure form. The emergence of societality means *ipso facto* that we exclude certain sexual objects from the objects socially allowed for sexual desire. Human sexuality is constituted as sexual affect from the start. Yet it is clear that, in its genesis, this affect did develop from the sexual drive, and was built upon the drive: the sexual affect, like all affects built upon drives, is less universally expressive and also less totally expressive than the original affects (i.e., those that are not built upon drives). Thus it is not possible to identify unconditionally the phonic expressions, the facial expressions, the gestures belonging to the sexual affect. The expressions result from the building in of more idiosyncratic, higher orientative feelings (taste), or emotions, unlike the expressions that belong primarily to the affect, as with rage, fear, or shame. We know how many primitive cultures do not know about kissing, and even many coital positions are quite idiosyncratic. As I have said, the same applies to all affects built upon drives. In the case of curiosity as well, it is only the observing attitude of the face that is expressive (the inquiring face is already idiosyncratic); similarly with appetite (we lick the corner of our lips, we smack our tongue, etc.). Nowhere do we find an expression that is totally and universally identifiable.

But sexual affect not only cannot be delimited "downwards" unequivocally, it cannot be delimited upwards either. Production for the satisfaction of the sexual drive as a need is at the same time production for the satisfaction of the affect, but this production is not limited to the affect. Production aimed at sexual attraction always contains at least the rudiments of *aesthetic* taste. Furthermore: the emotion of attraction is usually connected with the sexual affect. Linton draws our attention to the fact that even in primitive societies where marriages are arranged, attraction that is not merely sexual is taken into account. Not to mention contacts before marriage where it is mainly these personal attractions that play a dominant role. As for love (which is also built on the sexual affect), according to Rousseau's witty observation, it is the very antithesis of the sexual drive, because it excludes all objects of sexual desire but one.

The Affect of Fear

We must distinguish between the startling reflex and the fear affect; for the trinity stimulus—feeling impact—expression which is typical of all affects is not typical of startling—the moment of feeling impact (*Gefühlstoss*) is lacking. The startling reflex may, of course, initiate such a feeling impact, but this appears after the fright—expression, and is a sign of fear provoked by fright. It is equally possible; however, that it will not elicit a feeling impact and the concomitant feeling of fear. Thus, if a friend of mine suddenly covers my eyes with his palms in the street, I become frightened (I react with the startling-reflex), but at the same time I hear and identify his voice. Hence the startling reflex does not belong to the "family" of affects, but is nevertheless related to them. The basis of the relationship is that the startling reflex is expressive, and furthermore, this expression is universal (typical of all humanity); moreover, the expression may be repressed (even if only in part), and then it is no longer the entire body that is expressive: but the eye reflex remains in any case, and it cannot be intentionally stopped.

Fear is one of our most expressive affects; the expression of the feeling is characteristic of the species in general, but what elicits the feeling (the stimulus!) is always socially given. The formation of fear has two sources: a) personal experience (I have been stung by a bee—I am afraid of the bee); b) social experience acquired through communication—if we know it is dangerous to fall out of a high window we are afraid even though we had never tried it. Prior knowledge (the communication of the social experience) has a much greater role in the case of the fear affect then in any other case.

The affect of fear (like all affects) is provoked by the stimulus that is present. Fear directed at the future, or at the past, is not an affect, but an emotion (and has no expression of affect). Of course, the emotion of fear may suddenly turn into the affect of fear (for instance when something we were afraid of in the distant future suddenly comes to pass), but it is not necessarily so at all. A feeling that can be formulated as follows: "I am afraid that my son's marriage will not work out," could never become a fear affect.

Fear affect may be provoked not only by an object known to be dangerous (for instance a murderous weapon aimed at the person), but also by an unknown object (in general, an unknown stimulus also), precisely because we are unable to place it cognitively, because we are unable to identify it. We are afraid of it, because we do not know that it is not dangerous, therefore it may be dangerous. The same trigger stimulus may arouse fear or may not arouse fear, depending on whether we know or don't know what it means to us. Thus, should I hear a knock on the door at midnight. ... If I await my beloved I feel happy, he has arrived! If I am not expecting anyone, then I am seized with fear: who can it be? A stranger. I keep feeling fear until I can identify him, until I know whether he is dangerous or not. With the non-affective fear this cannot happen, I always know of what it is that I am afraid.

Here we must deal with a peculiar type of fear, anxiety. Anxiety is undoubtedly characterized by the fact that I do not know what it is I actually fear, that the specific meaning of fear is not clear to me. Is anxiety an affect? Can it be classified under the category of the fear affect?

In general anxiety is defined as a fear without object. But if this fear is without object, if it does not have a trigger stimulus, a stimulus present, then theoretically it does not satisfy the criteria of the family I have designated as the category of affects.

Before proceeding along these lines, let me state in parenthesis: in patients suffering from anxiety visceral-endocrinological signs characteristic of fear, for instance, the increased production of adrenalin, have been found. This makes it probable that we are dealing with an affective phenomenon. Now let us take a look: is it true that anxiety is fear without object? In one sense it surely is: one does not feel anxiety because of a knock on the door, a wolf, a weapon, etc. Anxiety is continuous; tension is not provoked by a stimulus or by an object. Nevertheless, I derive a conclusion that is the opposite of the one usually derived: namely, that anxiety does have an object. Moreover, what is characteristic of anxiety is precisely that everything, or at least many things, can become its object. An anxious person is the person who does not see clearly the meaning of the majority of stimuli, and therefore experiences as dangerous those stimuli (and their multitude), which are not experienced as dangerous by others. A person is anxious if the majority of signs—or at least a considerable number of them—are "unknown," "alien" and he does not know if they are dangerous or not. It is not true that the anxious person is afraid of the Nothing; the anxious person is the one who is afraid of Everything.

I believe it is easy to conceive all this if we begin with temporary anxieties. Everyone is anxious in a completely unknown environment (because he does not understand, does not know, what is dangerous and what is not): country children feel anxiety when visiting a big city alone, for the first time, and every city boy feels the same if he goes alone into the dark forest for the first time. The hypochondriac is also anxious—not because his anxiety has no object, but because everything becomes his object (every sore throat, headache, or stomachache equals cancer).

If it were not so, the correlation of anxiety with certain social conditions would not be comprehensible. If anxiety were the fear of nothing, if it had no object, then why would anxiety become more general under certain social conditions? If we disregard the primitive cultures basically dependent on natural factors, then we can say that the more obfuscated the social relations in a given era, the more difficult it is to know what is dangerous and what is not, the more the individual feels himself threatened by social forces functioning independently of his selection and decision, the more frequent and general anxiety becomes: because the greater the number of objects—i.e., stimuli—that can become dangerous, and can provoke in us the feeling of anxiety. It is no accident, therefore, that the problem of anxiety first received a philosophical formulation in Kierkegaard, and that it became general almost to the point of triteness in the twentieth century.

It is because of these factors that I classify anxiety essentially in the group of affects, not as a separate affect, but as a variety of fear.

The Affect of Shame

Shame is the social affect par excellence; the affect derived from our relationship to social prescriptions—we feel that we have departed from these prescriptions. Its expressions are blushing, lowered eyes, head turned aside or lowered, a humiliated bearing of the body.

In the case of shame stimulus is just as much present as with other affects; this stimulus, however, is not the act we committed, but rather that "they are seeing us," the "eye" of the community, the immediate presence of a public. Shame as an affect is independent of whether we have been put to shame with or without good reason, and also independent of whether the reason is significant or not: we had departed from the prescription, the eye of the community is upon us, it condemns us, derides us, or merely "sees" us, that is why we feel shame. Of course, opposite affects (and emotions, orientative feelings) may dominate and obliterate our shame, as in the case of all affects. With the feeling of shame, however, this may be even more difficult than with other feelings. How many persons proud of their poverty nevertheless attempt to "hide" at the opera if poorly dressed in the midst of an elegant crowd; how many autonomous characters nevertheless feel involuntarily ashamed if they or somebody in their environment create a scene! We are ashamed of our physical defects, even though we know that there is no "sin" involved, that we are not responsible.

What provokes our shame and why, is at all times regulated by social prescriptions; after all it is precisely the departure from these prescriptions that constitutes "the shameful thing." Hence shame—and putting others to shame—is always an instrument in the process of socialization. The more complex the society, however, the more problematic this instrument becomes. Darwin distinguished the so-called "shame cultures" from the "conscience cultures." In integrated cultures in which morality (the subjective relationship to ethical values) has not developed the feeling of shame is the regulator of morality. Where there is morality, however, that is actual virtue; the regulatory role of the feeling of shame in relation to virtue is taken over increasingly by the pangs of conscience. Bad conscience is not an affect but an emotion (cognitive-situational feeling). It relates to the act itself, quite independently of whether the act was public, whether it was "seen." It is true that the public character of the act may also have an effect on bad conscience, the feeling of regret; it is not, however, a primary factor but rather a secondary one. Since bad conscience is not a deviance from regulation by custom, but rather a regulative feeling concerning the deviance from the moral norms accepted by myself, it is undoubtedly of a higher order than the affect of shame. The feeling of shame (and putting somebody to shame) begins to play a problematic role in the process of socialization when (and where) the ethical norm differ from the regulation of customs, or the regulation by custom loses in ethical content. The child who has been put to shame too often rarely becomes a morally autonomous adult, and will tend to become conformist.

Of course, emotions may also build upon the affect of shame, and the most important among these is the one we may designate as "secondary shame." This type of shame has nothing to do with deviance from the regulation of custom, and yet we are entitled to consider it a feeling of shame. The feeling I am referring to is what I feel while I am revealing myself—when I declare my love, or when I talk to someone about myself. An aspect of the affect of shame is present: we seem to undress, expose ourselves, if not in public, at least in front of the Other. Even the expression of the affect of shame may be preserved in part: we speak with bent head or, should we look into the Other's eyes, we may even blush. (The feeling of shame derived from nakedness may be purely affective or may also be of an emotional character.) But the following is also a feeling of emotional shame: "I am ashamed that I hurt his feelings" or "I am ashamed of being so rich"—in such cases there is no expression of shame at all.

The Affects of Gaiety and of Sadness

In practice, it is difficult to experience the affects of gaiety and of sadness in their "pure" form, for most of the time various emotions of joy and of sorrow are built upon these affects. The purest form of these affects appears during childhood, and this is when we may follow the familiar trinity of stimulus feeling-impact-expression (the expression often follows the stimulus and is total)—it includes phonic expression, facial expression, and gestures or may involve the whole body—as in jumping for joy or collapsing with sadness. The mature adult keeps these affects mostly "to himself" and thus their expression becomes partial. Because of the "contagious" nature of the affects, however, the forms of total expression may again appear in a larger company, or in the midst of a crowd. Think of the New Year's Eve parties when, under the influence of a general inebriation even strangers fall into the arms of one another. (Let us note, by the way, that the consumption of alcoholic beverages opens largely the way for the pure affects.)

The affects of gaiety and of sadness have secondary forms just as the affect of shame. Sadness, as emotion, is at the same time a predisposition for certain stimuli to elicit the affect of sadness; the sad person may break into tears at the sound of a song. Laughing may be the expression of gaiety too, just as crying—as we have seen—may be the expression of sadness. This does not mean, however, that crying and laughing are necessarily, and invariably expressions of affects. Undoubtedly, crying as well as laughing bears some relation to the expressions of affects in general. These forms of expressions are also universal; they are to be found in every culture. They have a communicative function, they are the conclusion of the sequence: stimulus—feeling impact, they are contagious. In spite of the fact that they may be repressed (for instance, by other emotions, or by turning away from the object of the stimulus), there is something compulsory about them. They are just as easy to recognize and difficult to simulate (while preserving the semblance of sincerity) as expressions of affects in general.

Yet, as I have said, not all crying or laughing is an expression of affect; they may be the expressions of the most diverse cognitive-situational emotions. Think of crying as sign of relief or of being moved, think of laughing out of pleasure at someone's discomfiture, or out of despair. Emotional crying and laughing are expressions of personality, hence they are idiosyncratic.[10]

Orientational Feelings

Orientational feelings are yes-feelings or no-feelings with regard to any aspect of life, including action, thinking, judgment, etc. Orientational feelings (yes-feeling; no-feeling) are not to be confused with what we usually refer to "good feeling" or "bad feeling." These latter categories, as we shall see further on, originate from the application of general value orientational categories to feelings. This difference can well be illustrated by the examples presented by Wittgenstein in connection with the feeling of conviction. Conviction is a typical yes-feeling (I feel it is so; I feel it will be so; I feel that I know, etc.). The feeling of conviction may be expressed in the following statement: "the weather will stay nice"—at the same time it is a good feeling. But the following statement may also be a matter of conviction: "the war will break out—and I say this with horror, by no means is it a "good feeling." (Of course, if I happen to be a professional soldier and yearn for war, it may be a good feeling.) It is also with a feeling of conviction that I may say: "there is an error in the computing!"—and this is likewise not a good feeling (it may be connected with irritation, dissatisfaction, etc.).

Further, orientational feelings (yes-feelings; no-feelings) should not be confused with feelings of joy or of sadness. No-feeling may also refer to joy ("I shall come to regret it"), and yes-feeling may refer to sadness: for instance in all those cases where sadness, or the event that provoked it, was deliberate. Let me quote Heine once again: "You, proud heart, it was you who wanted it!"

The formation of orientational feelings is a consequence of the complete demolition of the instincts. It is in full measure the social objectivations that are the shapers and leaders of orientational feelings. We are certainly not born with orientational feelings. Their sole, exclusive source is experience. Without the experience gained through social objectivations we are completely unable to orient ourselves. The wider the experience, furthermore, the greater the scope of action of the individual within the prescriptions of objectivations, the greater the role played in our lives by the orientational feelings. When and where systems of customs completely prescribe our actions at all times, we have no need for orientational feelings. (Of course, this is merely hypothetical, as there can be no such all-inclusive prescription in practice.) When and where this occurs to a lesser extent or barely, we have increasing need for orientational feelings. Adults are guided by their orientational feelings in a much wider area than are children; and under complex social relations there is a greater need for these feelings than under simple ones.

I have said that the orientational feelings have come about as a result of the demolition of instincts. Nevertheless, these are the feelings we are in a habit of calling "instinctual." We say "he has good instincts" about the man whose yes- or no-feelings are in some respect practically sure. This undoubtedly refers to the fact that behind the development of sure yes- and no-feelings there is some inborn predisposition. Everyday experience shows that undoubtedly there exist such inborn and at the same time idiosyncratic predispositions. These, however, never refer to the yes- feeling or no-feeling itself, but merely to the fact that some individuals have an inborn capacity for developing surer yes- and no-feelings in some area and others in other areas. Think of good diagnostician, who may not necessarily have "good instincts" when it comes to the stock-market or to love. At the same time, and this is essential, no one can become a good diagnostician without having studied medicine, and no one may have good "instincts" at the stock market without experience and some previous acquaintance. It is not possible to develop any kind of orientational feelings without acquiring experience, cumulating knowledge prior to it.

Orientational feelings play a role in all aspects of human life, and they are universal. They lead—or at least they lead partially—in living up to expectations or deviating from expectations; thus when I adjust a man's necktie, because it was not tied correctly, or when I turn a portrait hung upside down for a similar reason. They lead—or, they lead among other factors—with regard to our own personal strategy, or tactics, or at least individual moves in life, and they may be aimed at our most diverse feelings themselves (thus, with regard to the feeling: "it is not in order that I am not feeling sad enough").

In what follows, while emphasizing the universality of orientational feelings, I would like to point out certain systems of reference in which orientational feelings have played a significant role throughout history.

1. Orientational feelings in direct action, in work, in everyday activity in general. I want to group under this category the types of action which relate to the realization, the attainment of a given (fixed) goal. This kind of orientational feeling appears (and its guidance is necessitated) when not all the steps leading to the attainment of the objective had been prescribed, and if, at the same time, we have appropriate experience (prior knowledge) at our disposal.

We want to reach a village. We reach a triple fork in the road. "We feel," that the road on the left is the right one. (If there are signs at the fork then we have no need for orientational feelings, nor do we need them if we had done the road a thousand times. On the other hand, no orientational feeling manifests itself if we do not know approximately where the village might lie or what kinds of roads usually lead to villages. Without some prior knowledge we can only be led by blind chance.) This is the yes-feeling that I shall call a "feeling of probability."[11] It is the feeling of probability that leads us in the majority of our daily activities (when to wake up, how to reach our workplace in time, how to cross the street, etc.). Without the guidance of the feeling of probability we would not at all be able to carry out our innumerable activities, the reproduction of ourselves would become impossible.

Now let us analyze the following statements: "I feel that one more effort and I will manage to lift it!"; "I feel that if I tighten this bolt the machine will work!": "I feel that if I begin to sow today, the harvest will be at its best!" All three statements formulate a yes-feeling pertaining to the accomplishment of work. In all three cases the goal is given, the road leading to the goal is not completely but approximately prescribed, and the yes-feeling is built on prior knowledge (either of the individual or of the collectivity).

The orientational feelings belonging to this group are generally background-feelings.

2. Orientational feelings in thinking. The yes- or no-feelings playing a role in thinking are difficult to abstract, in practice, from cognitive processes in the strict sense of the word, since they are always the background feelings of these processes. Nevertheless this separation is necessary if we want to stress the functional independence of the cognitive process within the whole process. Thus, for instance, all judgments have a "yes" or a "no" form (I aver or I deny something and by so doing I assume responsibility for my assertion or my denial)—but this yes or no should not be confused with the orientational feelings; their function is cognitive quite independently of the extent to which they are accompanied by feelings, including orientational feelings. If I should look out the window and say: "it's raining now" or "X is nice" then I have made in both instances an assertive judgment (the judgment has a yes-form, and I accept responsibility for its truth), but the first statement may be altogether indifferent (perhaps no orientational feeling is connected to it), whereas the second feeling is undoubtedly accompanied by an orientational feeling; what more, the judgment is precisely the expression of this orientational feeling.

Among the various forms of thinking orientational feelings play the greatest role in problem-solving thinking. Such is the feeling of "I must seek the solution in this direction" (or the same in the form of a no-feeling). The background of every so-called "intuition" is a yes-feeling—the cognitive process of the sudden perception of the solution is always accompanied by the feeling of "yes, it is so!" or "I have hit upon it!" The background of every realization of evidence is also a yes-feeling: "it is obvious, isn't it?" The method for solving the problem is also accompanied by yes- or no-feelings: thus when I say that such and such a procedure is "beautiful" or "elegant." Every prediction based on probability is also accompanied by orientational feelings. The feelings indicating conviction or lack of conviction I had mentioned previously play an important role here.

Yes- or no-feelings accompany the reception of cognitive information as well. Such is the feeling of "that jibes" or "that does not jibe." The nature of the feeling is determined not only by the content of the information, but also and largely by its source. Information originating from an authority is more likely to be accompanied by a yes-feeling than if the same information should have a non-authoritative source. In the case of no-feelings (doubts) relating to information originating from an authority, there is a much greater need for prior knowledge and experience, then in the case of yes-feelings (faith).

If faith and/or doubt remain in the background, either in the instance of problem solving or in that of reception of information, they fulfill a positive function as do all yes- and no-feelings. But these same orientational feelings (and only these) are not only background feelings, but may also get into the center of consciousness. If this should happen the aforementioned orientational feelings fulfill a negative role in the thinking process. Whether I believe a priori that which originates from a person or an institution that is an authority accepted by me, or whether I a priori disbelieve everything that originates from a person or institution that is not an authority accepted by me, in either case my thinking is blocked. Feeling either inhibits or leads the initiation and carrying out of cognitive processes. (Of course, the authority can be myself for my own benefit; I have yes-feelings only with regard to those solutions which correspond to my earlier solutions.)

3. Orientational feelings in interpersonal contacts. In interpersonal contacts the significance of orientational feelings grows proportionately to the widening of contacts, to the multiplication of its relations. If I should meet with a stranger today and afterwards say: "I like this man" or "I don't like this man," then the yes- or no-feeling orientates in a way it never could have orientated in those times when people lived their entire lives among people they knew from birth. The same applies to the no-feeling accompanying the declaration "this man will never make a good soldier" or to the yes-feeling accompanying the following one "it will be possible to make a man out of this child." All these examples concern knowledge of men in some way. But yes- and no-feelings are far from being knowledge of human character, although they are the points of departure for all such knowledge of human character. Yet feeling can provide erroneous information as well, we may discover that "the first impression" formed about a person has to be modified later, selected out. Nevertheless, I can assert that under more complex social relations man's social homeostasis is impossible to maintain without orientative feelings in human contacts.

The more individuality evolves, the more variegated types of orientational feelings play a role in a person's life. It is unnecessary to waste words on the significance of faith and doubt in this context. Let me mention, however, a very important feeling: tact. A lot of prior experience is necessary for tact (we do not meet with tactful small children), yet it can evolve only, when our action in a given situation is not fully prescribed. When every moment of expression of pity is regulated there cannot be tact, in this regard. Where the regulation is not complete, or where it does not exist, the feeling of tact plays a rather important role.[12]

4. Orientational feeling with regard to the *sensus communis*. The *sensus communis* guides the taste of individuals belonging to a society (a social stratum, a community, a nation) at the most diverse levels. The "guidance" at various levels is far from being equally forceful (it may be strong at one level, looser at another, and the guidance may even vary according to strata). Where

the guidance of *sensus communis* is unconditional, yes- and no-feelings play a role only during the process of growing up. Where they are conditional, looser, there the orientational feelings become all-important with regard to the *sensus communis*.

What dish do we like? The one that is prepared the way we used to cook at home. The majority of people react with a no-feeling to unknown taste experiences. At the same time the gourmand will notice the slightest deviation in the manner of preparation, and his yes-feelings relate only to the most perfect form of the dish. Fashion guides in the manner of dress or of interior decorating, the conventional guides in human contact. The more *sensus communis* guides only "generally," the greater the role of orientational feelings. The area of movement granted to orientational feelings by the *sensus communis* may even vary according to sex—thus it plays a much larger role in dressing with women then with men.

The yes- and no-feelings have an even more prominent role in their relation to the *sensus communis* concerning value objectivations of a higher order. This is the role performed by *aesthetic* taste with regard to *aesthetic* values. Even in cultures where the *sensus communis* is strong, i.e., where it "assigns" those forms irrevocably (or even the "correct" proportions that were, for instance, the canon in ancient sculpture) which are the measure of beauty, the yes- or no-feelings of individuals in the evaluation of works of art is extremely significant; in these cultures too a sure judgment based on "good taste," on experience, on knowledge, on "general culture" is preferred. The looser the *sensus communis*, the greater the role played by what we call *aesthetic* taste, and the more prior education is required.[13]

That which is usually referred to as "moral feeling" has a function similar to that of *aesthetic* taste in its relation to moral value objectifications. The idea that moral feeling "is born with us," reiterated so often in the 18th century, is absurd. No one can have moral feelings before the acquisition of values and before the acquisition of certain experiences. If we do not know what is judged to be good or bad in a given society (or stratum), the yes- and no-feelings which lead to good "sense"—and which are usually referred to as "moral feeling"—do not develop in relation to our own decisions or in relation to the acts of others. The "instinctivity" of the moral sense is just as secondary (that is, learned) as the instinctivity of orientational feelings in general.

Moral feeling, just like *aesthetic* taste, has an important social function even when there exists a fixed hierarchy of values. Already Aristotle described this fact under the category of phronesis. Its significance increases during the period of the disintegration of *sensus communis*, and later, just as in the case of *aesthetic* taste, it becomes problematic with the total disintegration of *sensus communis*.

5. The Orientational Contact Feelings. The orientational contact feelings do not belong in the same family as the orientational feelings, but are closely related. These orientational contact feelings are: love and hatred (sympathy-antipathy, attraction-aversion). Why do I call these contact feelings the relatives

of orientational feelings? First of all because their social function is primarily that of orientation. They orient us in the choice of the persons it would be good for our personality to be together or in contact with, also regarding the person (of the persons) we should avoid. Love is a yes-feeling in relation to another person as personality, hatred is a no-feeling in relation to another person as personality; the first is a yes feeling regarding the being of that person, the second a no-feeling regarding the being of that person. (Or, in an extreme case: a yes-feeling regarding that person's non-being.)

Furthermore, orientational contact feelings are related to orientational feelings because their source is also experience, system of objectivation, knowledge. Motherly love does not stem from the so-called "maternal instinct," and only the suckling of the infant can be considered a remnant of instinct, but this bears no relationship to love as an orientational feeling (it does not orient in anything). Motherly love, like other kinds of love, is a feeling regulated and led by social prescriptions. If, however, the object, form, and measure of love were completely determined, there would not be any orientational feeling (there would be nothing in which to orient). Such complete regulation, however, does not exist anywhere; even in the most thoroughly regulated societies the individuals we may choose to love or not love are the overwhelming majority; and even with regard to those we are obliged to love, there is considerable area of movement as to the extent of love. The situation is the same as in the case of every orientational feeling: the more complex a society, the less or the looser the prescriptions relating to love, the greater the role of orientational contact feelings.

Orientational contact feeling (like every orientational feeling) may be more or less yes, or more or less no. Thus we may speak, within the category of orientational contact feelings of the antinomy sympathy-antipathy, or of attraction-aversion; these contact feelings are not primary, however, but secondary: they have come about as a result of emotional differentiation. And this differentiation is particularly significant nowadays. Thus it is important to differentiate in the case of our yes-feelings (even from the point of view of our actions and our behavior): are we dealing with sympathy, attraction, or love?

After all this, why don't I classify the orientational contact feelings into the "family" of orientational feelings? First of all because orientational contact feelings (like all contact feelings!) are not feeling occurrences, but feeling dispositions. So far we have had no dealings with feeling dispositions. Drive feelings, affects, and orientational feelings alike were feeling occurrences. The category of feeling disposition will play a central role in the case of emotions (cognitive-situational feelings).

By "feeling dispositions," I mean those feelings which may bring forth the most heterogeneous feeling occurrences—either simultaneously or in a sequence—and these feelings are all the consequence of feeling dispositions. These feelings are always accompanied by a specific behavior. We may only speak of feeling dispositions if it has a more or less long duration; how long should it last before we are prepared to accept the disposition as authentic depends to a large extent on the type of feeling disposition, but also on *sensus communis*. Wittgenstein is entirely correct in stating: if you loved him for only one hour, you did not love him truly—such a statement makes sense; if your tooth ached for only one hour, then it did not really ache—such a statement does not make sense.

Undoubtedly, however, there are ages when love does not count as authentic unless it lasts a lifetime, and there are ages when a love that lasts two months already counts as quite authentic (yet, a friendship chat lasts only two months, hardly). Although I have classified the concept of "feeling disposition" under the general category of dispositions, I do not mean at all that the characteristics of a feeling disposition correspond in all respects to the characteristics of a physical disposition. If we say about a substance that it is inflammable, this is a disposition to burn: the inflammable substance is "disposed" to burn. In comparison to this, however, the feeling disposition has a specific differentiation: namely that it is auto-igniting. If a man is in love this constitutes not only a feeling disposition which makes him "disposed" to react to everything in connection with his love (to be happy if she be present, yearn for her when in trouble, be sad if she is distrusting or feel pain if he should lose her); it also means that he himself creates again and again the emotional situations. The man in love does not need a special indication in order to live feeling occurrences in accordance with his feeling disposition; he wants to think about his love, or to be always together with her in imagination, he evokes her image in the midst of the most heterogeneous activities. If he should be creating something, he also thinks about to what extent the creation shall please her, during significant activities he practically "evokes" her as a person particularly important to him, what he has to say he says it to her, he speaks to her even if she is not present. This constant "auto-ignition" is the specific trait of feeling dispositions as opposed to all other dispositions.

But it is not only because of their being feeling dispositions that I have not classified the orientational contact feelings within the family of the orientational feelings. But also because as contact feelings in general, by their very essence, they are emotional relations. They are typically emotional relations, although not invariably so. Love, as a mutual feeling, develops bonds. (Hatred is likewise usually mutual.) The fact of being mutual, of course, does not imply equality. Here, as in all cases, there may be equal or unequal relations.[14]

What I have said in connection with the grouping of feelings in general, however, also applies to the present groupings: there is no such thing as a "pure" group. Love and hatred may orient us not only with regard to persons, but also with regard to communities, institutions, objectivations, principles. It makes sense to say: "I love romantic music," and this is not in the least synonymous with a judgment of *aesthetic* evaluation ("romantic music is beautiful"). I may love a person and hate, another, I may love a way of life and hate another. In such cases love or hatred are a "transition" between orientational feeling and orientational contact feeling. On one hand they are not feeling occurrences, but feeling dispositions, on the other hand they do not create bonds. Yet there are loves and hatreds which may not be classified under orientational feelings. Such is "philantrophy" or "misanthropy," since they do not have an orientational function—as purely spiritual feelings they may be considered emotions. (To stay on the subject, I shall classify all spiritual feelings, including the love of God, among the emotions.)

Cognitive-Situational Feelings or "Emotions Proper"

I have made the case that orientational feelings are purely social. Indeed, all emotions "proper" are purely social. The significance of yes- and no-feelings—as we have seen—increases proportionately to the widening of the range of experiences, and to the complexity of society; at the same time, they become differentiated. But while all the types of orientational feelings (even if not every specific yes- or no-feeling) are present in germ and play a role at least during the process of growing up (such as taste orientation, knowledge orientation, action orientation, social contact orientation, orientation in living up to expectations or in not living up to them), the actual emotions, or at least their majority, are idiosyncratic in all respects. They have traits in common, but no typology. Nevertheless, not all emotions are present in every culture whereas certain emotions develop under certain social structures, other emotions develop better under other conditions. For instance, the feelings of bad conscience, devotion, the desire for independence, humility, love of mankind have not always existed. At the same time, the feeling content of emotions performing the same function (intensity, depth, and the behavior implied) also varies. Love was different in antiquity, in the Middle Ages, and during the 19th century. Furthermore, emotions arc highly idiosyncratic. While the feeling of fear, of rage, or of hunger is essentially the same with all persons, and the idiosyncratic differences are partly physiological and partly stem from emotions aimed at or built upon affects or drives, the love of Romeo, of Miranda, of Lady Macbeth, of Brutus, of Cleopatra—in order to remain within the same historical period—are idiosyncratically different feelings. What more, the same emotions of the same person are also different: Romeo's love towards Rosa is different from his love towards Juliet.

Therefore, we may assume the following: drive-feelings and affects will always exist and will remain essentially the same; and the role of orientational feelings increases with the growing complexity of human relations. Yet we may not assume that all emotions that exist at present will necessarily exist in the future, not even with regard to those that have existed hitherto under some form in every culture, or in the majority of cultures.

Emotions are partly feeling occurrences, partly feeling dispositions. Some emotions we may consider "pure" feeling occurrences (for instance, being moved, devotion), whereas others are always feeling dispositions (first of all the emotional contact feelings, but not only those, also jealousy, envy, philanthropy, and in general all those emotions that are usually described with the term "desire" or "love" such as desire for vengeance, love of knowledge, etc.). There is a considerable number of emotions, however, about which we cannot decide whether they be feeling occurrences or feeling dispositions, in other words, that occur in both forms: thus with pity, contempt, trust. I must add that from the point of view of the common and fundamental traits of emotions it is entirely irrelevant whether they are feeling occurrences or feeling dispositions. In what follows, in the analysis of these common traits, I am entirely justified in disregarding this difference.

1. Emotions are not universally necessary. We cannot say about a single one of the emotions that they play a necessary, indispensable role in the biological preservation of the species or of the individual, in the social reproduction of the human species, or in the social homoeostasis of the individual. We cannot even say that a single one of them has at any time fulfilled (for instance, at the origins of the human species) such a function. (The feeling of sympathy or love, as we have seen, is also an orientational feeling and not always an emotion.) But we can say about each one of them that they have been (or still are) indispensable organic constituent parts in the functioning of certain—although different—ages, social strata, or classes. Still, social coexistence would be impossible without the existence of emotions (I do not mean one or another particular emotion, but emotions in general). If only because every culture must regulate the drive feelings and the affects (first of all the affects of rage and of fear), and this regulation unavoidably implies the evolution of certain emotions. Whether the sexual affect is channeled or sublimated into love, feeling of comradeship, or desire to possess, depends on the system of norms of a given culture. The channeling of the sexual affect can lead to the most variegated emotions, but it always does lead to some kind of an emotion.

2. Emotions are always cognitive and situational. It may be objected with reason that this does not constitute a specific difference. After all there is cognition in the case of drive feelings and affects as well. At a certain degree of intensity the affects always become conscious (we know that we are angry, that we are afraid, etc.). The drive feelings likewise become conscious at a certain degree of intensity; we know that we are gasping for air, that we are thirsty. The feeling of hunger may often manifest itself not directly, but indirectly (stomachache, feeling of weakness, etc.) still it is not necessary for anyone to use complicated means to lead us to the realization that the reason for this feeling is that we are hungry. It may seem paradoxical that this kind of consciousness is not at all typical of emotions in general, in other words of those feelings which we had decided to call "cognitive." How often does it occur that we do not know that what we feel is a feeling of inferiority, or contempt, or envy. People may be fully justified in saying: "I thought I was in love, but I was wrong" or "I just discovered that I had despised my father all my life!" But could someone say that "I have just discovered that I have felt disgusted at the

sight of blood all my life?" If I did not feel disgusted before, then I was not disgusted.

Furthermore, it was precisely about the affects that I had said they are always situational. After all they are elicited by a stimulus, and this stimulus is always present, therefore it is my situation. It may seem paradoxical again that in the case of emotions, which I have called par excellence "situational" feelings, this is far from being so. Emotions do not require a stimulus; they may refer to the past, or to the future. If the object of fear is not present, there is no fear affect. But if the object of our love is not present, we may feel even more in love.

What do I mean, then, by the cognitive and situational character of emotions? Let us start from the model of "reading" emotions; the recipient interprets the meaning of feelings from the signals of feelings (expressions). Suppose we are talking with someone about the weather. During the conversation we glance at him. We ask him: "why are you so happy?" or "what are you so angry (irritated) about?" These are undoubtedly sensible questions. But it would not make sense to ask him "why are you so moved?" or "why do you have a bad conscience?" If I see that his eyes are shedding tears when he receives an award or listens to music, I may say with justification: "this man is moved," but if I see tears in his eyes, I can interpret this in many different ways; perhaps even non-emotionally: something got into his eye.

The affect is, then, always elicited by a stimulus, but the affect itself is independent from the stimulus that elicits it; I may recognize and identify it without having any idea what kind of stimulus elicited it. But I cannot recognize an emotion (and I cannot even ask about it) without knowing and interpreting the situation. Why?

Let us analyze this same process from the point of view of the person who feels. Let us take the following feeling: "I felt found out." Let us compare two declarations. "Z told me that I have a bad opinion about X because I am jealous of him. Since I felt found out, I became embarrassed." "Z told me that I am only playing indifferent, actually I love him. Since I felt found out, I became embarrassed." In this case we are dealing with the selfsame chain of emotions, that of being found out and being embarrassed. Yet we are dealing with two different, specific feelings. In the first instance "feeling found out" is definitely unpleasant, in the second rather pleasant.

That which causes a particular emotion, the thing towards which we feel a given emotion, belongs to the emotion itself, whether we are dealing with different emotions, or the different "nuances" of the same emotion—actually also different emotions. The content of the feeling cannot be separated, in principle, from that which elicits the feeling and from the interpretation of the feeling. For instance, to the feeling of contempt belongs the evaluation, the interpretation of the other person's personality, actions, the thing because of which I despise him, to the feeling of forgiving that to whom, why, when, and how I forgive. The forgiving of Fielding's Amelia is full of goodness and lenience, that of the Joseph of the Bible is a forgiving full of triumph, that of Prospero a forgiving of resignation.

Since in emotions as feelings the references (references to persons, situations, etc.) are inherent precisely because they are so idiosyncratic, it often happens that we do not know what we feel. And just because cognition is part and parcel of feeling itself, the quality of feeling undergoes a change when a person realizes what he or she actually feels. We all know how a person's behavior and even feelings change, if he discovers that he is actually in love with X, or that he is no longer in love with X, if he discovers that he no longer believes in God, or does believe in God, that vengeance is still alive in him, or has already vanished from him.

Everything I have said in the first chapter about the antinomy of feelings refers to emotions alone. Precisely because of their situational, cognitive, and idiosyncratic nature, we do not dispose, for reasons of principle, of sufficient emotional concepts for their expression; we can only approximate them by classifying them under concepts. This is why we attempt to describe them again and again, and often in a different manner. This is why we cannot "read" the meaning from the Other's sign with accuracy only satisfactorily from a pragmatic point of view.

But this same cognitive, situational, idiosyncratic nature of the emotions may bring about a reverse situation in the relation between the individuals "transmitting" and "receiving" the signal. It may happen that the Other cannot "read" the signals, but it may also happen that the Other can interpret the meaning of the signals accurately, although the transmitter has not been able to do it. Bedford mentions that it is possible to imagine a situation where everyone knows that X is jealous except X himself. This may derive from several causes. For instance, that X had never been jealous or has never felt jealousy in this way, and thus he is unable to classify his feeling under the concept of jealousy. Or that X despises the feeling of jealousy and, in an inauthentic way, does not want to interpret his feeling as jealousy but prefers to rationalize: "this is not jealousy—I do not hate him, despise him because of jealousy, but because, etc."

Therefore, emotions are not so-called "simple feelings," nor even "combinations" of affects. The "it hurts" and the "it is good" do not combine to "add up" love as their "sum" but may become the feeling contents of an infinity of specific emotions; similarly, fear and shame together do not "add up" and become a bad conscience. We may combine simple feelings and affects as much as we like, we will never arrive at a single specific emotion.

3. Every attempt to subdivide emotions fails, precisely because of their heterogeneity and their idiosyncratic nature. We cannot say that emotions are needs, nor that they are not needs (for some emotions are, whereas others are not, for they may be in the case of some persons, but not with others). We cannot say that we produce for them, or that we don't, for we produce for some, and not for others. We cannot say that habit increases or decreases emotions, because some are strengthened by habit, while others are weakened; habit may strengthen them in the case of one person and may weaken them in the case of

another, or on another occasion. We cannot say that they are regulated by custom, because some are sometimes regulated (for instance, the feeling of mourning), whereas others are not or may change according to the occasion. Indeed, we may say that ethical norms have a decisive role in the regulation of emotions (and there is a moral emotion with special status, the feeling of duty), but even this does not apply to all emotions, and certainly not at all times. We may add, furthermore, that they may orient equally with regard to the present, the past, or the future, but there are certain emotions to which even this does not apply. Thus the emotion of mourning can only orient with regard to the past, whereas the emotion of hope is aimed at the future. We may also say that emotions, as opposed to affects, are not "contagious" and that their expressions are idiosyncratic, and this applies to every emotion. We must recognize, however, that the result is very thin. Nor could we expect anything else. We must not be astonished if the attempt to categorize something essentially idiosyncratic fails.

4. The differentiation of our emotions is at the same time the accumulation of our human wealth. Our wealth in feelings is part of our personality. We are potentially the freest in relation to our emotions, since the emotions themselves have no biological basis whatever (at the most, certain affects may predispose us in the direction of certain emotions, but even here our scope of potentiality may be considerable with the help of the values we have chosen). In reality, however—as I shall explain later—this is not necessarily the case. What more: only emotions may be quantified and may become alienated, our drive feelings or our affects never. Neither the world of our drive feelings, nor that of our affects, nor that of our orientational feelings may impoverish in general, but our emotional world may impoverish. This is why I consider the analysis of emotions the most important within the whole theory of feelings. If instead of emotions we should focus on the affect of rage or of fear, on the feeling of hunger or its examination on what light stimulant should be considered pleasant and which unpleasant, then we have avoided the real and decisive issue: the role and function of feelings in the constitution of our personality.

5. Every emotional concept, as must be clear from what I have said already, is actually a category: the grouping of an infinite number, qualitatively different, specific emotions. Of course there are narrower and broader categories. The broadest emotional categories: pleasure and pain (spiritual pain). What feelings are contained in these categories varies even according to the language. Furthermore, feelings that are often functionally equivalent may be classified under different categories; here again according to language. In German I may say *es tut mir Leid* or *ich bedauere*, but I can only say *es tut mir Leid für Dich*, or *ich bemitleide Dich* but never: *ich bedauere dich*. The latter in English would be "I am sorry for you" or "I feel pity for you"—thus the feeling can be classified under the category of sadness (not pain) or pity.

I cannot undertake here the analysis of emotional concepts. It would be possible to write a book about each one of the emotions (Scheler undertook a thick volume about the essence of sympathy and its manifestations). Thus I shall mention only a few emotions with the sole purpose of distinguishing them from non-emotional feelings.

The fear-emotions are built on fear affects, but in such a way that the affect may pale altogether. Fear-emotions (as opposed to affects) have no universal expression; this expression may be idiosyncratic, or may not show at all. The main types are as follows:

a. Fear, as in the feeling "danger is threatening me in the future." For instance, "I am afraid that I will have to have my appendix operated on." This kind of fear-emotion may become transformed into an affect. (Let's say on the surgical table.)

b. Fear, as in the feeling "I do not dare." Thus "I am afraid to undertake this enterprise" or "I am afraid of this relationship." Fear refers here to the uncertainty of the result (and is built on the affect concerning the unknown, the alien).

c. Fear, as in the feeling "I am concerned about." This type of fear does not relate necessarily to myself; it is the farthest away from the fear affect, and seldom assumes the form of an affect. For instance, "I fear that this peace will not last for long."

d. Fear, as in the feeling, "I don't want this." To mention an Aristotelian example: "I am afraid of baseness." (This is not the same feeling as "I am concerned about 'x.'")

e. Spiritual fear: for instance, the fear of God. Spiritual fear, like all spiritual feelings, is an emotional disposition. This emotional disposition, as feeling occurrence, may also involve the affect of fear.

f. There is only one existential fear, the fear of death. We must distinguish it from the fear of death as affect (a fear that occurs immediately before death, or while facing death). The existential fear is a feeling disposition (there is no person who feels it constantly), yet the affect of fear may also appear in its feeling occurrences. Existential fear has two forms: the fear of our own death, and the fear of others' death (the death of those we love).

The emotions of joy are not built on the affect of happiness. We may be happy without the emotion of joy; for instance, when good jokes are being told in company, and the gaiety "catches up" with us. On the other hand, we may feel the emotion of joy without being happy. What more, emotion of joy may be accompanied by the typical expression of the affect of sadness, by crying. Yet joy may play the role of the feeling disposition of the affect gaiety; the emotion of joy often makes it possible for us to react with gaiety to the most insignificant stimulus. The main types of emotions of joy are as follows:

a. Joy, as the achievement of a goal: "I am glad that I finished my work" ("I enjoy it").

b. Joy, as the fulfillment of desire: "I am glad that I received a nice dress" or "I enjoy that we can finally be together." Both examples show that grouping certain emotions of joy together does not at all imply that we are dealing with feelings of similar quality.

c. Joy, as the successful realization of my will (a combination of the preceding two): "I am glad that I managed not to show my irritation" ("I enjoy it").

d. Joy with regard to chosen values. Thus, "I am full of joy that justice triumphed." Joy, unlike fear, does not have a single form in which the feeling refers exclusively to myself.

All the statements above also make sense if we say: "I am glad that he finished his work" or "I am glad that she received a nice dress" or "I am glad that they can be together finally" or "I am glad that he did not show his irritation." But if we say "I am afraid to undertake this job," this only makes sense when referring to myself. The statement "I fear that he undertakes this job" does not belong to this category, but to the category of "I am worried about."

e. There is a form of joy which can only refer to someone else. This is glee at someone's misfortune: "I enjoy that he exploded out of anger." The following statement would not make sense (there is no such feeling): "I enjoy that I burst of anger."

We may say about all the emotions of joy that insofar as my whole personality is involved, i.e. they represent no merely partial involvements—they may also be described by the emotional concept of happiness. The synthesis of the main types of joy verifies our starting point: joy is not built on the affect of gaiety. Let us recall: when the emotion of fear becomes intense, the affect of fear invariably appears, even if only partially. But even the most intense joy (happiness) is not necessarily related to gaiety in any way. "I have been happy all my life, because I am an honest person"—is a sensible statement, and does not in the least imply that I have been gay even once in my life.

I will merely mention, because I cannot analyze in detail that the emotion of sorrow (sadness, depression, regret) is likewise not built on the affect of sadness. If I am subject to the affect of sadness, this does not mean that I am emotionally sorrowful. If I see a kitsch movie (a typical stimulus for the evocation of sadness), I take out my handkerchief, because I fall under the influence of "contagion." In the meanwhile, however, I may be irritated, or even amused by my attitude. Yet the relationship between the emotion of sorrow and the affect of sadness is closer than the relationship between the affect of gaiety and the feeling of joy. The feeling of intense sorrow always elicits the affect of sadness. If I should say "how sad was my life" then it may justly be presumed that the affect of sadness has dominated me a number of times.

This distinction becomes evident in the expressions as well. Joy may be accompanied by the expression of gaiety (even totally, but most of the time partially), but this companionship is by no means exclusive; it may be accompanied by expressions typical of fear or of shame (although only partially). One may become pale, may blush, may tremble with joy, one may even faint. Or it may be accompanied by the expression of sadness (crying because of joy). Sorrow likewise is not necessarily totally expressive; it may be so partially or barely. The degree of expression (just as in the case of pleasure) is

idiosyncratic according to individual and situation. The expression of the
emotion of sorrow, however, stem without exception from the expressions of the
affect of sadness (or are the modifications of some of their traits). If we are
sorrowful we cannot laugh; the so-called "dark laughter" is not the expression of
sorrow, but of despair.

The emotional contact feelings (love, friendship, comradeship, the feeling
of solidarity) are feeling dispositions as all contact feelings are. The particular
characteristic of emotional contact feelings is that they differentiate just to the
same extent they may get integrated. The emotional contact feelings are the only
ones about which it is possible to say that they may all coalesce into one. There
is feeling which contains as an organic unit love, friendship, comradeship, and
solidarity. This does not apply to orientational contact feelings, not with regard
to the totality of orientational and emotional contact feelings. Although *odi et
amo* does exist, it cannot contain friendship or comradeship. One cannot feel
friendship and antipathy towards the same person.

The differentiation and integration of emotional contact feelings is one of
the most important component of human emotional life. Of course, this also
applies to affection, insofar as it develops into an emotion. We know that every
spiritually-rooted affection is an emotion, but so is all affection to which
emotional contact feelings are connected: thus friendship with affection,
affection with feeling of solidarity, affection with love.

Here we meet immediately with an important problem I have not touched
upon as yet: the problem of depth of feeling. It is generally known that intensity
and depth of feeling are two quite different things. Every feeling without
exception may be intense or less intense (stronger or weaker), but not every
feeling can be "superficial" or "deep." In general we can say that neither in the
case of drive feelings, nor in that of affects, nor in that of orientational feelings,
can we differentiate "deep" from "superficial." (While we can clearly
differentiate intense feelings from less intense ones.) One may feel very hungry,
but cannot feel "deeply" hungry; he may feel very angry, but cannot feel
"deeply" angry; somebody may have good or bad taste, but not superficial or
deep taste. Even our moral feeling cannot be deep (although we may
occasionally describe it that way), but our feeling of responsibility may well be
deep, we may feel deeply moved, we may have a profoundly bad conscience, we
may have deep or superficial joy, we may have a deep or superficial mental
pain, sadness, or despair. Lastly, but not least, we may feel a deep or superficial
friendship, love, solidarity, comradeship, etc. Only to the orientational contact
feelings among the non-emotional feelings (since they are contact feelings), may
we apply the distinction "deep" and "superficial" with justification.

Only cognitive and situational feelings can be "deep," that is those spiritual
feelings in which the "natural" and the "inborn" have no part. What, then, do the
terms "deep" and "superficial" refer to when applied to feelings? A feeling is
deep when it sets our whole personality into motion: we feel deeply when we
become involved in something with our whole personality, either positively or
negatively. If we say about somebody that he deeply despises traitors, then what

we have really said is that betrayal repels him in his entire personality structure. If we place the following two statements next to each other: "X was vehemently disgusted by the sight of cruelty" or "X was deeply shocked at the sight of cruelty," then the first statement merely contains: cruelty, as stimulus, elicits a strong feeling of disgust in X; for all this X as personality may still approve of cruelty, and may even promote it as much as possible. (We know that Himmler was unable to attend an execution without becoming sick.) The second statement, on the other hand, contains: X is negatively involved in cruelty with his whole personality.

What does all this means with regard to emotional contact feelings (as feeling disposition)? It is possible that the same person should feel a love that is strong but superficial at one time yet, on another occasion and towards another person, his feelings may be deep. He may be involved with his whole personality in one person, and perhaps not in the other. And this, since we are dealing with contact feelings, is quite natural, since these contact feelings are based on reciprocity. It depends not only on ourselves, but also on the Other (or others) whether our feelings are deep or superficial. We may find out about a certain person that he or she is inappropriate for becoming involved in with our whole personality, or to become thus involved in the relationship with that person. The situation is similar in the case of friendship, or in the case of sympathy with emotional overtones. This is why Kierkegaard had said that the only "perfect" love is the love of God; we cannot be disappointed in the absolute, we cannot be disillusioned by it. Yet I do not believe that what man really needs are emotions without risk. Every emotional relationship involves risk, including the risk of not being able to "deepen" it, yet we must accept that risk.

What can we say, however, about persons who do not have a single profound emotional relationship? Here we have to ask a different question, although still merely with regard to emotional contact feelings. Namely, whether man is able to develop deep emotional contact feelings in general, whether in general he is capable of becoming involved with his whole personality in another person, in a relationship with another person. With this question, however, I have transcended the analysis of feelings and of feeling disposition, I have already asked about emotional character and the emotional personality.

Emotional Character and Emotional Personality

Every person has many kinds of drive-feelings, and experiences various affects and emotions innumerable times. But the greater part of these have nothing to do, or are only distantly concerned with what I call emotional character and emotional personality. Thus, for instance, the drive feelings in themselves may never become component parts of either of the emotional character or of the emotional personality. If someone has been starving for a long time, that does not mean that the feeling of hunger has become an organic part of his character; only those feelings, primarily emotions, which have come about as a result of the hunger experience can be built into the character (for instance, contempt for the well-fed, sympathy for the poor, a feeling of inferiority, perhaps an enhanced desire to enjoy, etc.).

Both emotional character and emotional personality are feeling habits. If we react with identical or similar feelings to similar circumstances, situations, or events, we become accustomed to these reaction types; or if our types of feeling reaction in general have assumed rigid, generalized, typical forms, in other words if prediction makes sense with regard to our emotional behavior (whether it is we ourselves who know in advance how it is we are going to feel and will act accordingly or in spite of it, or others know in advance the same thing), then we are dealing with character or personality feelings.

What is the difference between the emotional character expressed in character feelings and the emotional personality embodied in personality feelings? First of all, character feeling is the broader category. Every personality feeling is also character feeling, but not every character feeling is personality feeling. The emotional character is a value-free concept, the emotional personality is an evaluating concept. All those feeling habits to which we can apply the categories of Good and Bad are included into the category of emotional personality. Those habits of feeling which belong to our feeling character, but not to our emotional personality are not "binding." We are not responsible for them and they do not oblige us in any way per se. Those feeling, habits, however, which also belong to our emotional personality are "binding." We are responsible for them, and they invariably oblige us to something.

Thus, for instance, the affects that have become habit are in any case an organic part of the emotional character, but do not belong to our emotional personality. For instance, there are bashful persons but the "fact" that one is bashful is not a value in itself, nor is it a non-value. There are some who feel afraid at the sight of any danger, but always manage to counteract their fear, of which they are aware (they are not cowards); in this case fear is not a value in itself, nor is it a non-value—it is not "binding." Of course, certain affects may be the predispositions for certain emotional habits, but this relationship is very conditional. It is not necessarily the angry man who would be usually more vindictive or aggressive, it is not necessarily the bashful person who usually has qualms of conscience; it is not necessarily the man disposed to gaiety who is of a "bright mood."

Those character feelings that do not belong to the emotional personality are usually "given" with the genetic code, or become fixed in infancy, before the formation of the moral personality. Apart from the affects (which are concrete reaction-types), such are the types characteristic of the general forms of feeling-reaction. There are persons with a nervous or a calm disposition, irritable or less irritable, persons who react strongly and persons who don't; the *Verlaufsform* (the course) of the feeling may be different on the whole. These differences (or their combination) are what the so-called "typologies of temperament" try to grasp and describe. Undoubtedly temperament belongs to emotional character and not to emotional personality; hence it is not "binding."

At the same time, every emotion, if it becomes emotional habit, is part of the emotional personality. Every emotional habit is an "attribute" of personality. Of course, such habits evolve. Let us recall what I have said in connection with "superficial" and "deep" feelings. Deep feelings (in which we are involved with our whole personality) play a really significant role in the formation of feeling habits. The most varied superficial feelings, or even emotions, may fulfill and do fulfill rather often, a figure function in our consciousness, yet they are selected quickly and do not become part of our habits (of our whole personality). How often do cruel people feel pity, for a few moments, towards their victims, only for that feeling of pity to vanish as quickly as it appeared? How often are feelings of pure friendship mitigated for a moment or two by resentment, only for the feeling to vanish again? It is true that even deep feelings do not necessarily become character feelings, especially in the case of those persons whose emotional personality, whose structure of emotional habits is "readymade" and has become relatively rigid. The inauthentic feeling of repentance of Dostoevsky's heroes is undoubtedly a deep feeling of this sort (when people feel that their whole personality is involved in it), yet it is inauthentic, because it is not followed by a transformation of the emotional structure, of the emotional personality.

1. Even if the feeling processes that are characteristic of temperament do not belong to the emotional personality, the circumstance that a person's feelings are superficial rather than deep, or that these feelings are rather superficial in certain regards, are the constituent parts of the emotional personality. As we know, all those attributes which lead to evaluative predictions can be classified under emotional personality. A person who is generally superficial emotionally is unreliable (general evaluative prediction). If, in contrast, a person falls "madly" in love with a different person every month, but his feeling of comradeship is profound, lasting, and always active, then we must evaluate him as unreliable in love, but we have unconditional faith in him as a comrade.

2. Every specific emotional habit may lead to evaluative prediction. The person who feels envy once or twice has not become thereby "an envious person." But the person who, in a similar situation, is always subject to envy is an envious person and will generally act accordingly. A person is sympathetic if, when witnessing suffering sympathizes mostly with the sufferer and, again mostly, expresses this in action. (Similarly there are persons who are haughty, jealous, vain, "freedom-loving," humble, kindly, selfish, persons "who can feel pleasure in other's successes," etc.)

3. The way a person usually channels (regulates) his own affects may also lead to evaluative prediction and belongs to the person's emotional personality. Aristotle, in his theory of the moral "medium" started out primarily from these affects. Such is, for instance, courage (with regard to the affect of fear), and the "moderation" felt to be so decisive by Aristotle, in the spirit of ancient morality

(but today losing its significance gradually), with regard to sexual and feeling affects. The regulation (channeling) may apply not only to affects, but to emotions as well, for instance to fanaticism or tolerance.

4. Our relationship to our emotional expressions may also lead to evaluative prediction, and likewise belongs to our emotional personality: whether we are open or hypocritical, sincere or insincere. Furthermore, similarly with our relationship to the emotional expressions of the Other person: there are people who are fully confident and easily convinced, and there are people who lack confidence in others.

Everything I have said so far warrants two qualifications. On one hand, neither one, nor two, nor many emotional habits can exhaust or account for a man's personality. An "envious person" is not only an envious person, but is characterized by a number of other "attributes" or types of reaction. If we describe a person by means of one of his emotional habits (or even with the help of several emotional habits), then we must always bear in mind that we are abstracting from the totality of his personality. This abstraction, however, is necessary, because it regulates or "leads" our expectations, our behavior and our evaluations.

Furthermore, the evaluative prediction is always conditional. The personality feelings, once formed, make it probable, that under certain circumstances the person will feel the same and will act accordingly. But we may never conclude with absolute certainty regarding future feelings and behavior. For one thing, as a result of the influence of other emotional habits, in some cases people may even feel and act in contradiction to some of their emotional habits. A selfish person may feel and act unselfishly; a brave person may act in a cowardly way, a vindictive person in a forgiving way. Prediction becomes especially uncertain if a person encounters a situation he has never encountered before; in the case of great shocks, in borderline situations, during sudden changes of his social being. What more, our emotional habits may become entirely transformed; our whole personality structure may alter from a certain point of view. This is what we call catharsis. While in prison, Julien Sorel sheds his ambitions like clothing. It is in the course of suffering that King Lear learns to feel something he had never felt as a king: empathy with other sufferers.

5. The *Lebensgefühl*, mood, and caprice: all of these are feeling predispositions. This concept is altogether different from the "feeling dispositions." Our feeling dispositions come about always in the presence of a specific object: there is love towards somebody, love of humanity, desire for power. Feeling dispositions are, therefore, primary involvements. Feeling predispositions, however, are feeling dispositions with regard to any object. These feelings predispose us to feel certain feelings rather than others, to feel certain feelings more frequently than others, certain feelings more intensely than others, certain feelings more profoundly, others superficially.

I. The *Lebensgefühl* is a feeling predisposition characteristic of an entire life or of a larger period of it. Such are the lust of life, melancholy, spleen or, as background feelings to cognitive behavior, optimism, and pessimism. The *Lebensgefühl* may have various sources. These are:

a. Data received with the genetic code, feeling "inclinations" born with us. These inclinations may, of course, be inherited. Remember Goethe's poem: "Von Vater hab ich die Statur (Des Lebens ernste Führen) / Von Mütterchen die froh Natur / Und Lust zu fabulieren."[15] Here Goethe is referring to two different life-feelings: a background as well as a figure feeling. Seriousness in guidance of life—the *Lebensgefühl* as a background feeling—this he ascribed to paternal inheritance. Whereas his "gay nature"—the *Lebensgefühl* as a figural feeling— he ascribes to maternal inheritance.

b. Personal life experiences, perhaps traumatic experiences, especially in childhood. The new experiences and traumas experienced by a character already formed seldom alter the *Lebensgefühl* itself (they alter the mood, rather). Thus, for instance, whether a person is led in his actions and choices by the feeling of self-confidence, or by the feeling of insecurity in face of himself and with regard to the world; whether in the course of his life it is the yearning for security or the yearning for something new that predominates, all this is predominantly the consequence of childhood experiences.

c. Social experiences, including the fashions of *Lebensgefühl*. Since I will analyze this problem in detail in the second part of this book, I will merely mention here that, while social experiences are the ones that shape the fashions of the *Lebensgefühl*, these fashions themselves become "popularizers" of the *Lebensgefühl*. The popularization aspect is connected mainly to important individuals—such as the Byronic spleen, the Rousseauean sentimentalism, or the Wildean cynicism, to mention a few well-known historical examples. I must add, however, that although Weltschmerz, melancholy, optimism (the old "keep smiling"), or sentimentalism may be general "fashions," individuals vary in how "appropriate" they are in conforming to the required model of the *Lebensgefühl*, as a result of other sources of the *Lebensgefühl*. Furthermore, these types of *Lebensgefühl* are mostly specific to strata. Thus the *Lebensgefühl* that originates in childhood experiences, inasmuch as there are a great number of similar traits in the childhood experiences and traumas of individuals belonging to the same strata, undoubtedly plays a role in the formation as well as the amplification of the Lebensgefühl specific to a stratum.

II. Mood is an emotional predisposition that lasts a greater or lesser time, and which always originates from a specific situation or is connected with it (perhaps to a sequence of similar specific situations). The same person may have the most varied moods, lasting or not so lasting, depending on the circumstances. That a person in some given moment has such and such a mood is not necessarily characteristic of his personality. If, however, the individual is "inclined" to certain moods rather than to others, then we must always seek the common denominator of these moods in the *Lebensgefühl*.

We consider our moods justified if we know the cause that had elicited them; similarly, we do not consider them justified if we do not know what may have elicited them. Let's assume I am depressed. Nothing interests me, nothing can cause me joy, I often think about suicide. If I had lost someone I truly loved shortly before, or if my plans had collapsed then I deem my depression justified. But if nothing had happened that can explain my depression, then I will not consider it justified. Then I must undertake "detective work." I ask myself, why? I seek: perhaps there is some cause which may justify my state of depression after all, only I am not aware of it. (Beware now! For it is never for the motivation we must look, but the cause!) In contemporary times we turn mostly to the psychologist; maybe he can discover the cause of the depression (perhaps in an experience repressed into the unconscious, perhaps in an illness).

Or perhaps I find that "I feel so nervous." (I react to everything in an irritated manner, I cannot remain still, I am often seized with trembling, I have no patience for anything, I hurry, etc.) Again: if for weeks I have not received a letter from my daughter, then I know why I feel nervous (I deem the feeling justified). If I have no cause to feel nervous, then I undertake "detective work"--the search for a cause—as in the preceding case.

Such a mood is the state of inquietude, the state of happy restlessness, the state of satisfaction, the state of "excitement" (although the last concept is usually applied only to situations where the cause is known), the state of enthusiasm, etc.

III. Caprice is a feeling predisposition that lasts a short while and which either does not have an eliciting cause, or the cause is of an *ad hoc* nature, insignificant and external from the point of view of the personality. Caprice may be predisposition in a single direction; for instance, when we rage for every little thing, when we are prepared to find fault everywhere. The Hungarian expression to "rise with his left foot" (or the American: to "get up on the wrong side of the bed) refers to caprice without a cause. The person may also feel merely irritable, and in the most diverse directions (the quick succession of exhilaration and depression). Every person has moments of caprice from time to time (and although I call them "moments" they may last for hours). A "capricious person" however, is a person who experiences such moments often; caprice becomes one of the traits of his emotional character. All emotional predispositions only become "binding" through the mediation of the emotions built upon them.

6. Passion is not a separate "family" within the typology of feelings. Only the emotions among all the feelings may become passions. We cannot be either passionately hungry or passionately ashamed, we cannot have a passionate headache; we cannot be passionately afraid of loaded weapons, we cannot be passionately considerate, we cannot have passionate taste. Even the sexual affect can only become passionate if some emotion is built upon it (attraction, love, desire of possession, desire of prestige, etc.). If love or hate should become our passion, then they no longer orient, but function as emotions.

Yet not all emotions may become passions. There is no such thing as passionate pleasure, nor passionate sadness, nor can we be moved passionately, nor feel passionate relief. Only emotional dispositions may become passions (and even the sexual affect-emotion only if it is an emotional disposition). There are passionate love and friendship, passionate desire for revenge and jealousy, passionate love of justice and desire for learning.

Furthermore, not even all emotional dispositions may become passions, only the ones in which my whole personality is involved which are connected, at the same time, to some intense desire. Thus envy, which is unquestionably an emotional disposition, does not normally assume a passionate form. I may become envious of something I do not desire at all; for instance, when somebody is happy with a man I never wanted. If he should be happy with someone who was also the object of my desire, then I am not envious, but jealous. A physicist may be envious of a successful critic, although he never yearned to attain success in critical writing (it is not at all involved in critical writing), but feels scientific jealousy with regard to another physicist who achieved better than which he meant to achieve himself.

With all this it may seem as if I contradicted myself. Let us recall: I described emotional disposition as a state of "auto-igniting fire" from which various simultaneous and successive feeling occurrences and types of behavior derive actively and reactively. Well, this is precisely why feeling dispositions, and only feeling dispositions, may become passions. A feeling disposition becomes a passion if auto-ignition is always present, when the subject is constantly in a state of "burning," because every stimulus, every event, every object and thought relates only to the object of the feeling disposition, i.e. the subject relates them only to this object. Jealous Othello can think of nothing but his jealousy; whatever happens to him (think of the appearance of the Venetian ambassador), he relates it to his jealousy, he loses his capacity to become involved in anything else. When Timon of Athens becomes misanthropic then everything that happens merely feeds his misanthropy. Don Juan looks at a woman only to see in her the object of his desire (if he had not satisfied his desire with her previously). Everything reminds Harpagon of money, he fantasizes about wealth, he cherishes his wealth, Juliet thinks about Romeo night and day, her feeling of love does not get into the background of consciousness even for a moment.

It is true that such passions, at least lasting ones, are rather rare (they are not so rare in the short run!). "In the long run" it would not be possible to live in such a way that the basic feeling remains always in the focus of consciousness: remember what I have said about the homoeostatic function of feelings; strong passions either gnaw away the person or he becomes tired after a while. Thus passion in the long run is not characterized by the disposition being constantly auto-igniting with regard to the object, to the person, but rather that from time to time, for short durations, it gets into the center of consciousness with particular intensity—in other words, that it feeds "passionate states."

Everything that I have said so far about passion also refers to another of its determining traits. The passionate feeling-disposition always dominates our personality, that is it forces into the background all those emotions and emotional dispositions which do not belong to its own feeling occurrences. The passionate feeling disposition extinguishes in us all those emotions and feeling dispositions that do not pertain to it, or that contradict it. While Julien Sorel is absorbed by the passion of making a career, he is incapable of true love; as soon as his basic passion dies out, he immediately becomes capable of it. Or as Father Goriot says: "I loved them so much that I returned to them like the gambler to the gambling table. My daughters were my sinful passion, they replaced everything for me, even love." All this applies to passions elicited by ideas as well, which I shall call, in deference to Kant, "enthusiasm."

How do passions evolve, when do feeling dispositions turn into passions? Undoubtedly, passions pertain to those desires which I am going to call—in the wake of Marx—fixed desires (*fixe Begierde*). Fixed desires are brought about by needs we cannot satisfy. It is the unsatisfied state that fixes the desire, and transforms it (if we are dealing with a feeling disposition) into passion. Of course, fixed desires pertain not only to feeling dispositions; eating may also be a fixed desire, if the person is continually starving. As we know, however, only feeling dispositions may become passions; and will only become de facto passions if they are "fixed desires." In the case of Julien Sorel ambition became a passion because he was born a peasant lad in an age when incredible obstacles would pile up in front of the success of such a person; the love of Juliet and Romeo became passion because they were the children of antagonistic families (otherwise they would have lived happily until they died). Alienated needs, as they are quantitatively infinite and therefore can never be satisfied, may play the role of "fixed desires" at all times, and consequently alienated passions may pertain to them at all times—as I shall discuss in detail in the second part of this book.

The evaluation of passion has changed many times in the course of history. In antiquity passion was unequivocally condemned. From the point of view of ancient thought every passion is "hubris," a sin or transgression. During the Middle Ages the evaluation of various passions differed; Christian thinking only approved of the passionate love of God. In common thinking, however, the desire for vengeance, or the "amour passion" were also evaluated positively. The problem of the unified evaluation of passions in general already belongs to the realm of problems of modern society. To refer to two contradictory stands: Goethe in his maturity condemns all passions as such, even if he feels attracted to the feeling disposition that has become passion. (See for instance, the figure of Aurelia in *Wilhelm Meister.*) On the other hand, Hegel votes in favor of passions; he argues that nothing great has been accomplished in world history without passion. The arguments used in the evaluation of the relationship between passion and knowledge are also contradictory; passion "makes us blind" or "passion makes one perceive more."

Unquestionably we may not deny passions the attribute "grandeur," even when dealing with alienated passions. Every passion comprises a kind of greatness, something significant; and we shall see the reason for it. At the same time, however, there is always a problematic aspect of the passions; and this aspect has something to do with forcing the emotions not pertaining to passions into the background, or extinguishing them. Passion and variety of feeling (wealth of feelings), assuming that the passion lasts a long time, are contradictory. At the same time (to speak of the relationship to knowledge): although it is possible that passion—in relation to its object—makes us see more, in another sense it certainly makes one blind. What is more, typically passion makes us blind even with regard to the object of the passion—remember once again the passionate love father Goriot feels towards his daughters. And this also applies to the passion for ideas; enthusiasm leads not infrequently to fanaticism.

Why did I speak of "grandeur" in connection with passion? Because passion is also and incessantly commitment. Commitment is one species of involvement: the involvement of the whole personality in one feeling disposition. If I am committed, then I "invest" my whole personality into a relationship, an affair, an idea, a desire, a project; I stand or fall as a person with this relationship, affair, project, or the attainment of that desire. Every passion is commitment. But the question is: is every commitment also a passion? I must answer in the negative. Because we must distinguish passion and "passionateness." My emotion becomes passionate if it is intense and deep, and if I consciously accept responsibility for it. This does not mean that the passionate emotional disposition must repress my other emotions or emotional dispositions; I may be passionate in more than just one emotional disposition. I may have a passionate love for justice, but it will not prevent me from loving my friend passionately, or nature, or my community. Of course, here too priorities may exist, and I may develop a hierarchy. The point, however, is that passionateness does not preclude wealth of feelings, on the contrary: there can be no wealth of feelings without passionateness.

Notes

1. Lazarus, J.R. Averill, and E.M. Opton Jr. "Toward a Cognitive Theory of Emotion" *Feelings and Emotion: The Loyola Symposium*, ed. M. Arnold (New York: Academic Press, 1970), 211. (FE)

2. FE, 20.

3. Wundt, Wilhelm *Grundriss der Psychologie* (Leipzig: Wilhelm Engelmann) 1888. "Where, on the other hand, a series of feelings succeeding one another in time unite into an interconnected process which is distinguished from preceding and following processes as an individual whole, and which has in general a more intense effect on the subject than a single feeling we call such a succession of feelings an emotion." C. H. Judd translator: Wundt, Wilhelm. *Outlines of Psychology* (Leipzig, Alfred Kröner, 3rd ed., 1907), 189.

4. Leading back to simple feelings is not the only kind of reductionism we encounter in the theory of feelings. For instance, Buytendijk derives all feelings from the feeling of love. Nor can all theory of emotions that is based on feeling-emotion quality be considered reductionist.

5. Tomkins, Silvan, *Affect, Imagery, Consciousness* (New York: Springer, 1962), vol. I, 31.

6. "... in actual experience it is not possible to separate the hunger drive from the interest to look for food at a particular place, and from the need to go to that place; and it follows from this that there is no objective frontier between drives, interests, needs, and habits." A. Gehlen, *Studien zur Anthropologie*, 56.

7. Tomkins, 88.

8. "... must be conceived as non-practical detours of feeling impacts (such as do not alter external world in any way). *Claessens, Instinkt, Psyche, Geltung* (Köln: Westdeutscher Verlag, 1968), 107.

9. By and large, there is now a consensus regarding the visceral and endocrinological processes that form a basis of the drives. The same applies to the neuro-physiological localization of the drives. It seems certain, for instance, that the hypothalamus plays a decisive role in the regulation of hunger, whereas the *formatio reticularis* plays a decisive role in the regulation of sleep and wakefulness. In the case of emotions the results are far more uncertain. No one can locate or define endocrinologically what it is to love, to hope, to despise. In the case of emotions—since we are dealing with cognitive situation feelings; we can only speak of "total action." If, however, research has been limited to the affects, localization is altogether justified. Although very much has happened in the past thirty years regarding the exploration of the physiological basis and course of the affects, the results are still rather perplexing. Thus there are some, although they are decreasing in number, who believe even today in the theory of James-Lange, that is in the purely visceral description of affects. Since Cannon it is more and more with the brain that neuro-physiologists have tried to locate the seat of the affects. According to Papez, both expression and feeling are located in the brain, but in different parts of it. Bard and Stanley-Jones have sought the center of the affects in the hypothalamus, whereas Lindsley and Tomkins in the so-called "activating system" of the formatio reticularis. McLean has sought it in the so-called lymbic system; Magda Arnold mainly in the hippocampus within the lymbic system. The location of individual affects, or their endocrinological description is even more problematic. The sexual affect has been located in the hypothalamus, but also in the precuneus. For a while the interpretation according to which fear is accompanied by an emission of adrenalin, and rage by an emission of noradrenalin, was generally accepted (Fletwood, Diethelm). Since then, however, Funkenstein found traces of noradrenalin in the blood with subjects affected by fear. The theory of Selye, according to which the same specific syndrome may be elicited by unspecific stimuli (cold, illness, fear, humiliation, etc.), became widespread. The difficulties are most assuredly caused by the fact that there are practically no "pure" affects in the case of adults, and therefore they cannot be isolated. The experiments of Schachter have confirmed that the same drug can cause varying affects if the situations are different (i.e., with differing stimuli). But experiments with animals are irrelevant; in animals there is no hiatus, the expressions differ, etc.

10. I will not deal here with the complex series of problems connected with laughing and crying. Consult H. Plessner's interesting work, *Lachen und Weinen*. I discussed this issue in a chapter of my recently published *The Immortal Comedy* (Lexington, 2005).

11. The detailed analysis of this type of feelings is in my book *Everyday Life*, English edition from Routledge & Kegan Paul, 1987.

12. For a detailed and beautiful analysis of consideration see György Lukács, *Az esztétikum sajátossága (Aesthetics)*, II, 1.

13. Taste itself has become problematic in modern bourgeois society, precisely with the disintegration of the *sensus communis*. On this issue see my study written jointly with Ferenc Fehér, "On the Irreformability and Necessity of Esthetics" *Philosophical Forum*, Boston University, 1977.

14. For an analysis of equal and unequal contacts see my *Everyday Life*.

15. From father I received my attitude, the serious guide of life, from my little mother the gay nature, and the yearning to invent stories (my prose translation).

Chapter III.
How Do We Learn to Feel?

To recall what I have said in the first chapter: man learns the tasks of the world from the time of his birth starting out from his own organism. The world provides the tasks to be internalized. Everything thus acquired, becomes my Self, the subject, "my own world." Man relates to the world and the aspects of this relation are internalization, objectivation, and self-expression. All three are simultaneously action, thinking and feeling. The capacities of man become differentiated and, at the same time, they become reintegrated, along with the formation and development of the subject. It is during this differentiation and reintegration process that man learns to feel.

I must add, however that the ability to feel, think and act are inborn, but feeling is philogenetically the primary process with reference to the realization of these abilities. At the moment of our birth we do not act as yet, nor even think, but we do feel. The cry of the newborn is undoubtedly an expression of feeling. Feeling in itself, therefore, is neither learned nor acquired. The cry of the human child, at the moment of entrance into the world, as analyzed so many times, is a "sign" of the relationship between the demolition of the instincts and human feeling. It seems that this may account for the fact that crying—as opposed to laughing—can later become the expression of each of our specific emotions. Not a single animal species "enters" the world with expression of feeling. The expression of feeling at the moment of birth signals the breaking away from nature. Everything I have said about feelings in the first chapter of this book, especially about its selective and homeostatic function, is related to the philogenetic primacy of feeling. The condition for learning purposeful activity and thinking in the case of a being not guided by instincts is feeling. At the same time, however, the formation of the types of feelings necessary for homeostasis and selection (in a given society, in a given environment), is a precondition for action and for thinking. A new-born baby that has come into the world with a serious defect in thinking ability may still feel, but his feelings will never fulfill the functions of homeostasis and selection, since they cannot be differentiated adequately with the tasks and cognition cannot be reintegrated into the feelings. *Thus the fact that man feels is not acquired. But each particular feeling is in some way related to learning, or is learned outright.*

The drive feelings as biological signals are not learned, it is true, but the process of their differentiation is tied to learning. First of all we must learn what it is we feel, inasmuch as we "cannot help ourselves" without such knowledge, since we are not beings guided by instinct. The identification of feelings often goes together with the understanding or interpretation of feelings. As I have mentioned, there are persons who feel that their stomach aches or feel ill when they are hungry and at the same time know that they are hungry. It is true that this knowledge does not alter the quality of the feeling, but it is indispensable to the formation of an adequate behavior. If in this case he did not know that he is hungry, homeostasis would become impossible.

We must learn, furthermore, with regard to the drive feelings also the differentiation within the feeling. First of all with regard to the intensity of feeling: thus we can be very hungry, or only slightly hungry, etc. This is not as easy to learn as one imagines at first sight, the reason being that affects are built on top of drives and the ability to separate the drives from the affects is part of the process of learning. A child may say he is very hungry, but if we should place in front of him something for which he has no appetite, it becomes immediately obvious that he wasn't so hungry after all. A strong sexual affect is often confused with the sexual drive. This often happens in a state of inebriety, which considerably increases the sexual affect, but not the sexual drive.

Furthermore, we must learn the behavior in relation to drives; and this reacts to the feelings themselves, especially to their intensity and the periodicity of their appearance (of course, only within certain limits). Freudian literature has analyzed this problem in depth. We know that regular or irregular breast-feeding already has an influence on the periodicity of the drive of hunger and the learning of the behavior in connection with urination and defecation plays a role in the formation of psychic character.

In the case of pain—a relative of the drive feelings—it is likewise not the feeling that we learn, but the identification of feelings first of all. The learning of identification is more complex than in the case of drive feeling; in the case of certain types of pains—where the ability to locate is not inborn, but presupposes the acquisition of that ability as well. The determining factor in the learning of the ability to locate the source of pain is verbalization. Every parent feels relieved when the child becomes able to say what it is that hurts, where it hurts, etc. The ability to approximately locate bodily pain belongs among the conditions of our homeostasis; precise location is not essential for homeostasis and there are people who never learn it.

Another important factor with regard to bodily pain is the ability to describe (designate) the specific nature of pain. Of course, verbalization is also a precondition to this process. We must learn to tell whether something "pricks," or "burns" or "lances," we must be able to distinguish cramp-like pain from continuous pain. How much experience is needed for such knowledge, how much "trial and error" is involved in learning it, I need not waste many words on this subject.

Inasmuch as bodily pain, as opposed to drives, is expressive and yet affects do not build upon it, learning has a much more reduced role with regard to the intensity of expression than in the case of drive feelings. "It hurts very much" is so strongly expressive that it becomes evident to the Other without further effort on our part. The person who is convulsed with cramps or screaming in pain "speaks for himself." Of course, even in connection with the feeling of pain we have to develop the expected "behavior." This behavior (which is, by the same token, expression!) influences the feeling itself, within certain limits, or at least the evaluation of the feeling as more intense or less intense (in practice we cannot separate the two). There are cultures where woman in parturition are expected to scream, others where they are expected to grind their teeth. The expression, as I have said, reflects upon the feeling or at least on the evaluation of the feeling. In the former case the woman will speak of terrifying pain, *post festum*, in the latter of great, but bearable pain.

In the case of affects we must learn not only the identification of feeling but, in addition and primarily, their object. Those stimuli with regard to which the affects must "react" are usually culturally defined. The infant digs into feces with pleasure; he must be told many times "ugh!" and "disgusting!" until feces should become a stimulus provoking disgust. Little children have to be told not to go with "strangers with candy" on the street, because that is dangerous; and then they begin to be afraid. If someone is raised in a culture where nudity is natural, he will never feel shame about nudity. All this applies also to those drives upon which affects are built; in every case where the differentiation of the drive feelings from the affects built upon them is not the determining factor, the learning of the specific (and culturally given) object plays a role. ("What is the specific food that would abate our hunger?")

In analyzing the affect of fear, I said that its formation may have two sources, information according to which something is "dangerous" and individual experience. The latter is also a learning process, but one that applies to the learning of animal affects, while the former is exclusively human and plays a primary role in the "learning" of the objects of our affects. Furthermore, we must also learn "to read" other people's affects. This learning process begins even before verbalization. An older infant already reacts differently to a happy or angry face or attitude; and often responds with a smile to the first and mostly with frightened weeping to the latter. But he may react to rage with aggression as well and to fear (to the fear of another child) also with aggression, or possibly with perplexity. Verbalization, however, makes even the reading of affects "more exact"; at the same time only verbalization makes possible the identification of the Other's expression with our own feeling: the acquisition of the knowledge, that what I feel and what is expressed by the Other's expression, are basically the same affect.

The expression of affect, however, as I have previously mentioned, is not learned. What elicits the affect in me is a consequence of learning. But once it has elicited the affect then the affect (every specific affect) may be rendered manifest and channeled only through expressions of affects that are inborn and universal. And this indicates the limits of learning affects. There are but universally human affects. Every person must acquire these (and must learn how to "read them"), "lest he perish." If we were to say that the rage elicited by injus-

tice is different from the rage that seizes someone during a life and death struggle with a wild animal, then we would be right insofar as we understand rage
within its cultural context, in its relation to the whole of the personality and to
the whole of the emotional world. But we are wrong if we consider "pure affect"
and its expression; because from this point of view rage is always the same feeling and it is not learned.

I have talked about the necessity of acquiring affects "lest we perish." Of
course, there are persons who are more "inclined" to certain affects and less to
others (there are persons, for instance, who are not disgusted by anything). I do
not assert that the presence of every affect is essential for the preservation of
every individual (this is not even true about the drive feelings—think of sexual
drives). But I do assert that at the time of the formation of the human race there
was a need for them and that there is more or less need for them even today, not
to mention the self-preservative function of the "reading" of affects.

Orientational feelings and emotions, however, are learned completely and in
every respect. Each of the orientational feelings and emotions is the consequence of the reintegration of cognition and action into feeling, the resultant of
this process. The Self builds its "own world" in its relation to the world, through
the processes of internalization, objectivation, and self-expression and intends to
maintain it and expand it in the given world on the basis of which it selects in
perception, thinking and action; then the actual feeling components of this "own
world" are always orientational feelings and emotions (emotional habits). Naturally: drive feelings and affects also select; and I have mentioned several times
the decisive role they fulfill in homeostasis. But if these were the basic components of the Self, then every Self would be emotionally identical; the difference
would stem only from the uniqueness of the biological organism. During the
development of the Self drives and affects become organic parts of the emotional character and the emotional personality and this is why I had termed them
in these discussions "abstractions." The Selves live in a world in common; but at
the same time each Self is a separate world. That our yes- and no-feelings developed on the basis of what experiences, in which area or areas of life, with
what intensity and what our emotions are like: this is what our Self, its social
homeostasis and its selective function are based upon. Of course, the Self may
be more or less idiosyncratic; but we know from reliable researchers in the eth-
nology of pre-civilized peoples (much has been done along this line by the
American "Culture and Personality" school) that even in the case of completely
identical activity types, even without division of labor and even with a given
fixed "basic personality structure," there is no culture so "primitive" in which
the individuals do not differ from one another with regard to emotional character.

Although I may have given the impression, at the starting point in my
analysis, that in the whole attitude of humans I would assign the primary role to
feeling, I now arrive to the opposite conclusion. Although feeling is philogenetically primary in comparison with thought and action, only the feeling can fulfill
the actual function of feeling, into which cognition and action have reintegrated.

The most important constituent of humans, as opposed to animals, is that they are purposeful and conscious beings, beings acting intelligently. Man's world of feelings is a human world of feeling the world of feeling of the subject—by virtue of the circumstance that his feelings are purposive feelings, cognitive and situational. Indeed, there is no knowledge without feeling, there is no action without feeling, there is no perception without feeling, there is no recollection without feeling—but all our feelings as feeling either include the factor of cognition or at least are related to cognition, goals, and situations and only become relevant as feeling through interaction with these.

Let us survey the process of the formation of feelings (their differentiation and integration), that is of the formation of the Self. We learn to feel; but how?

The new-born feels, but its feelings are undifferentiated, as we may surmise from their expressions. In the opinion of Allport they have only two types of feelings: distress and excitement. Gehlen analyzes the formation of the hunger feeling as follows: "Wir haben keinen Grund anzunehmen, dass der Hunger des kleinen Kindes ihm anders gegeben ist, denn als schmerzhaftes Unlustgefühl. Die Orientierung dieses Gefühls an wiederholten Eindrücken und Bildern der Abhilfe schafft erst mit der Zeit ein gerichtetes, konkretes, d.h. zusammengesetztes Bedürfnis, nämlich ein solches, das, sobald es fühlbar wird, in den Phantasmen der Erfüllung sich meldet, das also jetzt als bestimmer Antrieb, als Hunger-nach-solchem fasslich wird,"[1] Gehlen concludes, and he is no doubt right in this, that the differentiation of the feeling of hunger drive occurs simultaneously with the formation of affects built on the hunger drive. If the drive feelings were given differentiated at the beginning of the newborn's life, then the behaviorists and the orthodox Freudians would undoubtedly be justified in claiming that all other feelings are connected to drive reduction; in other words that the drives exist first and all other feelings derive from the reduction of drives and from the manner and form of their reduction. But if Gehlen is right—and I believe that practically all known facts support his train of thought—then the "building up" of feelings on the reduction of drives is an untenable theory. Then we must assume that the formation of certain affects, what more of certain emotions!—is simultaneous with the differentiation of drive feelings and is even a precondition of the latter.

The formation of the subject begins at the moment of birth. The newborn is thrown into the world; or, if you prefer, he is thrown into freedom. He pays increasing attention to the response of the world and this world begins to become object-like for him at about the age of six weeks, that is, when it begins to assume the form of object. The three month old infant is already beginning to distinguish objects or "things" from the subject-object; he increasingly distinguishes the important subjects (such as the mother) from the unimportant ones. As soon as he is able to integrate his movements somewhat, he becomes engaged in purposeful activity. The infant begins to pay attention to the results of his own activity. Parallel to this "he discovers" his own body and distinguishes it from all those objects which are not appurtenances of his body. He is involved in all his activities, in all his observations; the specific quality of involvement, however, differentiates depending on the object of involvement, on what type of activity is the involvement in question connected with. The differentiation of feelings, hence their learning, is an organic part of the universal learning process.

Among the expression of feelings of the infant it is the smiling response that has been analyzed most thoroughly. According to Dumas the smile of the newborn is not yet actual smiling, it is not expression of feeling, but the consequence of the spontaneous play of facial muscles. Undoubtedly: the smile of the newborn is not reaction, hence it is not really a smile. Nevertheless it cannot be denied that the germ of feeling disposition is already present in it. For the infant in a state of "distress" is unable to smile. The smile of the newborn is a readable "sign"—at least for the adult—it is the sign that "everything is all right."

Actual smiling develops at the age of two to five months; this is the first expression of "contact" feeling in man, one might say the first expression of feeling of social relationship. The smile is directed first of all at the representative Other (for instance, the mother), initially as a matter of response (the infant "smiles back"), later as an initiative as well. The experiments conducted by Brackbill have proved convincingly that this first contact feeling (and its expression) has nothing to do with drive reduction; he approached his infants only after they had satisfied all possible drives. (They had been fed and changed.) He never took part in any way in this procedure of satisfaction. When, however, he smiled at the sated and clean babies, they responded with a smile the same way they respond to the mother who suckles them and changes their diapers. Thus the smile response was not built on drive reduction, but derived directly from the relationship between subject and subject (social relation). Hence the smiling response is already the expression of an emotion or, if you prefer, the response of the first, as yet undifferentiated emotion.

Our first emotion—the still undifferentiated emotion—is therefore "entering into contact" with the world. In the first smile of the infant we witness the birth of the subject-subject-object relationship; I smile at You, because You are you, because You are non-I.

Piaget has analyzed beautifully the differentiation of the smile, as well as the differentiation of the emotion that has become explicit in the expression of smile. The infant smiles when he encounters a familiar toy and he smiles at the expected and unexpected results of his own efforts. The smile of the one-year old is very much differentiated; we can distinguish between the smile of gaiety, relief, triumph, recognition, love, pleasure. The formation of the idiosyncratic character of the smile expression has begun (with the possible exception of the gaiety smile, insofar as the affect is "pure"). It is already the emotional character that is reflected in the idiosyncratic smiles.

We can follow attentively the same process in the case of the expressions of crying (although the material on which we may base our arguments is much scantier and less elaborate than in the case of the smiling response). The crying of the newborn is an undifferentiated expression of feeling; but that of the baby gets more and more differentiated. The various types of crying appear gradually:

the crying out in pain, the cry of rage, the cry of anxiety, the cry of displeasure, the demanding cry. At the same time these assume partially idiosyncratic forms. The mother of the newborn establishes the cause of the crying always by trial and error; she attempts to change his diapers, to feed him and, if all this does not help, she says "surely he must have a stomachache." But the mother of an older infant no longer has recourse to the method of trial and error; she can determine from the cry itself what the cause is, what type of feeling is being expressed. Witness of the increasingly idiosyncratic character of one or another of the types of crying is the fact that those who know the infant can tell immediately what is expressed by a certain cry, whereas those who do not know the child are unable to read the various cry "signs."

Here, too, we may assume that the various feelings do not originate with drives. If the baby cries because he wants people to pay attention to him, that does not stem from the fact that people paid attention to him when his hunger was being satisfied; if he is used to being picked up when crying, he will cry even if sated. And this type of crying does not even stem from hunger for entertainment; this hunger (including the affect of curiosity) can be amply satisfied by the active "discovery" of his environment. Of course the emotion expressed in the "demanding" cry—and those not built on drives—is itself still undifferentiated. Innumerable specific emotions will evolve from it in the future and each one of them is cognitively and situationally different: the feeling of helplessness, the feeling of abandonment, the feeling of loneliness, the desire and will for contact, furthermore forms of behavior in which feelings play merely the role of background—such as extortion, aggression, persistence, complaining, etc.

As I have already mentioned, the acquisition of verbal thinking is like a cornerstone in the learning of feelings and in the most varied relations. I argued that some drive feelings and other feelings (for instance, feeling of pain, feeling of unpleasantness, rage, etc.) become differentiated even before verbalization. But the differentiation becomes complete with verbalization. Let us recall what I have said about the drives; because of their essence, they are least expressive in facial expression in modulation of voice. Hence, in the case of humans, the differentiation cannot become complete before verbalization. The human child who, as opposed to the young animal, is not a being guided by instincts, who is "thrown into" the world by his birth, can only let the world know about his drive feelings, before the formation of verbalization, through expression. The drive feeling, which is essentially directed at ourselves ("seek the solution!"), cannot be addressed to himself in the case of the helpless infant, since the infant "cannot seek the solution." The hungry infant cries, hence his hunger behavior (which, precisely for this reason is not yet a typical hunger behavior), is expressive. As soon as the child learns to say "I am hungry," however, the hunger drive ceases to be expressive. The child who can speak no longer cries if he is hungry or thirsty, but communicates his feeling; the "whining tone" that accompanies the communication and that is so frequent at the beginning is a remnant of the expression, which gradually fades away.

The denomination of the feeling is decisive not only because it is a condition for its identification (its conscious identification for instance, I know that it is my head that aches, I know that I am a bit thirsty or very thirsty, I know that I am angry now), but also because in general the objects of the affects cannot be socially given without denomination. Of course, the designation of the stimuli of the affects—the stimuli that are socially indicated—begins well before the development of the child's verbal thinking. The adult operates with words even in this case, but the words function not as verbal signs but as signs of feeling. If we should say "ugh!" to the infant digging in feces, then it is not the word itself, but the accompanying expression of disgust that has the primary task of developing the affect of disgust in this context. We warn the infant who does not speak about touching the hot stove with a frightened shout (that is, with an expression of feeling) whereas, in comparison, the words used by us do not play a significant role. In the course of the development of lingual behavior denomination of the stimulus called upon to elicit the affect gains ground increasingly. The more the emphasis shifts to denomination, the less need for the denomination itself to be expressive. If we explain to a three-year-old that should he fall out the window, he would break his neck, that is, that it is dangerous to lean out of the window, we no longer rely on the expression of fright or of fear; we only show expression of fear if we ourselves are afraid, for instance should we catch the child precisely in the act of climbing out the window. It is the denomination that enables the formation of the affect on the basis of intelligence rather than on training. We can indicate to the child (and we usually do) those "groups" of objects and persons that are disgusting or dangerous and we indicate those acts in relation to which he should feel ashamed. The function of verbalization in the case of rage or curiosity is just the opposite. Here it is essential to designate those "groups" which cannot become the objects of the affect, according to social prescriptions. (Whether the limitation of curiosity is or is not desirable from the point of view of the development of the child is another matter with which I cannot deal here.)

The designation of the objects of the affect based on intelligence (rather than training) makes it possible for the affect to become independent of personal experience; it also allows the development of fantasy with regard to the affects. In the presence of a stimulus the affect may manifest itself in such a way that we only imagine the consequences, without ever having lived through them. Thus a child may be seized with panicky fear in the presence of a "sugar daddy" even if no such person has ever done him harm.

The "conceptual elaboration" of the stimulus eliciting the affect has, however, a limit. This limit is the affect feeling itself. If someone has never experienced a certain affect, then the denomination of the feeling does not suffice to bring it about. If someone has never experienced fear, it would be no use telling him that this or that is dangerous, he will not learn to feel fear thereby. For in the learning of affect personal experience is primary. Only in the case of someone who has already experienced rage does it make sense to say that he should not feel rage because of this or that; only in the case of someone who has already experienced fear does it make sense to say that this or that is dangerous. It is not possible to teach someone an affect if that person has not had prior experience of that affect. Only the person who has experienced shame can know what shame is; only the person who has experienced disgust can know what disgust is. Consequently affects would evolve even if none of their objects were socially given. True enough, this is merely a thought experiment, because such human affects do not exist and even in thought it does not relate to the affect shame, which is social par excellence. I have been obliged, however, to make this hypothetical qualification, so that the distinction between affects and emotions may become clear from this point of view as well.

Although, as we have seen, some undifferentiated emotions evolve even before the appearance of verbal thinking; yet even at this time they invariably relate to intelligence activity. The smiling response is an "assumption of human contact," the smiling ahead (smiling at somebody) is already the active "provocation" of such a relation. The examples mentioned by Piaget (smile at the expected or unexpected result of our effort) refer to emotions all of which accompany the par excellence intelligence activity (I brought something about); at the same time the "situation" is already "built into" these feelings, they are modified by the intellectual "grasping" of the situation itself; thus the "expected" and the "unexpected" effects bring about two different situations and two different emotions. (The former contains the feeling of "familiarity," the latter the feeling of "surprise" or "wonder.")

The formation of verbal thinking, however, brings about a much more radical turn in our emotional life than in our drive feelings or our affects. While in the case of the affects verbal communication merely provides the objects of the affects, but does not create the affects themselves, in the case of the emotions the same verbal communication fills a role of primary importance in the process of formation of the feelings.

First of all we must learn what emotions and feeling dispositions actually exist. The process of understanding the affects takes place rapidly and is parallel to the "discovery" of their existence within ourselves, with greater or lesser intensity, since we feel them ourselves whereas the recognition of emotions and emotional dispositions is a successive and protracted procedure, which never becomes complete, perfectly finished. In the case of persons born into complex social structures this process of recognition is theoretically infinite (the only limit is the one imposed by the finite nature of our existence). Yet the "discovery" of the emotions and of the dispositions to feel is in no way parallel to the process of discovering them within ourselves. And this remains true even if we consider entire "types of emotions." Even the person who has never felt hatred must know that hatred exists, because if he did not, he would not be able to react to hatred, would not learn the relationship to hatred, would not be able to evaluate it, etc. The basic condition of existence, of social preservation, is to know many more emotions (types of emotions), than what we have had opportunity to feel ourselves. If a three-year-old should come home from nursery crying to the effect that "Sue has broken my doll and I did nothing to her!" then, after asking her about the details we are able more or less to interpret the behavior of her companion and we explain to her: "Sue is envious of you. If someone is envious that means that she cannot bear you to have nicer toys than she has, to receive new dolls, etc." And if we should experience "signs" of envy in this child as well, then we tell her: "Now you see, you are envious, just like Sue." But if we do not notice such signs—for there are children who are never envious—she must still know what it means to be envious. Let me refer once again to what I have said in the first chapter about the formation of one's "own world": from this the child will not know exactly what the feeling of envy means—he will be learning this continuously all his life; the knowledge that "envy" exists, is merely the point of departure of this learning.

Now let us place into parentheses the fact just analyzed, namely that we always know many more feelings than what we actually feel. With reference to those emotions we merely know, but do not feel, we cannot ask the question "how do we learn to feel?" We can only ask a different question: "How do we learn to recognize feelings?" If, however, we remain with the initial question, then we must note the following: the learning of a feeling is at the same time a process of "fitting together" the emotional concept and the feeling. I have borrowed the notion of "fitting together" from geometry; for feeling and emotional concept can never be "concurrent" (for every emotion is idiosyncratic, even individually), they can only be "fitted together."

"Fitting together" feeling and emotional concept may happen in two opposite ways. What is the first way of "fitting together?"

I have the emotional concept (I know it), but I have never felt the feeling. The feeling that forms in me is referred to the already known emotional concept, that is, "I fit it together." This may take place in many different ways. To mention the most important types: it is possible that the feeling breaks out of me suddenly and I identify it with the known concept slowly and with difficulty; it is possible that I desire to experience the emotion designated by the concept; I watch in myself to see whether it is in formation, I force its formation, I deliberately place myself into situations which will facilitate its formation, etc.; it is possible that I behave in accordance with a feeling and, "reading the signs" of my behavior, others will identify my feeling with the emotional concept I already know (this is particularly frequent if I evaluate the emotional concept negatively). Thus, in practice everybody knows that love exists before even falling in love, for the existence of this emotional disposition has been practically "pushed in front of the eyes" of children by everything from folksongs to prattle, to television; and so has its greater or lesser significance in the life of the individual according to age. There is no need to waste many words to show how crucial in the life of every person what I have called "fitting together" becomes: we often interrogate ourselves, "am I in love?"—"what I feel, is this what people call love?" "Yes, I think I am in love" and "This must be what people call love!" Or "no, it is not love after all," we may reply to ourselves. In the "process of fitting together" it is not the concept, but rather its content, its meaning that is crucial. The person who, let us suppose, became acquainted with the content of the concept of love by reading *Werther*, will not "fit together" with the concept of love feelings which others may already experience as love. This "fitting together," however, is by no means necessarily final; the learning of love seldom ends with the first love experience. Later on we may say: "I did not know then what true love is, but now I do." (Or, it seems that I am depressed, or it seems that I am in despair, although I have never felt despair before.)

Since emotions are cognitive and situational feelings, we discover them in ourselves not only when we first feel those that belong to a certain type, but each time we feel in a specific relation or reference. For instance: "Is it possible that I should feel pity for my foe? But I do feel pity for him!" "I have never felt commiseration in such and such a case, but this feeling 'fits together' with the already known concept of commiseration, or with those feelings which correspond to that concept," etc. Pity for the foe is the learning of a new feeling no matter how many times one may have felt pity for members of one's family or for friends.

Even if we should be quite familiar with the emotional concept before the appearance of the feeling, the feeling always modifies the content of emotional concepts. A feeling we have experienced is understood differently from one we have never experienced. This modification, however, does not necessarily imply that we are better able to read from the emotional "signs" of others, although that may imply it. Since, however, we experience every emotion in an idiosyncratic way, this process of concretization (for every feeling is a process of concretization) leads us to analogous understanding when "reading" other people's emotions. If the feeling of an Other (as judged from its expressions) is not quite the same as my own, then I am inclined even to question the very existence of that feeling. The more particularistically inclined the individual, the more likely it is that he can judge only by his own idiosyncratic emotion and emotional expression the feeling belonging to the feeling concept in the Other.

In the "fitting together" of emotions and emotional concepts the latter are decisive and no better proof of this is required than art. The arts, in the first place its verbal forms, are capable of evoking in us all the emotions we know. For what we are able to understand, could be evoked in us, regardless of whether we have ever lived through or have felt the emotions and feeling dispositions illustrated by the artist in our own life. We need never have been in Othello's shoes in order to experience his jealousy; in fact, we need never have been jealous at all. We need not have been madly in love to be moved to tears by the deaths of Tristan and Isolde; we need never have felt desire for vengeance in order to feel through Electra's rancor. Of course, this does not mean that we are jealous along with Othello, in love along with Tristan, or that we desire vengeance along with Electra, but rather that we are to empathize with these feelings, because we understand the situations that have elicited them and the feelings themselves. These same masterpieces which shake us may be indifferent or boring to a child, not because we have experienced the depicted feelings while they have not, but because we understand those feelings, whereas they can only barely understand them. Children barely understand these feelings not because

the emotional concepts themselves are simply unfamiliar, or only partially familiar, but first of all because children do not understand the situation of the
protagonists. And we know that emotions are situational and not only can they
be felt only along with the situation, but they can be interpreted simply through
the situation. The particularities of those novels that children can also enjoy and
live through do not consist in communicating feelings which the children have
felt, but rather in dealing with emotional concepts and situations which make the
emotions understandable to them and thus enable them to live them through.
The happy child can cry along with Oliver Twist because he understands what
Oliver suffers.

There is, however, another way of "fitting together" feelings and emotional
concepts: we feel something, but we do not know what it is we feel—we seek a
concept that "fits" our feelings. It is true that after the formation of verbal thinking we do not have any feeling we could not name and do not actually name.
The child says: "I am in a good mood," or "I am in a bad mood," "I am excited,"
"I am curious," "I like so and so," "I don't like so and so," "I hate so and so,"
etc. But seldom do we hear let us say, a six year old declare "I feel desperate" or
"I am filled with satisfaction" or "I feel inspired" or "I despise so and so" or
"while so and so is a nice person, I cannot say I really like him." Of course, this
does not imply that the feelings classified under the categories indicated are
completely undifferentiated even at that age. If we should tell the child a nice
story and he breaks into tears saying: "I became so sad," the adult may well explain "You are not really sad, you are moved." And possibly, on the next occasion, the child too will say: "I am moved"—and in this case he distinguished
between two feelings and has "fitted" them to different concepts. It may happen
that this differentiation is postponed. The process of differentiation may also
begin to take place within the feelings described as "I don't like" For instance,
"I don't like him because he is always clowning" (an instance of contempt), or
"I don't like him because the teacher gives him special treatment" (an instance
of jealousy) or, without further explanation "I don't like him" (pure orientational
feeling). It seldom happens, however, in the development of the child that,
should the need arise (and mostly even earlier!), he does not find within his
reach the differentiated emotional concepts that correspond to his differentiated
feelings.

As soon, however, as the growing person begins to "keep his feelings to
himself," the second way of "fitting together" plays an ever more important role.
(Later I will discuss the process of learning to "keep feelings to oneself.") The
intensity of the process and the age at which it takes place are largely idiosyncratic. Certainly it was rather typical of the 19th century that "fitting together"
took place to a considerable extent with teenagers; today emotional "infantilism"
is more frequent, but this particularity of the teenager has by no means ceased.
The half-child-half-adult begins to observe his own feelings and he begins to
realize that the feeling concepts he disposes of are not sufficient to express them
completely. The more complex process of "fitting together" feelings has started;
the person in question begins to use previously unused nuances in the repertory

of emotional concepts. The feeling "I like him" splits, it takes on many shades: I sympathize with him, I feel attracted to him, I feel friendship towards him, I adore him, I respect him, etc. "I am in a bad mood" splits: I am sad, I feel regret, my heart is aching, I feel desperate, I suffer, I feel depressed, etc. The feeling of not being able to express my feelings in all its nuances now appears; the process of circumscribing emotions begins. The dilettante poetry so freely flowing from teenagers has its source precisely in this need: we want to circumscribe, to express what it is we feel. Yet no matter how detailed the circumscription, we can only do it with concepts; the feeling concepts preserve their priority in spite of every attribute and adjective. (Only the true poet is capable of indicating a specific emotion in all its totality and in a way acceptable to everyone with the help of adjectives and attributes.)

The use of the nuances of emotional concepts, the circumscriptions of emotions and moods, of "supplying" them with attributes and adjectives, is by no means as simple as dotting an "i." I am not talking about the final point of an already completed process, but rather of the beginning of a new process. The denominated feeling is no longer the same feeling we intended to denominate and for which we had been seeking the right term. The denomination of the feeling is at the same time becoming aware of the concrete quality of the emotion, a process that partakes of the very quality of the emotion. If I should declare: now I feel depressed, now sad, now unhappy, now desperate, then, by making it conscious, I increase the differentiation. This is precisely what is meant by (although from only one aspect) the reintegration of cognition into the feelings. If someone should say to himself: "I no longer love this man," this sentence although pronounced only for her own benefit, cannot be retracted. Actually, precisely by becoming conscious of the "I no longer love him" he (she) ceases to love him. From this moment on he looks at the person differently, he lives togetherness in a different way, the "magic" collapses. By the way, the "magic" of words functions in a similar way during the "reading" of the emotion of the Other. If but once I should perceive the Other's feeling in a different light, this irretraceably influences my future reading. If but once I should say: "the kindliness of this person is merely outward appearance; in truth he is selfish and cold," then from this moment on I accept all his kindliness only with a grain of salt.

From the time of the formation of verbal thinking, but in germ even earlier, humans learn a significant proportion (but not every one) of the feelings together with the expectations, customs, and social evaluations pertinent to those feelings. This is obvious in the case of drive feelings and affects. For instance, the affective concepts need not even be "explained," because in any event everyone is more or less able to feel them or read them; at the same time there hardly is a feeling so difficult to "explain" as certain affect feelings. If the child lied or told on someone we tell him: "you should be ashamed of yourself!" or we may say, in the company of friends: "don't be bashful!" and he "learns" to feel ashamed in one case not in the other. But if we had to explain to the child what it means to "feel shame," we would undoubtedly be at a loss. In the case of emotions—at

least during childhood—learning is likewise combined with the learning of social evaluation. ("Don't be jealous of your brother," "It's not nice to be jealous
of your friend," "learn to respect this man, because he is a real hero," "trust only
those who have earned your trust" etc.) Yet it is not possible to form emotions
merely by enjoin of command. Precisely because we are dealing with cognitive
and situational feelings, the communication of the evaluation of feelings must
accompany the explanation of emotional concepts. Though schematically, yet
we must teach the child what it means to "envy," "to feel jealous," "to respect,"
"to trust." But even this is insufficient! We must explain what "friendship" is,
what it means to be a "hero," how one person can earn the trust of another. True
enough, even enjoining an affect at least appears to have conditions of knowledge. When we enjoin the child to "be ashamed" of himself for having told a lie
or for telling on others, we assume that the child knows what it means to lie or to
tell on others. But insofar as we explain the concept of lying and differentiate
the concept of telling on others, we have not formed an affect, but rather an
emotion; the eliciting of the affect, in this case, plays merely the role of the
means of teaching the emotion. (In the same way as if we said: "you should be
ashamed of yourself for having been envious, for having been jealous, for having been selfish.") With whom the eliciting stimulus is not being-caught-at-
lying, but lying itself is the source of the "bad feeling," this person will feel
"ashamed" even if no one sees him and everyone has forgotten about it; and this
is no longer the affect of shame, but the beginnings of a bad conscience.

Even the former example shows: The channeling and regulation of affects
plays the leading role in the early formation of emotional behavior. Drive reduction, which always remains the most important factor in the formation of animal
behavior (even the rudimentary intelligence activity of Köhler's apes is tied to
the consumable banana at the end of the task), takes part in the formation of
human emotional behavior only through the intercession of affects.

As long as and to the extent the formation of affects originates in personal
experience, they are not necessarily the source of emotions (as we know, the
affects of animals also emanate from experience). But whereas the instincts constitute the basis of animal experience, human affects are not based on instincts;
the "role" of instincts is taken over by the socially given stimulus. The socially
given stimulus (which by the same token are always specific situations) however, unavoidably give an emotional "coloring" to the affects. Along with the
learning of affects man learns the relationship to the affects in the prescriptions
pertaining to them; the relationship to the affects, however, is always emotion
creating.

Let us recall how Aristotle defined courage: a courageous man is one who
fears what he should, where he should, when he should, the way he should. We
may react with fear to certain stimuli (at the appropriate time and place), but not
to others. An important, but by no means exclusive form of the regulation and
channeling of affects (i.e. of their transformation into emotions), is self-control.

Every child must learn to dominate his affects. If someone has learned this
and has transformed it into an emotional habit, self-control no longer plays an

important role subsequently. If someone has not learned this or has not learned it in some respect, he has to practice self-control all his life (his emotions in this or that respect have not become emotional habits). The beginning of the regulation of affects, that is, from what age and how intensely, varies considerably according to culture. According to the observations Whiting and Child carried out on fifty-five tribes, rage is already regulated and channeled at a relatively early age everywhere; whereas the channeling and regulation of the sexual affect shows far greater variation (with regard to what is channeled and at what age; for instance, masturbation or sexual play with members of the other sex, etc.). I need hardly mention that the channeling of fear or of disgust exists all over the world.

The regulation of the affects by evaluation and by means of self-control goes along with the regulation of the expression of affect. Better said: the point of departure of the control over the affects is control over the expressions of the affects. In this or that regard we must not show our fear, our rage, our disgust, our curiosity. The expression of affect becomes partial; of course, only in those cases, where we judge the presence of affects to be negative. To the extent we internalize the negative relation to the affects in this or that case the expression will differ from the original expression of affect and becomes an increasingly idiosyncratic expression of emotion. Darwin was already aware to what extent expression influences the feeling itself (in this case, the affect). "The free expression by outward signs of an emotion intensifies it. On the other hand, the repression, as far as this is possible, of all outward signs softens our emotions."[2]

Darwin likewise noticed the fact that some expressions of emotions come about precisely as a result of the repression of certain expressions of affects and this fact is the "sign" of the appearance of emotional feelings taking the "place" of affect: "Again, some highly expressive movements result from the endeavor to check or prevent other expressive movements."[3] The "learning of feelings" by means of affects is not the only way to acquire self-control and, by the same token, the conscious "domination" over the expression. The process of tying certain affects to specific value situations (as stimuli) is already emotion creating in itself. I have already mentioned this in the case of "be ashamed of yourself, because you told a lie." Or: when we must feel rage, we are angry; anger is an emotion, because the quality of feeling of anger contains the reason of our anger and the situation in which we feel anger. Anger, of course, is not invariably "a raging anger"; but if it is, then its expression may be identical with the expression of partial rage (the same neurophysiological or endocrinological process takes place), although it usually contains something "in addition" to the expression of rage. The affect is likewise the instrument of learning emotions if, in the formation of emotional behavior (in its evaluative formation), we "make use" of one affect against another. From this aspect the role of the affect of shame is particularly significant. We tell the child having a tantrum "you should be ashamed of yourself," or "aren't you ashamed that you are afraid of a dog?" But a similar role is played (decidedly negative from the point of view of the formation of the psychological character) by the use of the affect of fear as a means. "I beat you, if you don't stop having a tantrum!" etc. Another not negligible means for the learning of emotions is the acquisition of the ability of the reading of affects. If the child has committed something and sees the angry, frightened, repelled, happy, or curious face of father or mother, then he sees the evaluation of his own act (and of the feeling behind it) as in a mirror and reacts to it with feeling (shame, happiness, sadness, fear). In the "reactive" feelings the affective quality becomes vague. We know that happiness is a pure emotion; but even the sadness, fear, or shame felt in these cases are far more emotive than affective.

As we know, we learn the emotions not only indirectly (by means of the relation to the affects), along with their evaluation (their preference, their selection, or their negative appraisal), but also directly. I have said that one condition of this learning is getting to know the content of emotional concepts (i.e. of their meaning) as well. The more developed the Self, the more idiosyncratic its feelings, the greater the discrepancy between the feeling occurrence and the emotional habit.

General moral norms pertain to emotional habits at all times. It is child's play to judge the emotional habits of others. At the same time our own emotional habits are "ready facts," we have learned these already. Here is where the second act of the learning of feelings begins: we must learn to "coexist" with our own emotional habits. Since I will return to this issue in connection with the discussion of particular and individual feelings, I just want to make a few remarks. There are people who never learn to coexist with their emotional habits: the consequence would be a permanent conflict with himself, a permanent feeling of guilt. There are those who learn to live in peace with their emotional habits in an inauthentic way. They live in peace with them, whether these habits are good or bad. There are those who learn to live with them authentically; and the precondition for this is critical self-knowledge. "To coexist with" is not synonymous with "to live in peace with." Such a person lives in peace with the emotional habits he deems positive and always endeavors to "balance" those deemed negative. This does not imply either personality split, or permanent feeling of guilt. But it means avoiding those situations in which his negative emotional habits may appear; furthermore, it means the conscious regulation of the behavior originating from negative emotional habits (I know I am extremely jealous by nature and just because of this I try to behave in a not jealous way); furthermore, it means refraining from judgment whenever the judgment stems from emotional habit ("I know that I am by nature depressive, but I must not judge the world on the basis of my own depression"); it means, furthermore, that I must not expect others to share my emotional habits ("I cannot expect my colleagues to share my passion").

The status of the one time feeling occurrences or feeling dispositions that do not have the character of emotional habit, is quite different in the evaluation. If it was true with regard to emotional habits that "I have already learned them," about the latter we may say: "I am beginning to learn them." (And there always are feelings, to the end of life, which "I begin to learn now.") Yet, in direct contrast to emotional habits, there are very few socially evaluative norms pertaining to individual feeling occurrences or emotional dispositions. (Of course, such do exist; I should love my parents, I should mourn my relatives, etc.) The evaluative norms (where they do exist) are so general that they can never be completely fitted together with specific, situational cognitive feelings; what more, the more differentiated, the less they can be "fitted together." At the same time the general norms are contradictory and the question arises: which should we apply to the evaluation of a specific feeling? Let us say: "You must not like a wicked person," "love your neighbor as yourself!" "love your enemies!" If I should like this or that person, does the evaluation of the feeling guide me in my feeling? And which evaluation? If I despise somebody for some reason, is the contempt praiseworthy or to be condemned? Is it right to despise somebody for this or for that reason! Is haughtiness expressed in contempt? Or is it justified pride? Or: contempt being the opposite of respect, if we want to respect, must we learn to feel contempt?

We cannot learn one time feeling occurrences and feeling dispositions along with their permanent specific evaluation. Evaluations may guide only as abstract norms (and indeed they do guide us); but it is often possible to apply to the same feeling occurrence different and even contradictory moral norms (as we have seen). Of course, this does not mean that particular feeling events cannot be "evaluated." On the contrary: their particularity resides precisely in the fact that in order to learn them we must in each case idiosyncratically evaluate them. In this case, "to learn to feel" also means to learn to relate to each one of our feelings and to judge our individual feelings idiosyncratically. True enough, the judgment is not a starting point, but rather the terminus, the result. The starting point is usually the yes-feeling or no-feeling. We have an emotion, the emotion differentiates, in one way or another "we fit it together" with its concept (perhaps we circumscribe what we feel) and, at the same time (one might say, during the fitting together) the yes-feeling or no-feeling regarding the given emotion appears. I come to suddenly realize that I am in love with X. Parallelly the no-feeling appears. It is not all right to be in love with X. Perhaps the evaluative judgment is also ready: I hold X to be a man without honor; and I evaluate negatively to love a man without honor. But it may also happen that I do not have any kind of judgment ready: I ignore why I have a no-feeling about being in love with X. In this case, either the no-feeling disappears or, if it endures, I must seek its cause: why do I have a "bad feeling" about being in love precisely with X. Then it occurs to me: this man is not being sincere with me and he is not sincere with anyone! This will seldom make my love vanish, but it becomes "evaluated," in this case evaluated negatively.

We should recall that the condition for the formation of relatively reliable yes- or no-feelings is experience in life. Small children seldom have reliable yes- or no-feelings and even then only in a rather restricted area. They likewise do not have a developed emotional character. The child barely learns to relate to his own feelings, to evaluate them consciously. Hence the basic role, in his case, is played by emotions accepted together with evaluation. (For instance, it is not nice to be envious; the kindhearted child gives his toys to his playmates, etc.)

The idiosyncratic evaluation of emotions (on the basis of yes- and no-feelings) develops only gradually; but it is already present, in the case of morally "normal" individuals, by the teens.

I began my analysis of the evaluation of emotions with the discrepancy between emotional occurrences and emotional habits. Let us remember that emotional habits are emotions we have already learned and with which we have to learn to get along from then on. It is simple to evaluate them on the basis of norms. On the other hand: every specific emotional occurrence "must be learned" again and again and must be evaluated idiosyncratically, even if the learning becomes simpler after the accumulation of life experiences (the formation of the assurance of yes- or no-feelings), although it will never become quite simple. Let us, however, go a step further. The already-formed emotional habit undoubtedly "plays a role," and not a negligible one, in the yes- or no-feelings that occur in connection with the feeling occurrences. Thus, the proud man generally reacts with a yes-feeling to his own feelings "expressing" his pride. We must not forget one thing, however; the emotional character, or emotional personality, is never "limited" to one or another emotional habit. Every person has a variety of emotional habits and these may even contradict each other during the "evaluation" of specific feeling occurrences. (Of course, there are emotional habits that are mutually exclusive; haughtiness and vanity, for instance; but vanity and kindness, or haughtiness and philanthropy do not exclude each other at all.) In the case of such contradictions, what I have called "secondary learning" becomes particularly important. The individual consciously relating to his emotional habits confronts one emotional habit with another and strives to "judge" his specific feeling occurrences on the basis of the emotional habits he deems to be more valuable. I will come back to the analysis of why the inauthentic personality is unable to accomplish this.

To learn to feel—as we have seen in several respects—from the very beginning means to learn to read feelings. It is simple to become familiar with the reading of affects, but learning to read emotions is a continuous task; we can never say "now I know," at most we may say "now I know it better." It is not merely the idiosyncratic nature of the emotions (along with the idiosyncratic nature of their expressions) that places before us new tasks all the time, but three other important factors. These are keeping our feelings "to ourselves," the authentic or inauthentic nature of the feelings and hypocrisy; in other words, three totally different factors.

Insofar as we keep the affects "to ourselves," emotions that are expressive (though idiosyncratically) will result. Repressed rage or repulsion is expressed. If we are somewhat acquainted with a person we can by and large notice when he dominates his rage, his fear, or his shame. The case of pure emotions "kept to ourselves" is different. Here the expression of emotion may be so indirect (or may be omitted altogether), that "reading" becomes impossible. Not seldom the person who has kept his emotions to himself and communicates them later is not believed. X may say to Y: "Years ago I used to be very much in love with you." Y may answer: "I don't believe it. You didn't show it in any way." And X replies: "I did not show it, because I did not want to trouble you with my feelings" and the reply may be accepted as authentic, although there is no proof of it at all. Or X may say to Y: "I feel found out by what you said." Y replies: "But you did not appear to feel that way!" And X replies: "I did not want to show it in front of strangers"; and this too may be accepted as authentic, although there is no proof of it. Whether the recipient of the communication (in this case Y) considers the declaration authentic or not depends on many factors, including his knowledge of human character. If he knows X to be a truthful person then he will accept the declaration as authentic. If the declaration flatters his vanity, likewise. If he is distrustful by nature, he will not accept it, etc. I must add, however: the need for reading feelings "kept to oneself" seldom arises—the breaking open of the so-called "incognito" matters only in the case of a few individuals very important to us.

To be able to differentiate authentic from inauthentic feelings is important in a much wider circle of communications and is decisive both from the point of view of response feelings and of behavior. We call authentic those feelings which express our emotional character and especially our emotional personality; whereas we call inauthentic those feelings which either are not in organic contact with our emotional character, or contradict it. Think of the "inauthentic repentance" so often illustrated by Dostoevsky. Undoubtedly this emotion exists, yet (equally undoubtedly) it is not authentic. At the moment when it is felt, it is truly felt and the expressions of feeling are also authentic; but since it does not emanate from the emotional character and does not even alter that character, it disappears without leaving trace. The person who evaluates the inauthentic as authentic will relate to the person who feels "inauthentic repentance" as if it were to have some effect on his personality in the future and thus exposes himself and others to risks (mostly moral risks).

Everyone knows that there is inauthentic forgiving; someone may forgive in the midst of tears, yet the desire for revenge will return within minutes. But even the desire for revenge may be inauthentic: the person forgives or forgets within minutes. Jealousy may also be inauthentic etc. Inauthentic feelings are particularly frequent when people follow "emotional clichés," whether in a positive or a negative sense. In such cases the inauthentic feelings may be quite enduring and their inauthentic nature is revealed only in moments of crisis or borderline situations, when it becomes obvious that it is not possible to rely on them. Think of Helmer's love for Nora, the inauthentic nature of which only becomes obvious when light is shed on it in a crisis situation. Yes- and no-feelings again play an important role in telling authentic from inauthentic feelings. The more considerable our experience with regard to a type of person the easier we can tell their authentic from their inauthentic feelings purely on the basis of "intuition." (Of course: yes- and no-feelings may mislead us, particularly if we apply them by analogy to types of persons we are not familiar with, which happens rather often.)

Hypocrisy, at least in its pure form, has nothing to do with the processes analyzed above. For in the case of the hypocritical person there is a discrepancy, often a contradiction even between feeling and behavior (expression), but in such a way that the behavior (expression) does not simply "cover" the feeling, but "pretends" a feeling that is not present. Hypocritical repentance is not "inauthentic repentance," but the pretence of repentance with the manipulation of guilt expression. There is no authentic and inauthentic affect at all (this distinction does not make sense here, because the affect—as we know—cannot be a binding character emotion), but there is hypocritical affect, although considerable acting talent is needed for such hypocrisy inasmuch as the pure expressions of affects are difficult to imitate. Emotional hypocrisy, however, is rather simple, precisely because of the idiosyncratic nature of emotional expressions. In addition, hypocrisy has a particularity as compared to the above-mentioned factors: it pertains only to the moral good, or at least to that which we consider the moral good. We may "keep to ourselves" feelings judged to be good or bad. Authentic feelings may likewise be good or bad, but there is no person whose hypocrisy would relate to the expression of some feeling he judges (or particularly which is judged by the system of norms) to be bad. No one pretends to be envious or ill-intentioned. LaRochefoucault was quite right in saying that hypocrisy is the homage sin pays to virtue.

Thus there is particular significance, in learning to read emotions, in the ability to recognize hypocrisy. For this reason as well, it is dangerous if vanity should become an emotional habit. The vain person becomes defenseless in the face of the hypocrite, because he is defenseless in face of flattery. But certain virtues may also make it more difficult to tell the difference between hypocritical expressions and sincere expressions: strong trust often misleads.

These three totally different attitudes, the "keeping of feelings to oneself," the authentic or inauthentic nature of feelings and hypocrisy in feelings, often combine in practice; they often connect or make room for one another. This makes the reading of expressions of emotions, that is, their interpretation and the comprehension of their meaning even more difficult. Everybody has to learn to read, to some extent, the signs of "covert" emotions, but no one is able to read them with dead certainty. If the reading of every emotional signal (and the interpretation of its significance) entails a risk, the reading of the signals of "covert" feelings is doubly risky. But since in general we cannot learn to feel without risk, we likewise cannot learn to read emotional expressions without risk.

We may forget what we have learned. We learn to feel; does this also mean that we may forget feelings? As is commonly known, there are two forms of knowledge: a "knowing what" and a "knowing how"—*Wissen* und *Können*. To learn to feel signifies the unity of these two forms of knowledge. Thus, to learn to "be moved" ultimately means to develop the capability to be moved and, at the same time, to know that we are moved. Since in the case of drive feelings the "knowing how" is the signal given by the biological organism, and in every culture each individual only has to learn the "knowing what," we can forget these feelings no more than we can forget to walk or to hold; in other words, the healthy organism never "forgets" in this regard. In the case of affects, too, the "knowing how" is partially not learned (the expressions of affects are not learned), but they are, at the same time, partially learned (the stimuli are culturally given and the expressions of feelings and, indirectly, the intensity of feelings are socially regulated). But the "knowing what" is always learned; hence in a certain sense it is not possible to forget the affects, but in another sense it is possible. There are two ways to "forget" (and both are relative). On one hand, it is possible to forget when it is always the same "stimulus" that is given for the affect. Likewise, such "forgetting" is possible when no stimulus is provided for the affect. The mercenary soldier "forgets" fear in the heat of battle (he becomes accustomed to the stimulus), that is, he no longer knows how to feel fear, although he can never "forget" that fear exists. If not a single stimulus in someone's environment is sufficient to provoke shame, he may forget to feel shame, but will never forget that shame exists. Let me illustrate the relativity of forgetting affects with an analogy (well aware that all analogies are lame): if someone has learned to swim as a small child and does not swim for 30 years, then we may only suppose he no longer knows how to swim; should he fall into the agitated sea he will most certainly swim again, for it is not possible to forget completely.

The orientational feelings have no organic foundation whatever; since they are purely acquired, they may be completely forgotten. Yet, the degree of oblivion is inversely proportionate to the acquired experience and to the measure of the assurance of orientational feelings. The greater the experience and the assurance of feeling, the more quickly can they be "learned again" or can be "learned over." To present another analogy: it is like the poem we have learned by heart and have recited innumerable times as a child; although we may forget it, we can learn it over quite quickly. Just as learning emotion was a rather complex process, forgetting them is also complex. Let me repeat what I have already said with reference to another problem: in the case of emotions the accord of *Können* and *Wissen* is but the end-result of the learning process. For one thing, we become acquainted with more emotions than we actually feel. For another thing, we often feel something without knowing what it is, something we cannot name. Hence, in the case of emotions there can be *Wissen* without *Können* and *Können* without *Wissen*.

The oblivion of mere *Wissen* is not the oblivion of the feeling, therefore does not pertain to our analysis. Feeling is also a co-determinant in this oblivion, that is, of the extent to which we are positively or negatively involved in the stored information. (Something I have already addressed in the first chapter.) The feeling co-determinant of oblivion is not synonymous, however, with the feeling designated by the concept. If it is synonymous, then we are dealing with forgetting not only of the *Wissen*, but also of the *Können*.

Emotional forgetting, therefore, is the forgetting of the *Fühlen-Können* capability of feeling; more precisely, the forgetting of the ability to feel something or to feel in a certain way. The forgetting of *Fühlen-Können* may be conscious, it may be painfully conscious or pleasantly conscious; a powerful yes-feeling or no-feeling may be involved in it. Of course it may be unconscious as well; we may forget our feelings by not acknowledging them, as if we left them behind "along the way." Tchekhov illustrates this beautifully in his short story "Rotschild's Violin." An old couple, selfish, greedy, heartless, always counting their "losses" and on the verge of the tomb, suddenly remember that they once had a beautiful daughter; they remember how much they had loved her—and all of a sudden they then realize that they forgot how to love. Emotions, much like a garden, require continuous cultivation, watering, if you prefer, as well as weeding out: in order never to forget some but to forget others as much as possible. In fact, everybody does this to some extent; which emotions he cultivates, which he "waters" and "weeds out" is solely his responsibility. In Balzac's *Father Goriot*, the young Rastignac is filled with the noblest feelings: pity, good-will, sympathy, loyalty, the yearning for true love. But at the sight of Parisian luxury "the demon of luxury touched his heart, the fever of the game took hold of him, his throat became dry from the thirst for gold," and he decides to weed out all the nobler feelings. The man Rastignac had already forgotten to feel pity, forgotten to love, forgotten to feel sympathy, forgotten loyalty and trust. Of course, the opposite may occur as well: a person may forget the desire for vengeance, forget envy, forget to laugh at the other's dismay. Until a feeling becomes an emotional habit it is always forgettable—pro or contra—and may be forgotten for good.

Emotional forgetting, however, does not entirely depend on the person who forgets. Emotions must be watered; but for that to be carried out not only a gardener, but water is needed as well. When all the resources in the world that may have fed an emotion dry up, even the best of gardeners cannot water. If someone should remark: "it was so nice when I could still feel happy about something," or "how good it was when I could feel enthusiasm about something," then it is possible emotion has dried up for lack of a resource (a "water") and not because the gardener had been negligent. If the fault lies not in the gardener, but in the lacking resource, then theoretically it is still possible to learn the emotion over again, although oblivion may be final even in this case.

Notes

1. We have no reason to assume that the small child feels hunger as anything but a painful and unpleasant feeling. The orientation of this feeling through repeated impressions and images of support grows with time into an aimed, concrete, that is assembled need, one that presents itself—whenever it reaches the level of sensibility—in fantasy images of satisfaction, that is it can be conceived as a concrete drive, as 'hunger-for-something-like-that.' Gehlen, Arnold. *Studien zur Anthropologie und Soziologie* (Studies in Anthropology and Sociology) (Luchterhand, 1964). 54.

2. Darwin, Charles. *The Expression of the Emotions in Man and Animals* (London: John Murray, 1872), 366.

3. Darwin, *The Expression of the Emotions in Man and Animals*, 354.

Chapter IV.
Value Orientation and Feelings

In the foregoing chapters, we have seen that when we learn feelings, we do so, for the most part, along with their evaluation. Insofar as we do not receive the evaluation "ready made," i.e. insofar as the feeling exists before the evaluative emotional concept, the feelings are nevertheless evaluated (one might say, they are hypothetically evaluated a priori) from the point of view of homoeostasis.

To feel means to be involved in something. To be involved means to regulate the acquisition of the world, departing from the preservation and expansion of the Self, and departing from the social organism. The feeling subject evaluates the species character proper for his own sake and involvement. The evaluation of the "species character proper" for one's own sake, however, entails at the same time the judgment of it: one judges what kind of involvement it is, how intense the involvement is that guarantees the homoeostasis of the social organism in a given environment. Without our feelings we are unable to maintain and expand ourselves, but not all feelings are appropriate for that purpose. The differentiation of our feelings is at the same time the reintegration of cognition. Our feelings can only perform their function if they include their own evaluation from the point of view of social requirements, of the system of customs of the concretely given culture. As Peters fittingly observes: "feelings are judgements."[1]

Hence, we evaluate our feelings according to whether they serve the extension of our Self in a given world, and according to which types of involvements actually hamper that extension. Or, if you prefer, our feelings are, too, the subjects of selection; we prefer those which can best perform the actual function of feelings in a given social milieu and we strive to leave out those which cannot perform this function well in the same given social milieu.

The preservation and extension of our Self is an extremely complex process. Human being is personality, with its own world and it is this "own world" which it strives to preserve and extend. Some feelings, as we know, must be acquired in order for a person to maintain himself in a given environment. The more developed the personality and the more complex the culture, the more variegated the ways and means in which the personality may "extend itself" and the more variegated the objects in which it may become involved. Yet its involvements may collide with one another (and such collisions occur, more or less, in every person's life); certain feelings are evaluated more highly than others, precisely from the point of view of the preservation and extension of personality.

But what is the origin of the "criteria" of evaluation? We evaluate our feelings on the basis of what? What are the criteria of selection? Every choice of value takes place under the guidance of value orientational categories, including the evaluation of feelings. Value orientational categories exist in all cultures; their formation proceeds along with the demolition of instincts. Without the value orientational categories "received" from society feelings would not be able to perform their function. As I have written elsewhere, "every existing entity can have value content. They function as values if they become generalizable choices either socially regulated and normative, or expressing a relation to social regulations and norms."[2] As well: "Something is a value if and only if our orientational categories are generally applicable to it in terms of social regulations and norms."[3]

What are the orientational categories with the help of which we evaluate feelings? In the first place, the primary value orientational category of good and bad. Furthermore, such secondary orientational category pairs as pleasant-unpleasant, Good-Evil, beautiful-ugly, useful-harmful, correct-incorrect, and true-false. We may also use, as we shall see, the secondary orientational category pair of successful-unsuccessful, but this pair is applicable not to the feelings themselves, but rather to their regulation or channeling (for instance, "he succeeded in dominating himself").

Theories of feeling often classify feelings according to certain orientational categories. Thus there may be good and bad feelings, Good and Evil (morally good or bad) feelings, pleasant and unpleasant feelings. But unless we emphasize the conditional applicability of this type of classification and its specific historical quality, we willy-nilly create the impression that the basis of our classification is some natural characteristic of feelings. In this connection, allow me to refer once again to my critical remarks about Wundt and Beebe-Center. They attempt to define pleasant or unpleasant feeling purely on a physiological (natural) basis. Of course, certain feelings do have a natural basis and social generalization itself is an expression of this natural basis (for instance, intense physical pain is bad feeling, thirst for air is bad feeling, or—to cite the example given by Wundt—an acute sound stimulus causes an unpleasant feeling). In the case of certain feelings, the evaluation of orientational categories has a natural basis, although not necessarily exclusively so. In the majority of cases even the use of the orientational category pleasant-unpleasant no longer has a natural basis, not to speak of Good-Evil, beautiful-ugly, correct-incorrect, etc. Thus repentance was a virtue in the Middle Ages—that is, it was a Good (judged to be morally Good) feeling. But Spinoza writes: "repentance is not a virtue," and he thereby expresses the conviction of the age that repentance is not, after all, a "good" feeling. Whether the reduction of experience or being satiated by experiences is pleasant or unpleasant depends on the age, on the class, on the social stratum, and always according to the choice of values. It is not the justification of classifying according to value orientational categories in general that I mean to question here (everyday thinking actually classifies them in this way); I only wish to stress that this system of classification is socially determined.

The evaluation of feelings on the basis of value orientational categories should not be confused with orientational feelings. A yes- or no-feeling with regard to something is neither good nor bad in itself, neither Good nor Evil, neither pleasant nor unpleasant. Let us recall the example given by Wittgenstein: we express with conviction the thought that war will break out soon. Indeed, this is a yes-feeling, but it is neither good nor pleasant. Yet it is correct, if war indeed breaks out. As we shall see, orientational categories may be applied to yes- or no-feelings as well as to any other feeling.

Let us survey the application of some value orientational categories to feelings. The primary value orientational category of good-bad may be applied to every feeling without exception and may replace (may be substituted for) every other, secondary, orientational category. It may be said that somebody has felt well what he should do (he felt it correctly), that forgiving is a good feeling (or Good feeling), that "it was good to be on the excursion" (I had a pleasant feeling), that "he controlled his feelings well" (he succeeded in controlling his feelings). "Jealousy is a bad feeling"—and it may be also said to be unpleasant, wicked, or harmful (i.e., bad may be substituted for any of these).

It is because of this particular function of the value orientational categories of good-bad that we often say about a feeling that "it is both good and bad." If a bad conscience is judged to be morally positive, it may be said that the feeling is both good and bad (since it is Good, but unpleasant). On the other hand, when the sexual affect is considered a "sin," then the feeling that comes about at the time of the appearance of the affect is both good and bad in the opposite way: it is pleasant, but judged to be Evil. This duality, of course, is not to be confused with doing or receiving something with "mixed feelings"; in these cases it is not the same feeling that is both good and bad, but different and contradictorily evaluated feelings refer to the same object.

There exist, however, two feelings to which we apply first of all the primary orientational category and with regard to which the secondary categories (and not every one) have merely a restrictive function. These are the feelings of joy and sorrow (not the affects of gaiety and sadness!) Why? Let us recall the first three types of the emotion joy. These are joy as the attainment of an objective, joy as the satisfaction of a desire and joy as the successful realization of my will (it may be mentioned, although I have not analyzed it, that these same forms, in a negative way, are the main types of sadness). Spinoza writes in the Ethics: "By joy, therefore, in what follows, I shall understand the passive states through which the mind passes to a greater perfection, by sorrow, the passive states through which it passes to a less perfection."[4]

As such, joy, no matter the circumstances within which it may appear, is the feeling which signifies that I have expanded my Self; whereas sorrow signifies, again with reference to anything whatsoever, that my Self has not succeeded in expanding; that my Self has become more limited. These emotions, therefore, never become ambiguous from the point of view of social homoeostasis (the

basic function of feelings), in spite of the fact that they have no natural foundation whatsoever. Joy and sorrow are reflective feelings and they reflect whether
or not I have succeeded in expanding my Self.[5] This is why we consider joy to a
good feeling, the good feeling *par excellence*, and sorrow conversely to be a bad
feeling *par excellence*.[6]

As I have said, however, the secondary value orientational categories (first
of all the categories of Good and Evil) play a restrictive function with reference
to joy and sorrow. The ever given norms have always morally prescribed in
what cases are we not allowed to feel happy. Thus happiness at the dismay of
others is judged negatively (an Evil feeling), as is every form of joy achieved by
transgressing the moral norms. We may opt for certain objectives, desires, or
ways of life as bearers of joy and we may exclude others. But there has never
been a moral norm or regulation (nor could there have ever been) which would
have made a principle out of the negation of joy, which would have judged joy
per se as an Evil feeling (although there have been times when enthusiasm has
been considered a harmful passion, when solidarity was considered a sin, when
blind faith or the desire for revenge were considered virtues). The function of
the most varied feelings is guidance in the expansion of the social organism (its
objectivation, self-realization, its process of appropriation of the world); the
primary function of the emotion of joy is to signal: this has been good, I should
continue this way, do it again. This is the reason why the feeling of joy is the
"good" feeling.

The secondary value orientational category pair is that of the pleasant-
unpleasant. We denominate a feeling as pleasant if we are partially but positively involved in the object of the feeling and unpleasant if we are partially
negatively involved. I say partially, for should our whole personality (our Self)
become involved, then this feeling can never be described with the help of the
category pair pleasant-unpleasant. I must, however, impose a restriction. The
above definition of pleasant or unpleasant cannot be applied to the drive feelings
without complications; and this is obvious, for we are dealing with two-step
feelings. Thus, the feeling of hunger is the "first step," the enjoyment of feeding
the "second step." When I am hungry, I am positively involved in feeding, as
well as when I "reduce" this feeling through the enjoyment of feeding. But I
must modify my definition, with regard to the "first degree" or "tension" degree
of the drive feelings: this is the only case when a partially positive involvement
may be judged unpleasant. Admittedly—and here perhaps I am making a restriction within a restriction—only if the drive feeling is tormentingly intense. In
every other case, I use the categories according to the general definition: and we
may speak of pleasant hunger, of pleasant fatigue, of pleasant sleepiness.

The feelings to which we attribute a "value of pleasantness" are socially
opted (and as such they are generalized, or may be generalized), or at least refer
to systems of rules or social selection. I say "opt" for when it comes to the
pleasant imperative norms do not apply (the "ought" does not apply to the pleasant feeling). For the same reason generalization does not necessarily mean that
the value judgment regarding the pleasant nature of the feeling may be brought

to the level of a generalization; generalization is mostly partial. It follows from all this that the pleasant-unpleasant pair of values does not refer (and cannot refer) to specific feeling qualities. The most varied types of feelings may be pleasant or unpleasant, provided we are partially positively or partially negatively involved and if our involvement can be generalized, even if only partially. (It may happen, of course, that we designate with the terms pleasant or unpleasant feelings that cannot be generalized and which do not refer to the generalization. In this case, however, the expressions "pleasant" or "unpleasant" are not used as value orientation.)

One may say: "This loud noise is unpleasant," or, generalizing: "loud noise is unpleasant"—meaning, loud noise should be avoided. One may say, "I felt unpleasant when I had to reject his advances"; generalizing, "to reject somebody's advances is unpleasant"; in other words, all those situations should be avoided in which I must reject others' advances. I may say "sunning was pleasant"; generalizing "sunning is pleasant" or "it is pleasant to bask in the sun when it is not too intense" (this is partial generalization); in other words, we may opt to sun, we may opt to bask in a sun that is not too intense, but one may not say, "we *should* sun." One may say "It was pleasant to be in his company—he entertained me"; generalizing, "the company of an entertaining person is pleasant"; that is, the company of an entertaining person should be opted. Still, one may not say: I *should* choose the company of an entertaining person.

Above, I have evaluated four feelings of different types, or of completely different qualities, with the concept of pleasant or unpleasant. In the first example, we referred to a perception feeling as unpleasant, a rather intense irritation (as we know, the theories of feeling that are based on merely physiological-natural factors use the terms "pleasant" or "unpleasant" only in this context). In the second example, the feeling or complex of feelings judged to be "unpleasant" is undoubtedly of an emotional nature (embarrassment, trouble). In the third statement the feeling judged to be "pleasant" is likewise complex: it includes perception feeling, but also drive reduction (rest). What is more, it also includes fulfillment of desire (joy), for instance, if my intention was to get a tan and I "feel" that I am getting well tanned. In the fourth statement the feeling judged to be "pleasant" may be the fulfillment of the desire for adventure, joy felt at the relief from boredom, gaiety, etc. (hence, drive reduction, emotion, and affect).

If only partial involvement is possible, then the only value orientational categories we may use in the evaluation of the feeling are the pair pleasant-unpleasant; furthermore, the good and bad primary orientational categories the function of which (in this case) is the simple substitution of pleasant-unpleasant. "Having sunned well" merely means "it was pleasant to be in the sun." But if one can become involved in something with one's whole personality, then the primary value orientational category of good-bad does not necessarily "cover" the pleasant-unpleasant, but may express the Good and Evil, or the beautiful and ugly. If one says: "I felt bad when I had to reject his advances," then this declaration may be synonymous with "I had an unpleasant feeling," but not invariably so. "I felt bad" in this case may mean (and what it actually means is revealed by the context) that I feel responsible for the situation that came about, I felt I had held out a promise I was not able to fulfill, etc. In this case we are dealing not with partial involvement, but with involvement of the personality and the "bad" is the application of the moral orientational category. Or if I should say: "it was good to be with him," because I had learned a great deal from him or because I grew to love him, then the "good" as a primary value orientational category either stands for itself as a result of the fulfillment of desire or the joy of having reached the goal (hence it cannot be substituted by the "pleasant"), or it signifies a moral good.

The value orientational categories of pleasant-unpleasant may only be applied to those feelings in which partial involvement is possible. Thus irritation may be unpleasant, but despair may not. It would not be possible to refer to the fear of death as either pleasant or unpleasant. There is no pleasant enthusiasm. We cannot say pleasant or unpleasant with reference to passion of any kind, since every passion involves the whole personality par excellence.

When I described the concept of involvement, I differentiated not only between partial and complete involvement, but also between direct and indirect involvement. To refer to an earlier example: if somebody becomes involved in a mathematical assignment by being praised for its resolution then, because the involvement is indirectly positive, we cannot call pleasant the feeling that takes hold of us while doing the assignment (and we don't usually call it pleasant). Tooth-pulling remains an unpleasant feeling even if we are indirectly positively involved in it. A feeling pertaining to indirect involvement may be good or evil, beautiful or ugly, correct or incorrect, useful or harmful, but—if it is positive—it does not constitute a pleasant feeling, nor does it constitute an unpleasant feeling if it is negative. It may be beautiful and good if, out of love of justice, we impetuously destroy what we had been working on for years. It may be correct, or even useful; but who would say that it is pleasant?

We resort to the Good-Evil secondary value orientational category pair in the moral evaluation (judgment) of feelings. Unlike the categories pleasant-unpleasant which are always nothing but optional (propose the option of certain feelings and the avoidance of others, but do not command nor prohibit), the moral norms referring to feelings, like all moral norms, are imperative or optional. From the point of view of their moral content, there are mandatory and prohibited feelings, recommended and not recommended feelings in every culture. The Good-Evil value orientational categories (whether imperative or optional), refer exclusively to personality feelings, or to the relation of the whole personality to certain of its feelings: for instance, to the emotions, emotional habits, emotional dispositions, furthermore, to whether the personality succeeded (and in what manner) in channeling its affect according to the expectations of society. Neither drive feelings, nor an affect in itself, nor orientational feelings in general may be Good or Evil. There are two orientational feelings, however, which constitute an exception to this rule. One of these is the feeling that refers to the moral *sensus communis* (the "moral feeling"); this is called Good, insofar as it conforms to the "correctness" of the given *sensus communis*.

The other is the orientational contact feeling pair of love-hatred, to which the value orientational category of Good and Evil may undoubtedly be applied as to emotional dispositions.

As we know, however, emotions are cognitive-situational feelings; the situation is always comprised in the moral evaluation of an emotional occurrence. There is but a single emotion (emotional occurrence) we may call morally Good—if we disregard its references, its specific object, its situation: the intention, desire, or will oriented at the moral good itself. Kant is absolutely right that there is but one feeling which we may describe as absolute Good, which may be judged as Good: the feeling the object of which is Good in the abstract or, to use Kant's terminology, the respect for moral law. Every other emotional occurrence or emotional disposition judged Good is Good or Evil in reference to something (its specific object, its place, its time, its intensity, its interpretation).

Thus the norms referring to emotions (emotional dispositions) are given along with their object. For instance: "You must respect your father and your mother!" "Fear God!" "Love your country!" "Forgive those who have forgiven you!" "Feel solidarity with your comrades!" "Feel sympathy for the needy!" "Don't covet the house of your neighbor!" "Do the good with pleasure!" "Do not despise mankind, you are part of it!" These are all norms with an imperative character. But optional moral expectations have the same character: the feeling of mourning at the death of a member of the family, joy at the success of others, sorrow at the sight of suffering, horror at the sight of cruelty, not to feel offended when someone has told us the truth, be friendly towards our subordinates, trust our friends, etc.

As I have already mentioned the same feeling occurrence may be subject of conflicting moral norms and expectations (imperative and optional) but emotional habits are always judged morally in an unambiguous way. The reason should now be clear. Emotional evaluation always depends on the situation. But if certain emotional habits have evolved this means precisely that the person reacts with the same emotion and pertinent behavior to innumerable different (similar, analogical, or divergent) situations; in this case it is the feeling itself that accomplishes the "abstraction" from the situation. Therefore, we may apply the moral orientational categories of Good and Evil to an emotional habit, disregarding the situation; envy is evil, vanity is evil, the man full of hatred is evil, the man who feels sympathy is good, the brave man is good, the generous man is good, etc.

Let me refer to a thought expressed earlier: there is only one "Good" feeling occurrence or emotion independent of the situation and of a specific object. The question is: is there such a thing as an Evil emotion, independent of the situation, of a specific object—in other words, the opposite of will directed at the Good?

I believe that such a thing cannot exist. "Evil feeling" can only exist and can only be understood with respect to its objects, to its references. There is no feeling the sole object of which is the Evil. Feelings judged to be morally Evil (and justifiably so) always refer to some specific goal, wish, or object (my own enjoyment, power, money, a means-object the purpose of which may even be good), but never to Evil itself. Even Richard the Third, who had "determined to be a villain," did it for the sake of power or, if you prefer, for the sake of the realization of his own personality. Of course, there is such a thing as "diabolical," but if someone identifies "diabolical" with the desire for Evil, he will not be able to recognize it, even coming face to face with it; because, to borrow the witty formulation of Erich Fromm, the human devil, the human diabolical, "does not have horns."

With reference to feelings as well as with reference to everything else, the Good-Evil value orientational category stands at the summit of the hierarchy of orientational categories. That is, if in the evaluation of our feeling Good collides with other categories (for instance with the pleasant, or the useful), then this feeling is judged primarily on the basis of the categories Good-Evil, for society expects us to prefer the Good feeling as opposed to the pleasant or the useful. This applies even in the case of those cultures where the pleasant-unpleasant or the useful-harmful play a de facto leading role in the evaluation of feelings. In these cultures social consensus equates the pleasant and the Good, or the useful and the Good. Certain Eastern cultures may serve as an example of the former, whereas modern society, particularly certain strata of it, may serve as an example of the latter.

When applying the secondary value orientational categories of beautiful-ugly to feelings, we run into a peculiar problem. For the orientational categories of beautiful-ugly "guide us" in the area of aesthetics, but not so in the case of feelings. If I say that "this table is beautiful" or "this table is good," the two declarations obviously differ; the first unquestionably refers to the aesthetical value of the table. Even the small child knows that to say of someone that he is a "beautiful person" is something quite different from he is a "good person." (In the case of the table, I used "good" as a primary value orientational category, in the second case as a moral value orientational category, but in both cases I contrasted it with an aesthetic value judgment *par excellence*.) With reference to feelings, however (and with reference to behavior expressing feelings) the beautiful-ugly guides not just in our aesthetic orientation, but in moral orientation. The "beautiful" feeling is mostly synonymous with the "Good" feeling and "ugly" is mostly synonymous with Evil feeling. The use of moral and aesthetic value orientational categories may differ only in nuance. We may equally apply the terms "ugly" or Evil to envy; and we may apply the terms "beautiful" or Good to sympathy. In common usage it is, at best, in the case of merit-feelings that we prefer to use the term "beautiful," while "ugly" may show a variation of a shade in the direction of Evil, but not dramatically so. The aesthetic character of the value orientational category of beautiful-ugly may only "intervene" in the appreciation when we talk not about the feeling itself, but about the form of manifestation of the feeling: for instance, if someone has "behaved in an elegant way," or if someone has "made an ugly scene of jealousy."

I do not mean to question the fact that in the course of the last couple of centuries and in certain areas of cultures a peculiar aesthetic function has evolved.[7] This aesthetic evaluative function plays a primary role not in the estimation of particular feelings, but rather in the general evaluation of the so-called "inner world." The categories of "beautiful soul" (see Goethe's *Wilhelm Meister: The Confessions of a Beautiful Soul*), or the "man with a beautifully formed emotional life" have become more or less part of common thinking. This application of "beautiful" to the world of feeling refers in the first place to the way of structuring of feelings—this is why it is only possible to speak of peculiar aesthetic value judgment. It is not about the Good man that we are in the habit of saying he is a "beautiful soul" or that he has "a beautifully formed emotional life" but about the one who is good in a special way, who has attained the moral content of his feelings through the careful tending of emotions, their careful cultivation, through the art of "gardening."

I must, however, warn about a complication to be discussed later: if, in the course of the cultivation, tending and formulation of feelings, that is, in the course of the development of their "beauty," the connections between the beautiful and the Good should become less close and only conditional, then the cultivation of "beautiful feelings" or the "beautiful cultivation of feelings" may even become morally problematic.

One proof of the extent to which we do not apply the aesthetic value orientational categories of beautiful-ugly to feelings, is that we do not even relate it to the yes-feeling referring to aesthetic *sensus communis*. Aesthetic taste is "good" (correct), but not beautiful! (*guter Geschmack, bon gout*—but not *schöner Geschmack*, or *beau goût!*) If we should want to stress that taste is directed at the selection, the enjoyment of the beautiful then we would say taste for beauty, *Geschmack für das Schöne, goût pour la beauté.*

All this, of course, cannot be explained by quirks of the language. Let us suppose, for instance, that the principle that is fixed in this particularity of language is the principle of the unity of good and beauty—*kalokagathia*—as worked out at the cradle of European thought, among the Greeks. We may suppose, furthermore, that it is the complete or partial identity of primary orientational category and moral value orientational category which made the analogical use of beautiful-ugly with moral value orientation necessary, in order to distinguish it, in the vernacular from the primary orientational categories. But I believe the answer goes deeper. Language "is right" in a sense. Let us therefore examine: do "aesthetic feelings" exist at all, that is do feelings to which the value orientational categories of beautiful-ugly may be applied as aesthetic categories *par excellence* really exist?

When Aristotle speaks of *catharsis*, the initial shock elicited by the tragic work, he describes it as the composite of two feelings: fear and compassion. I need hardly mention that neither of these is an "aesthetic feeling" although both have been elicited by an aesthetic object in this case. Kant relates the experience of beauty to the feelings of pleasure and displeasure (*Lust und Unlust*): these are likewise not aesthetic feelings (although according to Kant's interpretation, they are feelings that constitute the experience of beauty). To mention an example in common experience rather than in philosophy: let us listen to a Bach-motet, a

Beethoven-quartet, or a *Lied* by Mahler and then ask ourselves what we feel. We might experience the most heterogeneous feelings, such as being moved, feeling joy, mental pain, sorrow, sympathy, desire, melancholy, enthusiasm, "*Unbehagen*," comfort, excitement, or even the feeling of "being found out." What will be our expressions of feeling? The most varied: those of absorption, attention, gaiety, sadness, or even weeping and laughing. There is not a single one among these feelings and expressions of feelings about which we may say it is exclusively "aesthetic."

With an aesthetic experience the object that elicits our feelings is the aesthetic object (the beautiful). Identification with the aesthetic object, the "peak experience" (Maslow) that results from aesthetic experiences, the suspension of the Figure-Background relationship, the rise into the level of the species (Lukács), elicits in us feelings that are not necessarily intense, but necessarily deep; moreover, these feelings are deep and heterogeneous, compressed in time, simultaneously or successively (what is preponderant as regards the latter depends on the type of the art work; simultaneity plays a greater role should we enter a church, succession plays a greater role in the reading of a novel). Since, to cite Lukács again, self-identification with the beautiful, the work of art signifies self-identification with the species (and moreover, identification with the species being-for-itself), the feelings that appear during the enjoyment of the work of art are morally good feelings. The enjoyment of the work of art, of beauty constitutes ascent into the world of noble feelings; the reader who is impressed by the reading of Hamlet will love the hero and Horatio, will empathize with the good, will "feel" himself to be Hamlet or Horatio, rather than Claudius, even if he ordinarily feels more like Claudius. Hence language is justified in using the value orientation category pair of beautiful-ugly as synonymous with Good and Evil in the context of feelings.

But if we do not identify ourselves completely (only partially) with the aesthetic object (the beautiful), or if the aesthetic object has only partial significance, then the feelings elicited by the object will not be "beautiful," but pleasant. Listening to a Mozart symphony as background music, during work (i.e., when we are not paying attention) is pleasant (we are only partly involved); and tasteful decoration is similarly pleasant. Whether we are capable and to what extent we are capable of the "peak experience" depends on our emotional personality. The circumstance of whether we attain a "peak experience" or not is only very conditionally related to the orientational feelings that have come about in the sphere of aesthetics. Many people who have excellent taste never reach a state of catharsis, whereas not infrequently people completely unfamiliar with the arts—precisely as a result of their pregnant emotional personality— experience catharsis at the first encounter with a great work of art. So even if only conditionally, such a relationship certainly exists. The orientational feelings of the person who has often attained a "peak experience" when meeting with beauty become "refined," even though it is not certain that they orient us in every case in the direction of common sense.

Hence "aesthetic feelings"—i.e., feelings to which we might apply the beautiful-ugly value orientational categories as aesthetic categories *par excellence*—do not exist. So it may seem paradoxical if, in spite of all this, I assert that there *is* an aesthetic feeling (and not only aesthetic taste!). And this is none other than enjoying the reception of the Beautiful as such. This aesthetic feeling is a particular feeling disposition; a sensitivity by virtue of which—should we meet with beauty anywhere and at any time—this Beautiful will evoke in us the "peak experience" with all the pertinent specific feeling events.

The secondary value orientational categories of true-false generally judge or evaluate the situation adequacy and the object adequacy. These value orientational categories are applied to feelings in a particular way. Object adequacy does not exist in the case of feelings. We cannot say that the "true" feeling is the one that conforms to the facts. Conformity or non-conformity to facts plays a role only in the judgment of Other's feelings. And that, however, is primarily a cognitive process, even if the "reading" of the expression of feeling assumes a special place in the observation that constitutes the basis of the judgment. When we judge others' feelings, when we pronounce a judgment about their existence or non-existence, furthermore about their nature, we strive to force our own feelings into the background; the less we succeed in doing this, the less "objective" the judgment, the more easily we become exposed to error (a prejudice is an error from the point of view of object adequacy, no matter how much it may assist the individual's movement in his own social environment).[8]

In the evaluation of feelings as "true" or "false," only situation adequacy plays a role. If we do not feel something when and where we are supposed to, then our feeling is certainly "false." It may be a false feeling—even though not Evil, not unpleasant, nor "incorrect"—to hope for the renewal of a relationship that cannot be renewed; jealousy is a false feeling when there is no cause for it (quite independently of whether we consider jealousy in general Evil). The plebeian pride of Gottfried Keller's Green Henry was a false feeling (again independently of whether plebeian pride is judged to be Good or Evil, correct or incorrect).

Whereas we evaluate feelings as "false" primarily from the point of view of situation adequacy (false feelings are "situation inadequate" feelings), the designation of feelings with the value orientational category of "true" or with the opposite value orientational category of "false" does not refer, in general, to the situation adequacy. To what does it refer, then? After all, object adequacy does not exist in the case of feelings. Hence it must refer to something which can only be applied to feelings or the behavior expressing feelings. And this is subject adequacy.

We call (evaluate) those feelings true, which are subject adequate; and false (deceptive) those that are subject inadequate. True feelings stem from our emotional personality, or at least from our emotional character; whereas false (deceptive) feelings are not organically related to our emotional personality, to our emotional character. The feeling of mourning is deemed false (deceptive) when the "mourning" person did not care for the deceased—although the person may indeed feel the feeling at the given moment (he is not necessarily a hypocrite); the feeling of forgiving is false (deceptive), if the person has a vindictive character. Our love is true if, in general, we "know how" to love and if we are involved with our whole personality in the feeling; but it is false if, in general, we do not "know how" to love and our whole personality is not involved in affection (although the feeling is present). The evaluation of feelings as true or false, whether in the case of others or of ourselves, is basic because this evaluation makes it possible to sensibly predict expected behavior. True-false evaluation is, therefore, decisive here—as in all instances of the application of that value orientational category—from the point of view of knowledge.

The value orientational categories of correct-incorrect, successful-unsuccessful, useful-harmful refer usually and primarily to orientational feelings. This is obvious, since it is precisely the orientational feelings that are typical of the type of involvement which I have described in the first chapter as indirect. Let us recall the examples cited in the course of the analysis of orientational feelings. If we intend to reach a certain village, we become involved in this goal; and at the fork in the road we "feel" which one leads to the goal; that is, we have a yes-feeling, which serves as the intermediary in reaching the goal. We want to enter into contact with persons who are reliable, who are right for this purpose or that and we become involved in this process; the yes-feeling of "I like this person" again acts as an intermediary in reaching the goal. This is another reason why it is not possible to apply the value orientational categories of Good-Evil to the orientational feelings (with the exception of the moral feeling, but even here we prefer to speak of the "correctness" of a feeling). The goal itself may be Good or Evil, but not the orientational feeling. Should the orientational feeling appear not in connection with reaching a goal but, let us say, in the process of knowledge, then the involvement refers to the object of knowledge and the yes- or no-feeling functions as an intermediary much as in the previous case. If I make an assertion with conviction then I am involved not in the process of asserting, but in the object of the prediction, respectively the truth content of the assertion; in the case of intuition I am involved not in the intuition itself, but rather in the discovery (truth) I have arrived at by means of the intuition. In this case I refer to my orientational feelings as "correct" if they indeed lead to the truth, if my prediction comes true, etc.

Thus we may say: "His first impression was correct" or "generally, good intuition plays a useful role in science" or "people often owe their success to good intuition." Thus the value orientational categories of correct-incorrect, useful-harmful and successful-unsuccessful may all be applied sensibly to orientational feelings.

The value orientational categories described above and referring to orientational feelings are not of an imperative character—much as with the categories of pleasant-unpleasant. The "Ought" (*Sollen*) may not be applied either to the correct prediction, or to the useful or successful intuition. The useful, the correct and the successful are all optional. We started from the proposition that we usually apply the value orientational categories of correct-incorrect, useful-harmful, successful-unsuccessful first of all to the orientational categories. I must admit, however, that this assertion is not based on facts, but on a norm. The author is the one who has opted for a society in which the above value orientational categories are applied exclusively to orientational feelings.

This description, however, does not bear on the actual situation. In the modern societies it is *de facto* the useful-harmful, successful-unsuccessful value orientational categories that guide in the evaluation of feelings. Love and affection, friendship and comradeship, forgiving and envy, vanity and solidarity are actually all classed under the categories "useful-harmful." This means that people do not select and judge these feelings according to whether they are Good or Evil, true or false, beautiful or ugly, but whether they are useful and successful. It is not a matter of people being concerned about their own interest in spite of the norms (for in this case, useful is not an orientational value, because it is not generalized and does not refer to the social custom or norm), for this may happen in any case; but rather that the evaluation of emotions on the basis of whether they are useful or harmful becomes generalized and functions as a norm (if not imperative, at least as an optional norm). Even the child is already confronted with such norms as norms. "Do not make friends with poor children!" "Even the smell of poverty is repulsive." "If you always have a soft heart, you will stand to lose," etc.

In contemporary society, the place of the leading role of value orientational categories of useful-harmful is increasingly taken by the value orientational categories of correct-incorrect. The feelings (emotions, emotional customs) are evaluated in the first place according to what extent they contribute to adjustment. In the last chapter of this book I shall discuss how the criterion of adjustment may lead to the psychologization of morality, or may be the consequence of that psychologization. But whatever the extent to which the value orientational categories of useful-harmful, correct-incorrect take over the guiding role of the value orientational category pair of Good and Evil, the take-over will never be complete. The evaluation of feelings as Good or Evil survives in the abstract norms and becomes handed over as such.

When I spoke of "partial involvement" or "personality involvement" (i.e., complete involvement) while discussing pleasant feeling and Good feeling, I did not say a word about whether the pleasant feeling or the Good feeling (unpleasant or Evil feeling) fills us or not. Every feeling may fill or not fill (at a given moment or continuously) and this "filling" is completely independent of the evaluation of the feeling, of the value orientational category under which we place the feeling. One may be filled by the feeling of thirst for air (a drive feeling), by the fear affect, by physical ill-feeling, by a perception feeling, a feeling connected with cognition (for instance, inspiration) by an emotion, by an emotional disposition; being filled does not in itself say anything about whether we are dealing with partial or total involvement in the given case.

We have several concepts to express being filled positively: for instance, enjoyment, delight, happiness, being "passionate." If someone should say, "I enjoyed being on the sun," then this means that a pleasant feeling has filled him completely while sunning. Yet I must add: positive filling does not in the least signify the positive evaluation of being filled. If the feeling judged to be pleasant (and which fills) is morally value indifferent, then being filled is judged positively, of course only on the level of pleasantness hence it is merely optional. But if the pleasant feeling (judged to be pleasant) filling someone has a morally negative value content (is condemned, prohibited), then the state of being filled can only increase the negativity. Thus, if we should say about someone "he was happy torturing his subordinate," that is, that someone was filled with pleasant feeling at torturing his subordinate, then this is morally more negative than if we were to say: "it was pleasant for him to torture his subordinate." Being positively filled by the torture, humiliation, manipulation of other human beings is precisely what we call sadism. This kind of "being filled" is often judged negatively even where domineering over others is opted as pleasant (useful), not to mention those cultures (or strata) in which the unpleasant feeling is the opted feeling, that is where the "pleasant feeling" itself (and not only the state of being filled with it) transgresses norms.

As I have said, positive filling is possible with every type of feeling (even if not with every specific feeling). We may say: "X enjoyed writing a poem," in other words the feeling that accompanies the cognitive creative goal accomplishment filled him completely. We may say: "He enjoyed X's conference," in other words, the yes-feeling (whether it refers to the content or the manner of the conference, or to both), has filled him completely. We may say: "He enjoyed the tragedies of Shakespeare," in other words the feelings elicited by the "peak experience" have filled him completely. (By the way, in the case of "peak experiences" it is only possible to speak of the state of being filled.) We may say, "he enjoyed to carry out his duty," in other words the moral feeling has filled him completely. We may likewise say, "he was happy with carrying out his duty."

I must add, however, that the expressions referring to "being filled" are rarely synonymous (the terms joy and delight may be used as synonyms most often). The term "I am happy" usually describes the "filling" form of pleasure that is referred to the state of "being filled" by feelings judged to be good by the primary orientational category of good, rather than the state of being filled by feelings judged to be pleasant. If during a sexual act someone says, "I enjoy it" or "I am happy," then the former means I am filled with a feeling of pleasure and the latter, I am filled with a feeling of happiness (the achievement of a desire, the reaching of a goal, etc.). In this case the two may *de facto* go together, yet the two declarations cannot be substituted for one another. (The latter, since it is a matter of emotion, describes being filled by personality involvement.) The expressions "passion," "passionately" describe being filled only if at the same time assumption of responsibility, engagement occurs. One does not eat "passionately," no matter how much one is momentarily filled with the feeling of drive reduction or the satisfaction of an affect, but we can say one is eating with delight or pleasure. On the other hand, one may love passionately, even if this should represent for him neither enjoyment nor delight, because one may be filled by the true or Good feeling, without being filled with pleasure; passionate love or affection may even be "painful."

From all this we may conclude that the category of enjoyment as "being filled," cannot be classified under mere pleasantness. The state of being filled with feelings guided by other values may also be described by the concept "enjoyment." Yet there is a relationship between pleasantness and enjoyment: that which does not contain, even subordinately, the category of pleasantness, with reference to that I cannot apply the term "enjoyment," no matter how intense the state of "being filled." The use of the category "pleasantness," I repeat, does not necessarily mean that in the given case and with regard to the given feeling the opted value is that of "pleasantness," but rather that the given feeling refers or may refer to the social option of pleasant-unpleasant (the example of sadism).

We also have several concepts to indicate negative fulfillment; but only four of these that can be used exclusively in this context: unhappiness, repulsion, torment, and suffering. Unhappiness plays a role exclusively in the description of being filled with emotion negatively—as "being filled" with sorrow, regret. All the others, however, may refer to negative filling of the most varied kinds and realized with the help of feelings evaluated by the most varied value orientational categories. I may be repelled by having to take a bitter pill—in which case an unpleasant feeling fills me negatively. I may be repelled by a lowly bastard, or by my own act, in which case I am negatively filled by an Evil feeling. I may be repelled by a bad kitsch, by the thought of nuclear warfare, by death, by lies, by hypocrisy, or even by cold water. I may be tormented by a thought, by not being loved, or by the hot sun, if it be unpleasant to me. I may suffer from humiliation, from shame, from the suffering of others, from a stomach ache, or from boredom.

There are, however, a number of categories which we do not use exclusively in the sense of being filled (being negatively filled), but which may also be used in that sense. The most significant among these is the feeling of "hurt." Whether we use it in this role or not depends in general on the context (often on the adverb "very"). The statement: "it hurts very much that she has left me" refers to being negatively filled, as do these: "it hurts me very much that I have offended you" or "my tooth hurts very much," or "intense light hurts."

We have, furthermore, a specific emotion, the very concept of which comprises negative filling: this is despair. Since despair always means personality involvement, this category cannot be adequately applied to the state of being filled with an unpleasant feeling. (Nevertheless, in everyday usage this may occur in a variety of contexts, such as: "I am desperate because I am very hungry and lunch isn't ready"—this particular feeling is the result of an unfortunate "fitting together" of the meaning and concept.)

Whether or not we are filled with a feeling does not normatively alter an iota the hierarchy of the evaluation of feelings. If a pleasant feeling that fills us collides with a feeling that does not fill us but is positively evaluated morally (a Good feeling then, according to the norm), we must yield the advantage to the latter as if we were filled by it and not by the former. In the dilemma between the feeling of comfort and carrying out a duty the norm does not ask whether the rest or relaxation is merely a pleasant feeling or if it constitutes enjoyment, nor does it ask whether our feeling of duty is passionate or not; in every case it is the latter that is preferred, or even required. But whether we indeed validate the norm or actually follow the norm is affected by which of the feelings is the "one that fills." The more a man is filled with feelings evaluated as moral, the more virtuous he is. But when it comes to a choice, the more he chooses what he judges to be morally good as opposed to a feeling that "fills him," the greater his merit.

Notes

1. Peters, Richard S. "The Education of Emotion" in *Feelings and Emotions*, Magda B. Arnold, ed. (The Loyola Symposium: Academic Press, 1970), 188.

2. Heller, Agnes. *Towards a Marxist Theory of Value* (Carbondale: Telos Books, 1972).

3. Heller, Agnes. *Towards a Marxist Theory of Value*, 28. Since I have analyzed the value orientational categories in detail in this work, I feel it is unnecessary to continue to repeat the train of thought here.

4. Spinoza, Baruch. *Ethics*. W. H. White, trans., revised by A. H. Stirling (New York: Hafner, 1949), 124.

5. Since joy and sorrow are feeling-occurrences (and not dispositions), and since both are reflective emotions, they cannot be passions in principle. Spinoza's attempt to derive all feelings from these so-called basic passions (or, as he writes, from these "passive states") is a typical example of reductionism in philosophy.

6. In one case sorrow may constitute the expansion of Self: viz., during the reception or experiencing of an art work. In these cases we may enjoy our sadness.

7. I cannot say, for lack of the pertinent knowledge, whether the application of the value orientational categories of beautiful and good to the feelings is similar or different in great cultures such as those of the Indian or the Chinese, nor can I address how this has evolved in the course of history.

8. Since I have analyzed the above problem in my study *On Prejudice* (Budapest: Akadémiai Kiadó, 1966; German edition: *Alltag and Geschichte* Luchterhand, 1970), I refrain from analyzing it here in more detail.

Chapter V.
Particularist and Individual Feelings

In the course of the analysis of the phenomenology of feelings I have intentionally left certain questions unanswered. Now, as I conclude the phenomenological treatment, I will endeavor to eliminate these question marks. I have said that feeling equals being involved in something. The Self in evolution (the Self's own world) relates to the world "given" to it; with its feelings the Self (the social organism) selects in this world from the aspect of self-preservation and expansion. Of course, there is not but one way to preserve and extend the Self and there is not but one type of relationship to the world. Can we distinguish (and if yes, how?) the main tendencies of the various kinds of relationships? I must answer this question.

I have argued that we learn to feel. I described the process of learning feelings (especially of the most complex feelings, the emotions) as a process of fitting together, whether our feeling concepts are prior to our feelings, or our feelings prior to our concepts. I have left open, however, the following important question: how do new types of feelings come about, types of feelings we cannot fit together because the emotional concepts that might "fit" them do not as yet exist?

And I have maintained that we acquire the majority of feelings, along with their evaluation, insofar as we use pertinent value orientational categories. I have, however, also left open another important question: how is it possible that there are feelings we evaluate with orientational categories in opposition to, or at least differently from, the dominating (imperative or optional) customs and norms? I intend to answer these questions first of all.

Our Self is always and inescapably particular. We receive "ready made" certain given particularities along with our genetic code, the "dumb species character." These given particularities more or less codetermine our relation to the world. Certain tendencies, lesser or greater, towards certain types of self-realization and acquisition, a greater or lesser tendency towards certain affects (and their intensity), a greater or lesser tendency towards certain types of *Lebensgefühl* or moods—all these are undoubtedly innate. This signifies certain predispositions from the aspect of the formation of our psychic character, yet implies no predisposition whatever from the aspect of the development of our moral character.[1] Our particular standpoint also constitutes a limit beyond which we cannot pass. We can select only starting from the world of the Self; we are

143

never able to pass beyond the boundaries of the Self. As we are never able to reproduce the infinite world in our finite Self, we can never identify ourselves with the human species, a complete identification even with a single Other (object or subject-object) can only occur for brief moments, in the course of a "peak experience." It is always the Self that is involved in something and this something, as we know, can only be selected by the Self.

But the fact that our particularities and our angle of vision are inescapably given does not mean in the least that our relationship to our world is particularistic of necessity. It is true that when we relate to the world, it is unavoidably from a particular angle of vision that we relate. But this relationship has two basic forms in its tendency: the particularist and the individual relationship.[2]

The person relating particularistically to the world and to himself is characterized by complete identification with his own world (with himself). He develops the Self's own world by selecting from the environment on the basis of his particularities and particularistic point of vision. In the particularistic personality, selection is directed at mere self-preservation in the environment or expansion without conflict. In the course of such selection, the person identifies himself with the prescriptions and norms of his environment, or develops his own "we-consciousness." In its relation to the world, the expansion of a we-consciousness, elaborated without critical distance, will be a mere extension of the I-consciousness. Or, the I-consciousness will be a reconstituted variant of the we-consciousness from a particular vantage-point. The relation to my I-consciousness without critical distances (to my particularities, my point of vision, my psychological character, my emotional character) goes together mostly with the undistanced and uncritical relation to the prescriptions of the given world, its integrations, to the We-consciousness. In declarations such as: "I am the best father, because I have brought up my children to become good businessmen, or good noblemen, or good Christians," this double identification is reflected quite clearly. This type of declaration is typical of the particularist person. He is "always right," he does "everything well," he is always "innocent"—in other words, he is a personality who always obtains his justification from direct identification with the system of customs.

I have said that in the case of the particularist person complete identification is two-dimensional. It is possible, however, to identify ourselves with the prescriptions of the environment by confronting our own peculiarities, our own psychological character (for instance, the good Christian who feels continual remorse because of his gluttony or his sexual desires). Insofar as this behavior comes about as a result of an undistanced and uncritical identification with the environment, behavior also becomes particularist in this case. If, however, the values are chosen, then we are dealing with individual behavior; for instance, in all cases where a person relates negatively to his emotional personality (or his system of emotional customs). A great example of this is Augustine's relation to the world during his conversion. Furthermore, it is also possible to identify with our particularist Self, while the systems of habits and norms in general are being questioned (we question all customs and norms), or even consciously disregarded. This attitude is individual only (and conditionally) if people chose the unfettered realization of their own particularity (like Sade's heroes) and not when the choice of mere particularity itself becomes social habit (opted norm). In this case, from the aspect of its moral value content individuality is more negative than the particularist behavior, even if it shows "greater format." In the novels of Balzac we meet with some such individualistic egoists, for instance Gobseck or Vautrin; these, however, always remain islands in the ocean of particularist egoism.

The person relating individually to the world (and to himself) is characterized by distance both to himself and to the world. The individual is the one who selects from the system of customs of his environment on the basis of values chosen by himself. And he selects likewise individually (again, on the basis of his chosen value system) from among his own particularities, from among the constituents of his psychological character, preferring (opting) some and repressing or eliminating the symptoms of others on the basis of the choice of values. Of course, the condition of the formation of the individual relationship is that there must be a way to choose from the values. If we disregard the small pre-market community, then we may say there always exists a possibility for such choice. First of all, because societies are not homogeneous, but stratified, and the value preferences of various social strata (orders, classes) differ for the most part. On the other hand, since societies are usually not hermetically "closed" to the outside there is always the possibility that the individual born into a society might consciously prefer the values of another. Redfield gives an account of a native American tribe in which annual human sacrifice was part of the social system of customs. The son of the tribal leader assisted the escape of the selected victim one year and did likewise the following year. He had decided against human sacrifice (incidentally, he did not change the custom). How was this possible? Among the neighboring and related tribes, human sacrifice was not customary. Thus Petalesharoo (this was the name of the leader's son) had a chance to become acquainted with different values and to contrast these with the customs of his own community. The greater the contact between different cultures, the greater the possibility for preferring the values of others to those one was born into (or even the fresh choice of our own values on the basis of a conscious comparison). Thirdly, this is possible because the abstract and concrete norms always differ and often collide with one another and the individual is thus given a chance to contrast the requirements of the abstract norms with the concrete norms and make a choice.

Thus there are no "two human beings" in one. The essence of man is not the "nucleus" of the individual, upon which some kind of "appearance" is deposited; the relation of man to the world is formed in the course of the development of the individual, in his relation to the world. The individual relationship, that is the choice of values, the distance to ourselves and to the norms or customs of our environment on the basis of these pre-selected values is nothing other than the conscious relation to the world.

On the basis of these considerations, the first question-mark may be dismissed. Man may relate to the world in two ways, although this double relationship is not "pure," for in reality there are very many "transitional" relations. Regarding its tendency, the relationship of the Self to the world is either particularist or individual. According to what is most characteristic of the assimilation of the world by the Self, the self realization of the Self and its mechanism of selection, the feelings fill a particularist or an individual function.

If our relationship to the world were merely particularist, it would always be possible to fit the feelings together with the emotional feeling concepts. But insofar as we select heterogeneous values compared to our environment and we continue to live in our environment, our feelings either do not have a "name" or their quality is not covered by a single emotional concept. I do not know whether Petalesharoo gave a name to the feeling which motivated him to liberate the victims selected for sacrifice. The "naming" of feelings, the conceptual designation of new values, of the feeling consequences of new types of relations to the world, already takes place as the new relationship to the world becomes relatively more general. It is particularly typical of the modern period that the "naming" is carried out by so-called "representative personalities." (Think of spleen, or of the inferiority complex.) In addition to the appearance of new emotional concepts the redefinition of old emotional concepts on the basis of new feelings is essential. This process taking place at the social level (of the entire society or only some of its strata) is, of course, the resultant of individual redefinitions. "What does it mean to love?" "What does it mean to forgive?" "What does it mean to humiliate oneself?"—this is how the questions are asked. And actually this means something else (different from the customary interpretation) and must indeed mean something else (choice of values). The content, meaning, sphere of the old concepts change and we have made them appropriate for "fitting together" with feelings that are different or deviate from the former.

This line of thought leads us to the dismissal of the third question mark. It is an unquestionable fact that it is possible to evaluate feelings in a way and on the basis of value orientational categories, which contradicts the prevailing generalization. If the relationship of the Self to the world could be simply particularistic, this "reversal" could never take place. Let us recall that we evaluate with the help of value orientational categories not only if we apply the imperative or optative embodied in it, but also if our evaluation relates to these imperatives or optatives. This relation may, however, also be negative. I may consciously reject the positive or negative evaluation given a feeling in the imperative. Further, I may consciously reject the hierarchy inherent (generalized) in the evaluation of feelings. And moreover, I may consciously opt for certain feelings I had not opted for before and I may assign an imperative to feelings that have been only opted for until this time. Until such reversal of values is simply individual, it will be always judged negatively by the age, or even considered a sin; much as Tannhäuser was judged sinful in his time for having consciously preferred erotic pleasure in opposition to the customary norms. If, however, the redefinition of values meets the social needs it spreads rapidly, since it had been the expression of such a need. Saint Joan attributed high moral value to "patriotism," which at that time still contradicted the prevailing customary norms and was based on an individual choice of values. But in the course of history the feeling of patriotism climbed ever higher in the hierarchy of the socially generalized customary norms and there came a time when it evolved into a feeling judged to be one of the supreme Goods.

The individual relation to the world does not necessarily depend on the choice of a different set of values. This relationship may be constituted in the conscious fresh choice of already given values. Somebody may love his brother, because it is "customary," or may love his brother on basis of his own values. I have placed the problem of the choice of new values into the foreground because we can understand this process only if we have a clear notion of the potentials of the individual relationship to the world.

Hence, depending on whether a person's relationship to the world is particularist or individual, the feelings fill a particularist or individual function, and in two distinct ways. This dual relationship is expressed either in the feeling itself (with regard to the object, to the situation in which it appears, etc.), or in our evaluative standpoint with regard to our own feeling. I should point out that the individual and particularist function of the feelings is inseparable from their "binding" nature. In relation to feelings that are not "binding," particularity and individuality is not differentiated. Thus, theoretically, the drive feelings cannot be individual, only particularist. The affects likewise may not be individual in themselves (only particularist) but the difference between particularity and individuality already finds expression in the relationship to the affects. I may identify with my affects and I may set a distance between myself and them on the basis of my choice of values, or I may accept without distance the socially ever given stimuli that elicit the affects, or I may choose from among them after evaluating them. Thus the man inclined to fits of rage may identify with this inclination of his and may rationalize all his fits, or may distance himself from them and may condemn the actions that derive from his rage, or may repress his rage. It may happen that a person is only ashamed of the shame stimulus provided for him by his environment and of nothing else, whereas another person may evaluate these stimuli and select among them; this is truly shameful, but I do not admit that this other thing should be considered shameful. Think of those women who, having rejected the "female role" ascribed to them, insist: "Why should I feel ashamed for having declared my love first, there is nothing shameful in that!" Similarly, *Lebensgefühl* cannot be differentiated as a particularist or individual feeling, nor can, in most cases, mood. Here too, it is in the relationship to the feeling that the difference between the particularist and individual behavior is constituted.

With emotions, the various functions of the particularist and individual relations appear in both regards: they are expressed in the feelings themselves, as well as in the relationship to the feelings. There are emotions which do not have an individual function, which are purely and unambiguously particularist feelings. These are *vanity* and *envy*. Vanity and envy are *par excellence* the feelings

of identification with particularity. Of course, these as all other particularist feelings, may be extended to the We-consciousness. I may envy another family "in
the name" of my family, as I may become envious of another person after com-
paring him with myself. I must add, however, that while in theory envy and vanity may not function as individual feeling, I may evolve an individual relationship even to these emotions. When I feel that I am being envious, or recognize
that envy plays a part in my judgment, then I can still look at myself from a distance. The man with self-knowledge is capable of saying to himself: "you have
said it out of envy, make up for it or don't say it again!"

All other emotions may function as individual feeling even in their contents.
This applies even to feelings such as self-love. Feelings of self-love may differ
from one another qualitatively depending on what one loves in oneself. Self-
love, like all other kinds of love, may be total self-identification (I love everything in myself); such self-love is mingled with vanity, with self-pity. It may be
a self-love with a distance, directed at the values of our Self; this self-love is
mingled with pride, often spiced with self-irony. Since the object of the two
kinds of self-love is not identical (in one case it is the Self as existence, in the
other the Self a value object) the different functions of the two feelings also play
a part in the difference in quality of the two feelings. Or let us take a look at
"feeling offended." Feeling offended is different if elicited by anything which
questions our particular self-love (for instance, if someone should tell the truth
to our face, be frank about his opinion, or be ironical), or if it is elicited by the
Other's intent to hurt. The latter is the individual form of the emotion, since we
judge negatively—and rightly so—the intent to hurt. The difference between the
two "functions" of the feeling often finds expression in the language; in the second case we are inclined to use the term "hurt."

How sharply the particularist form of the feelings differs from the individual form in the case of affection (or love), furthermore in the expression of these
feelings in behavior should be rather obvious. Let us take a look at them first
from the aspect of the relation, with or without distance (value selection) to the
norms and customs. We love the one we are supposed to love in a "quasi-
natural" way according to the norms (customs), without reflecting on the nature
of our love, without questioning the worth of the persons we are supposed to
love (for instance, if we should love the girl our parents have betrothed us to at
the time of our birth, or the man the marriage agent procured for us): this kind of
liking or love is different from that other kind of love or affection where we
choose its object ourselves on the basis of his inherent human values. The former is a particularist feeling, whereas the latter may be individual, but not necessarily so. For the other aspect of the difference between the particularist and
individual relationship intervenes: do we identify with ourselves, that is do we
love the Other primarily in relation to our own particular Self, or do we love him
for himself, for those values for which we had actually chosen him. Maslow, as I
have mentioned, uses two different concepts to distinguish the two types of love.
The former is "deficiency love," the latter "love for Being" (D love and B love).
D love is "permanent desire to be loved," whereas B love is "love for Being of

another person."[3] Indeed, who does not know how different the two feelings are and how different the attitudes they imply! The person who loves only with reference to himself (in a particularist way), can love only as long as the Other belongs to him or her, as long as the Other loves him best. The main value attached to the beloved is belonging. If this should cease, so do affection or love; love shifts into hatred, into contempt. As long as the other belongs to him, the identification with the Other is unconditional. The Other is perfect and faultless and remains perfect and faultless as long as she belongs to him. From the moment he is no longer the extension of his own Self, all perfection becomes imperfection. There is no distance, only complete acceptance or complete rejection. The feeling of individual love is quite different. The person who loves as an individual, loves the Other for his own sake (for his being). Of course, this love too demands a response, as all emotional dispositions demand it. But love is not motivated by the other being "ours" or "becoming ours," but by the fact that the other is worthy of love and affection on the basis of her qualities. Individual love knows distance. No matter how overpowering the feeling of love he may yet judge the other person, may resort to irony, although it is true that this distance nevertheless assumes the unconditional acceptance of the other's personality. And if the Other is not "his," the distance does not increase; the acceptance of the whole personality—again on the basis of its worth—persists. Let us cite as a beautiful example of B love (individual love) Kleist's *Prinz von Homburg*: Natalie is begging the *Kurfürst* to spare the life of her beloved:

> Zu deiner Füsse Staub, wie's mir begührt, Für Vetter Homburg dich um Gnade flehen! Ich will ihn nicht für mich erhalten wissen—Mein Herz begehrt sein and gesteht es dir; Ich will ihn nicht für mich erhalten wissen—Mag er sich, welchem Weib er will, vermählen; Ich will nur, dass er da sei, lieber Onkel, Für sich selbständig, frei und unabhängig, Wie eine Blume, die mir wohlgefällt.

To make the example complete, Natalie has doubts regarding the character of the Prinz von Homburg and puts them to a test. And she throws herself at the knees of the *Kurfürst* for mercy when her beloved has overcome his character deficiencies—the arrogance of the spoiled nobleman and his panicky fear—and not without her assistance.

In order to find an example of D love in literature as well, let us recall the love of princess Eboli for Don Carlos, which is transformed by an offense against personal vanity into a desire for retribution. The emotion of love is not the same feeling in its particularist or individual function.

Of course, even with emotions, an individual relationship to the particularist feeling is possible (and rather frequent). In such a case the feeling itself is particularist, but the individual distances himself from his own feeling, mainly by not allowing the expression of his own feeling in adequate behavior or action. Insofar as the appearance of the particularist feelings and its negative evaluation happen at the same time, then this distancing may be accomplished even in the repression of the expressions of feeling; the individual keeps the particularist feeling to himself and does not cultivate it, but forces it into the background. In most cases, however, the individual's distancing from his own feeling is a delayed process; the expression of feeling persists, but behavior (as a consequence of the intervening self-distance) does not show it. The individual may feel offended if he is told the truth in his face: and his expressions of feeling may reveal this state. But he may say to himself, after some delay: "it was not nice of you to feel hurt, after all, what they had said about you was true; X was led not by the intention to offend, but by the love of truth or by friendship. Everyone needs to be confronted by himself every once in a while." And after this he will feel grateful to the person who has told him the truth in his face and will behave accordingly (and not according to feeling offended) towards that person. Flattery makes many people "feel good," even people who do not take it at its face value; but the individual—in consequence of the intervening distance—begins to feel irritated that flattery made him feel good and his attitude towards the flatterer will become one of distrust and skepticism rather than of trust and love.

The guide in the behavior of the individual is the *gnoti seauton*, even if he has never heard of the famous inscription of the Delphic oracle to know oneself. Let me refer to the phenomenon I had called "secondary learning" in the third chapter of this book. "Secondary learning" becomes decisive primarily with reference to emotional habits. This secondary learning characterizes exclusively the individual. As a result of knowledge of self the individual takes account of his emotional habits (which may have developed even before his individual choice of values, in childhood). Secondary learning consists in eliminating the symptoms of emotional habits judged to be negative, by choosing situations in which they cannot be realized, or by confronting "negative" emotional habits with ones judged to be "positive." Since, however, the individual is characterized by the will of self-building and self-change initiated by himself (and along with it the joy felt at successful self-building and self-change), his relation to the self cannot on the whole be negative. Precisely because of this, since he has initiated the self-change on the basis of his own selected values, he is not the object, but the active subject of the development of his values; thus he always approves his own personality on the whole. The distancing from particularist feelings, from emotional habits judged to be bad, not only does not contradict the self-enjoyment of personality, the two actually presuppose one another. True enough, with the particularistic person it may also happen that he should judge certain of his emotional habits negatively; but the source of his negative judgment is the uncritical acceptance of the system of customs and norms, or at least their acceptance on the basis of reselection. Then the person simply applies the prescriptions and norms not chosen by himself to his own personality and represses within himself all those feelings which deviate from or contradict these. Repressed particularist feelings, however, do not cease to exist as particularist feelings: they seek those "authorized channels" through which they may burst forth. The vain person who is forced to humble himself by his environment will not thereby cease being vain, not even if the humiliation was intended by him. His vanity "bursts forth" all the time whenever possible—even in the humiliation itself—for nobody humbles himself so perfectly, so exquisitely as he does. Since he cannot show offense in front of his superiors, he visits his hurt resentment on his subordinates. The constant exercise of self-control, and the constant self-torture whenever custom prescribes, far from stopping self-pity or the identification with the self, instead makes them more intense. The particularist gardener will cut down everything he finds inappropriate to the uncritically accepted system of customs, yet will let the weeds thrive everywhere else. The individual gardener will cultivate his garden on the basis of his knowledge of the world and of self-knowledge. He will cultivate the most beautiful flowers the given soil will permit. Everyone has an image of what man should be like. The particularist person says: "I am what I should be" or "since I cannot be what I should be, I am satisfied that I am exactly what I am." The individual says: "I try to be what I should be as far as possible; I must take advantage of all possibilities."

The approval of one's own personality is the need of everyone. Every person rightly defends the relative continuity of the Ego's own world; one function of the feelings, as we have seen, is precisely the insurance of this relative continuity, the regulation of the proportions of "preserving" and "expanding." Both particularist and individual feelings insure the continuity of identity and thus the homoeostasis of the person. Only each accomplishes it in a different way.

Defense mechanisms play a key role in the preservation of the "identity" of the particularist Self. Moreover, the function of particularist emotions is precisely to satisfy the defense mechanisms. If the other person does not love us, we hate him, we despise him. If one of our desires should not be fulfilled, it was not important, or it is unattainable, or it could not be fulfilled because of intervention or meddling by evil persons. Thus feelings insure the self-approval and identity of a person by reacting with particularist emotions to every danger threatening the identity. Naturally, particularist feelings also guarantee the expansion of the Self: and the area of expansion is the system of norms and customs accepted without reflection. The person who accepts everything prescribed, who expands in this particular sphere, does indeed insure his own homoeostasis for the most part; from this point of view the particularist feelings guide purposefully. The guidance of the particularist feelings ceases to operate in "borderline situations" (in the case of some catastrophy or trauma). In borderline situations the Self guided by particularist feelings invariably becomes subject to panic or lamentations ("why did this have to happen to me?"). In a traumatic situation the particularist Self is incapable of preserving the "identity" of the personality; the Self "falls apart," and personality disturbances such as neurosis or even madness occur. Laing has demonstrated beautifully (in his book *The Divided Self*) this emotional root of the madness of Ophelia. Ophelia had always been the dutiful daughter, she never chose, but accepted all rules prescribed by her environment (whether in connection with her father, her brother, or Hamlet). Hence she reacts with madness, with the very dissolution of her personality, to a traumatic situation. According to Laing, children who, like Ophelia, are always obedient, have an "underdeveloped" Self which tends to dissolve, especially in cases of trauma or catastrophe. Since catastrophes and traumatic experiences are rather rare in everyday life the particularist feelings—I repeat—generally function successfully in insuring identity.

Individual feelings, on the other hand, fill the function of the Self's social homoeostasis in a totally different manner. First of all, the individual does not have defense mechanisms or, if he does, he examines them critically and does not resort to them in action. The feelings of the individual are emotions evaluated on the basis of his own criteria of choice; even though he chooses his values, of course, from among the ones "provided" by the world, their constant intentionality, the fact that he is at the origin of the selection, the fact that he takes responsibility for them, all these insure the continuity of the Self. The distance from the self and, at the same time, the pleasure of building the self may lead to the self-enjoyment of personality and this is more than the simple self-approval of personality. Nor is this affected by an eventual fresh choice of values (as often happens); the intention still has its origins within us and the structure of the person remains individual. The self-knowledge, the relearning of the relation to emotional habits, the acceptance of the "soil" of the personality as something given, the fact that we mean to cultivate the most beautiful flowers possible from this soil, in other words the conscious acceptance of ourselves as the "raw material," is sufficient in itself to guarantee identity through every alteration, every self-change, every turn of fate. The Self of the individual (since it is as Self worked out in the conscious relation to the species) is always strong and its resilience is far greater than with the Self guided by particularist feelings. The individual can support solitude, can accept not being loved, will not panic in borderline situations and never asks the world: "why did it have to happen to me?" but rather asks himself: "what should I do to stand pat even in such a catastrophic situation?" The person guided by individual feelings does not dissolve in traumatic situations; Hamlet, as opposed to Ophelia, does not go mad— he only pretends to be mad and, as we can tell from the reaction of Polonius, with little success. Furthermore Hamlet is a beautiful example of what the well developed individual (what more, representative individual) is like. He not only questions his environment, but appraises the justification of his own revenge on the basis of chosen values. Moreover, he is a ruthless knower of self. Let us recall what he says of himself to Ophelia: he describes himself as vindictive, but to what extent this does not find expression in his behavior, to what extent it is not vengeance but the yearning for justice which guides him in his behavior and which he had chosen as norm, all this is brought out in the course of the drama.

Of course, even the individual needs to have his personality approved by others. But the particularist person expects that the approval of everyone and, furthermore, the security of his Self at the same time depends on such approval. For the individual the approval of significant persons (of those highly valued by him) is sufficient—and does not even expect the love, worship, or recognition of others. (The approval of Horatio was sufficient for Hamlet, because his friend was the only one for whom he had esteem in his environment.) In addition, the Self-strength of the individual does not derive from this approval. He does something not in order to have his personality approved, but rather would like to find approval (to be loved) because he is what he is, because he has done this or that. His "identity" is maintained even if nobody approves of him temporarily.

When I said that the feelings of the individual are determined by the distance between the Self and the reflexive evaluation of the "world" (on the basis of the conscious relation to the species), then I did not have in mind that the individual "feels less." On the contrary. Even if his feelings are not more intense than those of the particularist Self, they are, at any rate, deeper. Since individual feelings are *par excellence* feelings expressing the whole personality, these are, by definition, deep feelings at the same time. Furthermore, since the individual's world of feeling is conscious and reflexive, his feelings (individual feelings) are always either subject adequate (true); or, if they are not subject adequate, then at least he is capable of judging them. (Whether or not they are situation adequate is to be judged case by case; they are not necessarily more so than in the case of the feelings of the particularist Self. The feelings of the individual may also err.)

I am justified in asserting that the individual is more "prepared" for the so-called feelings of "self-abandon"—for giving himself to feelings—than the particularist subject, and from several aspects. I may also phrase this by saying that the particularist "self-abandon" is different from the individual "self-abandon"; the later is undoubtedly more reliable. Ericson (and others) attribute great significance to the capacity of self-abandon, and rightly so. The stronger the Self, Ericson argues, the more it is capable of self-abandon, because the less it fears (and the less it has to fear) that it will lose itself in giving. The weak Self is afraid of self-abandon, because it is always jeopardizing itself. If the beneficiary of the self-abandon proves unworthy, then the particularist person stands "robbed," and loses himself. On the other hand, the strong Self becomes stronger in giving. He has nothing to fear and does not fear; if the beneficiary of the self-abandon proves unworthy, he is not robbed for all that. Disappointment only makes him stronger.

Undoubtedly, the individual Self since it is strong, abandons itself without fear and without even stopping to think. The individual love is not anxious, not suspicious. On the other hand, the subject that feels particularist love or friendship is often "on guard," often suspicious; he seldom experiences the pleasure of the unconditional. Even so, the problem has other aspects we may not neglect.

First of all, it is not possible to say of the particularist Self that it is fully incapable of self-abandon. His self-abandon, however, is of the same nature as his particularist behavior in general. Insofar as he exercises self-abandon at all, he gives himself to such an integration, principle, person, or institution which is "ready made" in his environment, with regard to whom or to which self-abandon is included in the social norms, not chosen by himself. As a result of this, we are confronted with the seemingly paradoxical fact that the particularist Self always gives himself only to himself. This is a paradox because if he should exercise self-abandon for the benefit of his child, husband/wife, family, country (i.e., for the benefit of not-chosen value objects), or some ready-made principle, then he gives himself to a non-Self, to an object, or a subject-object. But—and the paradox finds its resolution herein—he only gives himself to an object or subject-object with which he has identified himself from the outset, or which is merely the extension of his own Self. The recipient of the self-abandon in the case of the particular Self is always the person, institution, or principle that constitutes the "We-consciousness." "My" child is the extension of my Self, part of me; "my" family is, likewise the extension of my Self; similarly with my country, my village, my cause.

So all this remains a paradox only if we do not translate it into experience. If we do, we will see that here too we are dealing with evidence experienced every day. Why did I say that the self-abandon of the particularist Self (however strong or intense it may be) is always addressed to itself? Because if the recipient of self-abandon separates him- or herself from the We-consciousness or does not identify itself with us, then self-abandon immediately ends; the Self either empties or is filled with opposite meanings. The recipient of self-abandon becomes the recipient of hatred, of resentment instead.

Coriolanus, the abnegated but previously zealous patriot, is immediately prepared to betray his country when he is not elected consul. He had been "rejected" by his country, hence ungrateful and self-giving love is transformed into hatred and desire for reprisal. What halts the hatred experienced by Coriolanus? The supplications of his family. The particularist Self structure remains, only now it is identification with another We-consciousness that reverses the intention. The mother who loves her child with particularist feelings remains self-giving even if the child should turn into a hoodlum, provided he loves her. But she speaks of unfaithfulness and ingratitude if the child should turn into an outstanding adult yet withdraws his love from her (even if he does it with justification). (In both cases we can observe the presence of the defense mechanism so characteristic of particularist feelings—ungrateful country, ungrateful child.)

If an individual abandons himself to a cause then his giving does not depend on what he might become through the cause; neither the recognition nor the non-recognition of his merits, nor any form of reciprocity will alter his self-abandon. One circumstance, however, may alter it: if he should find that he had misjudged the cause, or if the value it bore at its beginning begins to vanish after his self-abandon. Remember Beethoven, who tore up the dedication of his *Eroica* symphony addressed to Napoleon when the first consul had himself crowned emperor. What did this have to do with the relationship of Napoleon to Beethoven? The final formulation of the deeply individual B-love that does not expect reciprocity is a sentence of Goethe's creation Philine: "if I love you, is it your business?" And Kierkegaard felt the love of God to be the only perfect (individual) form of love because, "in front of God I am always in the wrong," since in this feeling (at least in Kierkegaard's estimate) a defense mechanism is theoretically not possible.

The problem of self-abandon, however, has a third aspect, the matter of the so-called investment of feeling. The more abandoned the feelings of someone, the more (and the more intense) feelings he "invests" in a subject or object. It pertains to the preservation of identity: a person does not easily renounce "an investment of feeling"; his entire constitution protests against the realization that he may have invested his feelings "mistakenly." In this regard there is no difference between the individual and particularist personalities: the "wasted" investment of feeling is painful in both cases alike. This is usually the great trap of individual behavior. The significant investment of feeling (I have given my entire life to this or that cause!) often makes even the individual "rigid," that is blind with regard to the change in value of the object of investment. But even if this should not blur his vision and he retracts the feeling invested, then indeed a "deflation of feeling" may occur (in the case of certain individuals, but not all), i.e., the loss of the capacity for self-abandon. The difference between the particularist and the individual Self in this regard is not in the possibility for the "deflation of feeling," but rather in the causes which may bring this deflation about.

When I have said that it is the individual who is capable of a more reliable self-abandon, furthermore, that the individual is not afraid of self-abandon, since he is not afraid of losing his Self, by the same token I have implied that distance and self-abandon do not in the least exclude one another. We may even have a distanced relationship to the person to whom we have given ourselves completely and without reservation. I have already referred to this in connection with B love. That Minna von Barnhelm dealt sarcastically with and even mocked Major Tellheim's typically male haughtiness was not a sign of lack of self-abandon, but rather an organic part of self-abandon. The person who knows how to tend his own garden of feelings will know how to tend well in those of others. Of course, the individual Ego cultivates the Other's "ground of feeling" the same way he does his own: he considers the soil from which the flowers grow as "given" and approves and appreciates the personality as a whole. The particularist person also cultivates the feelings of Others as he would his own; he either wants to assimilate the Other to himself, independently of the soil of the Other's feelings, of his emotional habits and thus uses force against the Other's personality, or allows the weed to thrive in the other's garden as well; the lack of distance also means lack of respect for the other's personality. But all this applies not only to the feelings of love, sympathy, and friendship: the individual practicing self-abandon to a cause is the "gardener" of the cause; the individual practicing self-abandon to a principle is the gardener of the principle. The enthusiasm of the individual does not go along with fanaticism. On the other hand, the particularist Self either assimilates, if he can, the cause or the principle, makes it the mere instrument of his own approval, or goes along fanatically with every facet of it: and he does not tolerate any counter-argument, any skepticism, no more than he would tolerate it against himself: he and his cause are one. The self-abandon of the individual is coupled with trust, the self-abandon of the particularistic Self is coupled with blind faith.

Let me return to human relations. We know that the need of the individual is not that everyone should love him and follow him; his need is to be loved by those who relate to him in the same individual way as he relates to them. Even if he is able to endure solitude, in no way does he prefer it; the person truly capa-

ble of self-abandon does indeed want to abandon himself. The lack of a relationship based on mutual respect and self-abandon leads to the "deflation" of feeling
even in case of the individual; what more, this makes even the "gardener's
work" he performs on himself the labor of Sisyphus. A person can only be a
good gardener of himself if he is helped in the task by others; no one has enough
self-knowledge not to require its perfection by means of the knowledge of men
provided by Others. There is no individual sufficiently developed who would
not benefit from being "rapped" every once in a while, or from being reminded
of the incompatibility of his feelings with a given situation. This is particularly
valid at the time of the formation of individual behavior. I might argue that in
general individual behavior (apart from exceptions) can only develop if a "good
gardener" stands next to one, either permanently, or during the crucial moments
in life. The great "novels of education" (such as Goethe's *Wilhem Meister* or
Keller's *Green Henry*) cast such "good gardeners" in a central role. Even when
they do not assume such a central role, the "good gardeners" are present, if only
at decisive moments. Without the immaculate probity of Mr. Allworthy, Tom
Jones would certainly not have become what he became. And to turn to everyday experience: do we not recall the significant phrases uttered by a relative, a
teacher, a friend, at key moments, which have played a determining role in the
shaping of the individual relationship to ourselves? In spite of all this, the work
we "perform" on ourselves remains decisive; without it, the most pertinent utter-
ances of the best gardener, or his most immaculate behavior, remains without
effect.

As I have said: the individual and particularist relationships to reality are
two basic tendencies. If I compare everything I have said about the particularist
and individual functions of feelings and about the particularist or individual relationship to one's own feelings with the world of feeling of those we know, then
we are justified in drawing the conclusion that, although these two tendencies
may be embodied "totally" in one person or another, the majority of people are
more or less particularist or more or less individual. We rarely meet with a particularistic personality who never has individually functioning feelings or who
never, under no circumstance relates to his own feelings individually. For instance, that is how even one of the literary prototypes of particularist behavior,
Tolstoy's Karenin, feels at the sick-bed of Anna. But individual feelings, or the
individual relationship to feelings in the case of the particularist personality are
exceptional and do not leave a lasting mark on that person's world of feeling, on
his behavior. On the other hand, the individual too has particularist feelings,
what's more, particularist feelings to which he is unable to relate individually at
a given moment (for instance, Hamlet at the tomb of Ophelia). But in the case of
the individual, it is the particularistic feeling (respectively the particularist relation to it) that leaves no trace in his world of feelings, primarily because he condemns them himself, *post festum*.

A person is born with particular capacities and his particular viewpoint cannot be transcended. The guiding function of instincts is taken over, in man, primarily by the system of social customs.[4] Thus one may say that the particularist

type of behavior is more "natural" than the individual type of behavior. Certain cultures and social relations are more favorable to the formation of individuality, whereas others are at cross-purposes with it. And the road is not equally steep for everyone. The inborn qualities of certain persons may favor the development of individuality, whereas the inborn qualities of others may make this extremely difficult. But there are few cultures and few inborn qualities which would exclude the formation of individuality *ab ovo*.

If is difficult to *become* an individual, it becomes ever easier to *remain* an individual. To respond to expressions of frankness with love, to reject flattery with contempt, to love those whom we love for their own sake, etc., all this requires an effort at the beginning, but eventually becomes increasingly "natural." Thus I am justified in speaking here of a "second nature," which questions and transcends the functioning of society as "second nature."

The majority of people, I repeat, are rather particularist with regard to their actions and even the majority of individuals remain individuals only in the tendency of their actions. We may experience day in and day out collisions between individual and particularist feelings, between the particularist and the individual relationship to the emotions (emotional habits). This may also take place in the form of "fluctuations of feelings": thus we triumph over our jealous hatred, but it again overpowers us and we triumph over it once again, eventually one of the two wins out and this results in action, then the other feeling wins and we attempt to neutralize through action our first action, or take responsibility for its consequences, etc. Who would assert that he has never experienced such "fluctuations of feeling?" What is basic from the point of view of a person's world of feeling is the final decision, the final behavior resulting from such fluctuations. Not only because we affect others with our final behavior, since it is this behavior we take into the world (although this is also a reason), but rather because this final decision influences our whole world of feeling, provides a predisposition (either particularist or individual, depending on the outcome of our final decision) for the probable outcome of future fluctuations of feeling; in other worlds, it shapes our emotional personality.

This kind of "fluctuation of feeling" arises not only in situations directly affecting our person; but also in situations of judgment. In case of judgment I must suspend not only the relationship to my own particularist Self, but the pertinent analogies as well. We need not read Tolstoy's *Resurrection* to discover how the defense mechanism based on analogies affects the stand adopted by certain members of the jury. If the particularist person discovers in the accused an analogy to the offense he himself had suffered, he will find it easier to vote guilty. The individual, however, is capable of self-analysis and self-distance, even when it comes to judgment. He does not suspend his feelings in general, only his particularist feelings and the particularist relationship to his feelings, in order to place in the forefront the self-abandon to the chosen values, whether they be love of justice, love of humanity, or considered pity. Even this "suspension" does not work in every case or in every instance. The success depends, among other things, on the "mobilization of reserves of feeling."

It is not only our particularist feelings that may collide with our individual feelings, but our particularist feelings and our individual emotions may collide with one another. The collision itself is particularist wherever the feeling requirements of unreflected customary rules confront the affects. Or, to employ Freud's vocabulary, when the Superego collides with the Id. Without a doubt, this type of conflict may give rise to complexes. And the example given by Freud also refers to this kind of situation: the collision of the sexual affect with the system of customs repressing it. Furthermore, the collision is particularist wherever all the conflicting feelings are particularist and the relationship to them is particularist as well. So it happens in the "fluctuation of feeling" between enraged jealousy and vanity, or when the hunger for D love collides with envy. ("That witch has cheated me! Foolishness! It is not possible to cheat me!" Or "He is richer and better recognized than I, yet he offered me his friendship," etc.)

Whenever individual feelings collide it is always a matter of collision of values; I have to develop the hierarchy of feelings on the basis of selection among values. "I love Plato, but I love truth even more." It is only this final decision of Aristotle that posterity has preserved, hence it is only in imagination that we may cover the road which led to this decision. Surely he did not arrive there without "fluctuations of feeling," since such fluctuations also exist in the collision of values of the individual. In the soul of the lion Carlos it is sometimes love for Elisabeth, sometimes love and faithfulness towards the Marquis Posa, or even self-abandon for the cause of liberty, that comes out on top in similar "fluctuations of feeling." Since the feeling of personality (and all individual emotions can be described as such) is always "binding," there can be no authentic personality without such fluctuations.

As I described in the first chapter, the conflict between particularist and individual feelings and between the particularist and the individual relation to the feelings is often interpreted as conflict between feeling and understanding. Yet, to refer to Spinoza again, reason can never conquer passion, only an even stronger and opposite passion can accomplish that. Our individual feelings may triumph over our particularist feelings if they are more powerful, not by reason of their intensity, but rather of their depth, of their authenticity, of their being embedded into the personality. The appearance of dichotomy between feeling and reason has its origin in the undeniable fact that individual feelings are more reflexive than particularist ones because they are connected to consciously selected values, because they presume the conscious assumption of individual responsibility and because their prerequisite is self-knowledge and self-examination. And all the factors we have listed here are cognitive, such as "reflexive," "conscious selection," "self-knowledge," "self-examination"! Should we then speak about dichotomy of feeling and understanding after all? I believe not. The essence of the problem is to be found in the fact that in the case of all individual emotions (or the individual relationship to the feeling) we are dealing with the reintegration of cognition. True enough, cognition reintegrates not merely into individual feelings, for all emotions are cognitive, whether individual or particularist. But in the case of particularist emotions we may speak of spontaneous reintegration, while the reintegration of cognition into individual feelings is intentional. Cognition does not stand in opposition to emotion; rather, the higher forms of cognition and emotion are interdependent.

Let me return for the third time to the topic of the secret of the effect of demagogy. The thesis against which I am polemicizing goes as follows: the demagogue appeals to the feelings rather than to understanding. As we have already seen, the demagogue means to elicit the affects first of all setting in motion the "contagion" of affects. Furthermore, he wants to create the "basic mood" which seems the appropriate predisposition for certain feelings. But now let me ask the question for the third time: for what types of feelings does the demagogue create this predisposition? And my answer is clear: for the particularistic feelings.

Let us throw a look at one of the "masterpieces" of demagoguery, the funeral oration Anthony delivers over the corpse of Caesar. Anthony incites the assembled crowd against Brutus and Cassius in a masterly fashion, in order to gradually elicit the affect of rage. He even makes use of the direct visual stimulus by uncovering the wounds of Caesar. At the three crucial moments of the speech there appear (for the sake of developing the proper mood and later for bringing the existing mood and affect to a climax) the direct plays upon the particularist feelings. First on the level of the We-consciousness: "he hath brought many captives home to Rome"; then by flattering the "wisdom" of the crowd: "you all did love him once not without cause," and finally by the reading of the last will, bringing in the theme of material profit: "To every Roman citizen he gives ... seventy-five drachmas." Anthony intentionally delays reading the will, for it is the particularist feeling of the desire for gain that is called upon to put the dot on the "i"; it can only be adequately exploited when the mood and the affect are already well founded. After this, directing the rage of the crowd against Brutus becomes child's play. The funeral oration delivered by Brutus is no less emotional, but he, unlike Anthony, builds on individual emotions: "believe me for my honor and have respect for my honor, that you may believe: censure me in your wisdom and awake your senses, that you may be the better judge. ... If then that friend demand why Brutus rose against Caesar, this is my answer: Not that I loved Caesar less, but that I loved Rome more ... his glory not extenuated, wherein he was worthy, nor his offences enforced, for which he suffered death." For Brutus has enough respect for the Romans gathered around him to attribute to them the same world of emotions that belongs to him.

Now, regarding the beautiful and the sublime, the happy and the unhappy individual: the individual, as discussed, distances himself from his world and also from himself. This means that he will not accept as true or valid all the norms and rules received from his environment, yet will use his own mind to decide which of them to accept or to reject. Moreover, he will not identify himself with himself in an uncritical way, he will not believe and feel that everything he is doing is right, unless it clashes with the rules he himself entirely condones. When Kant, in the third *Critique* (§40), describes the maxims of good understanding, such as, "think with your own mind" and "think in place of the other," he is in fact describing the way of thinking of an individual. Thinking, as we know, is also feeling. An individual who thinks according to those maxims of understanding feels well in doing so, even if he might feel the pangs of certain possible unpleasant consequences.

Yet from all this one should not draw the hasty conclusion that the individual is a happy and harmonious person, whereas the particularist is mostly torn and unhappy. One can perhaps maintain that a particularist person has a different idea of happiness than an individual one. But whatever his idea is, he can feel happy and in modern times (contrary to Aristotle's rendering of the ancient Greek ethos) to feel happy is tantamount to being happy. For there are no more objective, external criteria of happiness. Thus if someone feels happy because of his great wealth or because—due to his wealth and power—he is surrounded by flatterers, then we are not entitled to say that he is not. Maybe it is more difficult for an individual to be happy than for a particularist person or maybe he, in the above sense, does not aspire to happiness at all. Yet whether he is closer to it or farther from it does not depend on his being an individual personality, but on many other factors, among them his psychological character.

I distinguish among three layers of human character: the psychological, the moral and the intellectual character. The psychological character begins to develop at birth and develops fully roughly until the age of fourteen. The moral character begins to develop from the acquisition of language and develops fully roughly till the person enters his thirties. The intellectual character begins to develop together with the moral one and perhaps never stops developing. The moral and intellectual character can assume different relations to one's own psychological character, thereby distancing oneself from oneself. We already came across several cases of such a distancing. The emotional character is already a result of such a distancing of the moral and intellectual character from the psychological character or the lack thereof.

Whether a person becomes a particularist or an individual personality depends entirely on his moral and intellectual character. Surely, some aspects of intelligence are inborn or at least develop very early, far before the development of moral and intellectual character, but while such aspects of the psyche may perhaps condition, they do not strongly influence the intellectual and moral character. Whether someone becomes an individual rather than a particultartist personality does not depend on his formal cleverness, nor even on his concrete talents, except his moral talent. Becoming an individual on the one hand and developing a kind of moral and intellectual character on the other are mutually dependent.

Typology is no classification, but rather a guideline. It is in this sense that I distinguish between two types of the individual personalities: between the beautiful individual on the one hand and the sublime individual on the other. I owe the distinction to Kant, and first and foremost not to the classical Kant of the third *Critique*, but to the young Kant, the writer of the pre-critical essay about the beautiful and the sublime. The moral person, so says Kant in this essay, can be either beautiful or sublime. The beautiful person is a harmonious soul, because she can do the right thing while guided by her emotions. She does the right thing happily. Women can be like this, but men cannot; men must constantly fight against their psychological dispositions. Moral rectitude is difficult for them; their distancing themselves from themselves is painful; and this is why they become melancholic.

We can leave the Kantian gender distinction behind, although it was certainly typical of the early period of modernity. There are far more harmonious, beautiful female characters in early modern literature than men, and not only in the works of the Romantics, but also in their forefathers Goethe and Schiller, with characters such as Egmont or Don Carlos.

The sublime character is no less an individual than the beautiful soul, yet he is constantly torn internally. His distance to the world takes the form of world rejection, of fury or escape; and his the distance from himself can take the form of self-hatred or the feeling of guilt without reason and remorse. A sublime individual can be outbalanced just for minutes, for his mood normally swings between extremes, such as enthusiasm and despair, love and disappointment. A sublime person rarely makes peace with himself or with the world, whereas a beautiful person regains emotional balance even after disappointments and defeats. Thus the emotional household works in another way for the beautiful soul and the sublime soul. The first keeps her internal garden in order, whereas the sublime weeds everything out radically to plant things afresh. The beautiful person's self enjoyment is constant, yet ironical, whereas the sublime person rarely enjoys his own personality, yet if he does, then without irony. The beautiful soul can be pleased with life, grateful for having the opportunity to live; for the sublime soul life is a duty fulfilled. Both are models of moral and intellectual rectitude.

Notes

1. I will analyze this problem in detail in the fourth part of my anthropology, in connection with the discussion of the theory of personality.

2. For a more detailed analysis of particularity and individuality see my *Everyday Life* (London, New York: Routledge & Kegan Paul, 1984).

3. Maslow, Abraham H. *Toward a Psychology of Being* (Princeton: D. Van Nostrand, 1962), 39.

4. I explore this in *On Instincts* (Assen: Van Gorcum, 1979).

Part II.
Contributions to the Social Philosophy of Feelings

Introduction to Part II

To feel means to be involved in something.

At all times, human beings have tasks. They must produce and act; they must reproduce themselves and the social organism into which they were born, and they must solve individual tasks, more or less well. What types of feelings are formed, and of what intensity, as well as when feelings are formed and which of them become dominant is primarily a function of these tasks. "Paying attention" to feelings or the need for a conscious "emotional household" arises during the solution of these tasks. To what extent one becomes independent—for independence can only be relative—depends not only on the individual, but first of all on the age, and on the social structure which provides the tasks for the individual.

The barely structured, so-called primitive societies are composed of a typical personality character that dominates the whole society, varying according to individuals, but no more than varying. This is what Benedict calls the "dominant configuration." More exactly, there are at least two such dominant configurations, one for men and one for women. For instance, in the Comanche tribe, every man is a hunter. It is the task of hunting that determines their world of feeling and fixes the boundaries of the emotional household. But even here there are "alternatives" (Linton), in other words, possibilities for individual housekeeping, but only within the rather narrow confines of the task. What's more, society even guarantees a place for those individuals who, by birth, are incapable of developing a character appropriate to the norms of the "dominant configuration." In the Comanche culture, the men performing womanly tasks and wearing the apparel of women play such a function. Their structure of feeling differs from the dominant one. Redfield calls them the "contrary ones." But it is never the "contrary ones" who are characteristic of the world of feeling of unstructured societies, nor could they possibly be, since they are incapable of performing precisely the basic task of the given society.

In these societies the social prescriptions and, within these, the feeling prescriptions appropriate to the given task, are of natural character. This is a "second nature," a social structure which functions almost as nature. Spiro describes this process in appropriate terms: "Hence the paradox: although evolution has produced a species characterized by the absence of drive goal invariants, culture produces personalities who behave as if there were."[1]

The formation of a natural (*naturwüchsige*) division of labor implies decisive changes even with regard to the responsibility. In the wake of Marx, I call

165

"natural" the type of division of labor where the place occupied in the division determines at the same time the place occupied by the individual in society, and divides society into strata, estates, or classes being constituted in interest conflicts. Natural division of labor (the starting point of which is the fixation of the division between the city and the village, between physical and intellectual work) causes the dissolution of the unity of the tasks confronting the members of the society. The varying kinds of tasks shape varying species of worlds of feeling. Strata feelings and, within these, feelings of rank, make their appearance. The serfs had necessarily other feelings than the nobility not only because they were confronting different work-tasks, but also because these different tasks were accompanied by essentially different ways of life and, furthermore, because society attributed different values to these different tasks; the feelings connected with the tasks deemed valuable thus became rank feelings.

The more a social structure, class, or stratum is fixed and constant, the more constant the roles the sexes fulfilled, the more constant its world of feelings; whereas the more dynamic the society, the more dynamic its world of feelings. Further, the constant or dynamic nature of a society always has a bearing on the possibilities of working out an individual world of feeling. Theoretically in more dynamic societies there is more opportunity for the appearance of emotional individuals in large numbers. Suffice it to mention here ancient Athens, or the Italy of the Renaissance. Every age (whether its social structure is stagnant or dynamic) has its own dominating feelings. I mean feelings, or even dominating configurations of feeling and not just one feeling, which refer to different but equally characteristic dominating models of ways of life. In stratified societies the models of way of life are heterogeneous. These pertain to different strata, but may vary within the same stratum, as a consequence of the range of tasks available to it: for instance, the way of life of the regular clergy and of the nobility in the European Middle Ages. To what extent the models of the way of life are polyphonic; to what extent they present alternatives; and at what pace the dominating feelings change depends on the particular social structure; hence we cannot generalize in any manner.

It is always the given concrete task—whether unified, stratified, or individual—which forms the world of feeling and, within this, the dominating feelings, but never directly, always indirectly: through the intermediation of feeling-prescriptions, or feeling objectivations. The emotional behavior needed for the accomplishment of the given tasks expresses itself in norms of feeling. Pericles could not cry when he lost his son, because in Athens the task of leading the city was tied to the requirement for the repression of individual pain; this emotional norm was ascribed to the accomplishment of the task. Likewise, in ancient Sparta mothers were expected to feel joy when their sons fell in battle; to glory in battle (the greatest task and also the greatest value) this emotional norm was ascribed. Of course, the abstract emotional norms pertaining to the tasks allow for greater or lesser freedom of movement in fulfilling the norm, and the actual feelings do not necessarily correspond to the norms directing them. This, however, does not alter the fact that society mobilizes for the tasks with prescriptions regarding feelings, including the vetoing or prohibition of certain emotions, affects, or expressions of affect.

The norms or objectivations regulating the feelings (which pertain to them) have a moral content; and this is a matter of course, since human behavior is thus being prepared or mobilized for one or several value-tasks. But their moral content may be primary or secondary. It is primary in every instance when the norm regulates the feeling directly, as in the case of the Biblical command "love thy neighbor as thyself." It is easy to see why the norms regulating feelings directly become moral in a primary manner, for the regulation of behavior is accomplished in this case through the regulation of the intention, and the formation of the behavior that corresponds to the intention is dependent upon the will of the individual directed at the good. The moral content of the emotional norms becomes secondary when the regulation affects not the feeling directly, but rather the expressions of feeling and the formation of emotional behavior in general. Thus with certain rules of emotional behavior, the girl or woman must lower her eyes in front of the man; the nobleman must pay homage to the king, etc. I have already shown that the normative regulation of the expression of feeling and emotional behavior affect the feeling itself. But the mechanism of the transformation of feeling nevertheless differs in the two cases mentioned. And I must add that it is only in extreme cases that one or the other becomes exclusive, most of the time they support one another, or may collide with one another.

One form of the indirect normative regulation of feelings is the collective rite. The regulation strives to homogenize the intensity and quality of feeling of the individuals participating in the rite. The function of the rite in creating an atmosphere of feeling can be observed even today wherever rites (more or less) survive, for instance, in the rite of burial. With those who feel deep grievance, the rites scale the expression of grievance down; it is not "proper" to scream or to leap after the casket; those close to the deceased must control their grieving. But in the case of those who may feel indifferent, the rites scale the expression "upwards." They may not chatter, they must assume a sad facial expression, they must show pain or at least sadness. Thusly, there developed a homogeneous atmosphere of mourning behavior, the common mood of the burial ceremony which suspends all other feelings. All this, however, is but the remains of something that has played a basic role in traditional societies.

Until now I have spoken in completely general terms about the reciprocal relations of tasks, feeling objectivations, and feelings, as well as about the historical nature of feelings, about rank feelings and their strata, about the historical varieties of dominating feelings and alternative ways of life. Methodologically speaking, on such a level of generality, so far I have not gone beyond the phenomenology of feelings. I have assumed the historical nature of feelings, but I have not demonstrated it. Since, however, this assumption is part of the essence of my conception, I cannot be content with a mere assertion; I must demonstrate its validity. For such a demonstration, however, analysis would be an inadequate method; the sole satisfactory means of proof is narrative evidence.

The documentation of the historical nature of feelings, however, is a task that gives rise to peculiar methodological problems. In practice, history is inexhaustible, even if we resort to it only from a selected aspect. To document the historical nature of feelings in the whole span of history would not only transcend the limits of one person's capacity for knowledge, but even theoretically would prove impossible. It would be impossible not only because the limited nature of the empirical material available to us would belie such an undertaking (and it is only on the basis of written records that we can say anything about the world of feeling of a historical epoch), and not only because we inevitably construe and explain the existing empirical material on the basis of our present consciousness, but also because any human integration is unique and specific, and any sensible abstraction comprises innumerable other facts, at the same time. Thus the task of documentation must be defined and limited.

For the following, I chose the bourgeois world-epoch and this was, I believe, a plausible choice. This is an age we understand, for it is the past of *our present*. By "bourgeois" I do not mean "capitalist," for there is no such world-epoch, but what the German language knows as *Bürger* (burgher). I count this world-epoch tentatively beginning with the "Age of Reason" in Europe, although its patterns appeared earlier, and terminating around the 1920s in much of Europe and America. Nowadays, after Hannah Arendt, one refers to this epoch as that of "class society," whereas the epoch following it, our own world, is known as "mass society." I do not use this terminology, and not just because it was not yet in vogue at the time when this book was first written, but also because I do not deal with the present but only indicate some of its tendencies.

In the following, I do not pretend to present a sociology of the bourgeois or modern world of feeling, nor even a social philosophy of it. My objective is less ambitious. In the first part of this book, I presented a general philosophy of feelings and emotions. I emphasized consistently that emotions are situated, and that cognition is inbuilt in emotions. It follows from that line of reasoning that they are also historically situated, and that the emotional concepts, which inhere in emotions, are, at least in part, also historical. And especially historical is the emotional household, the structure of emotions and the way one actually deals with them. I tried to make a case for my hypothesis in referring to a few examples at the outset, yet they were haphazard examples, randomly chosen. Thus I had to build my hypothesis on more solid grounds.

To contribute to a social philosophy of the modern world by discussing its most conscious phenomena seems to offer such a solid ground. Since I will concentrate on the presentation of a few syndromes of the bourgeois world of feelings and emotions, I must abstract from the presentation of the historical processes, of which the changes in the emotional syndromes were but one of several manifestations. I will not survey exhaustively the social or other conditions for the changes in the world of feelings; I will only document key changes by the presentation of literature representative of this particular age. This method may give rise to some doubts. Foremost, it may incite the doubt as to whether the emotional world of fictional characters is, indeed, representative of the emotional world of average people in everyday settings. True enough, there cannot be a one-to-one correspondence between them. Yet I have attempted to pick literary works that have a bearing on the emotional life of their age, and in the main characters who people have recognized as presenting or embodying of their own feelings. The analysis will undoubtedly be stylized, yet will remain the stylization of the true feelings of certain decisive strata of the bourgeois age.

Note

1. Spiro, Mulford E. "Social Systems, Personality and Functional Analyses" in *Studying Personality Cross-culturally*, Bert Koplan, ed. (Evanston, N.Y.: Row, Peterson and Co., 1961), 105.

Chapter VI.
About the Historical Dynamics of the Modern World of Feelings in General

Modern society is the first "pure" society; natural or blood kinship no longer determine the path of the individual. At the same time it is a dynamic society, and increasingly so; the tasks to be dealt with change continually from the point of view of every stratum and class, often even within the space of a generation. With the disintegration of community ties the individual becomes an "accidental" individual (his class- or stratum-affiliation is of an accidental character) but, at the same time he becomes a free individual, at least potentially. *In abstracto*, his relationship to the tasks at hand is free, insofar as he may choose it; what's more, he may choose his own task.[1]

The series presented so far (and basic to any society until this modern period), namely task-objectivation-feeling-series, will be replaced by ever more complicated series, for instance, objectivation-feeling—the selection of the task; or task-objectivation-feeling—the reselection of the objectivation. Also possible is the reselection of the task or the heterogeneous system of objectivations-feeling—selection among the objectivation—the choice of the task or task-objectivation-feeling-new task—which is the selection of the adequate objectivation, or transformation of the world of feeling. And these series will become ever more idiosyncratic. When the task ceases to seem "natural," we witness to an entirely new phenomenon: the experience of the lack of a task commensurate to the feeling, to its nature, to its requisites. Extraordinary tensions may result between the social possibilities on the one hand and the world of feeling shaped by the chosen objectivation on the other. The "great heart" feels it is capable of accomplishing great deeds. The myth of the age of Napoleon originates first of all in the fact that the emperor opened up opportunities for great deeds to the "great hearts"; he provided them with commensurate tasks.

Thus the domain of feeling of the individuals in the modern world-epoch essentially differs from the emotional individuality in all ages when the task is given at birth. Feelings are less "natural" and are much more reflective; perhaps they are less sublime even than the rank feelings of organic societies. Nostalgia for lost simplicity and sublimity is not rare in the modern age: it is characteristic of Cooper's Indian tales and of the whole Romantic movement. But nostalgia is a typically modern feeling: the problematic individual looks back with painful yearning and respect to the non-problematic individual. This painful yearning is peculiar to the individual in the modern world-epoch; it marks the reflected nature of his feeling, of its no longer "limited" character.

The conscious shaping of the emotional world is only characteristic of the individual of the modern world-epoch, the no longer "limited" individual feels himself to be problematic and is aware of himself as problematic precisely for this reason, for he may engage in shaping the world of feeling that transcends the social limits, the possibilities into which the individual is born (which, of course, does not mean that he always actually transcends them). The emotional household likewise becomes individual; it is no longer a matter of the affects conforming to the prescriptions of customs and norms, but rather is connected to the conscious evaluation of individual opportunities and inborn qualities and, along with it, to the development of one's own individual capacities. (Which, of course, again, does not mean that submission to norms and customs ceases to be of paramount importance in the case of the particularist person.) When speaking of the modern age it is customary to refer to its prosaic features, the predominance of prosaic feelings over the poetic world of feeling. This cannot be accepted, however, as a generalization. The Shakespearean world so often contrasted to modern prose also happens to be a product of the birth of the modern world-epoch. The wonderful wealth of the domain of feelings, the individual dynamism of feeling we encounter in Shakespeare is already indicative of the individual of the modern age, if not of the modern world of feeling. He who seeks "simplicity" should not turn to Shakespeare, but rather to folk-tales. Undoubtedly, the modern world of feeling has indeed become prosaic in part. But this kind of prose should not be confronted with the alleged poetic character of more ancient times. The authentic experiences of prose does not originate in the "objectively" more prosaic aspects of modern society (for why would the world of the nobles eating and drinking themselves to death, or the world of the serfs tied to the soil be more poetic?), but rather emanates from the chasm separating the subjective world of feeling, the needs for inwardness, a fertile ground to unfold capacities, and the market selection preventing the realization of these capacities—what is usually called alienation. Indeed, organic societies did not know such dichotomy between potentiality and actuality.

The modern individual is the individual with historical consciousness. The individual of the modern age reflects his own feelings along with the age, and recognizes them as socially determined ones. The cultivation of the emotional personality and the historical determination of these same individual feelings go together, hand in hand. True enough, only as a tendency. The more evolved the individual of the modern age, the better he announces the historical nature of his feelings, what more, its commensurability to some specific task, or to the principle of an inexistent task.

The modern world of feeling, however, has a peculiar, distinguished trait (within the modern world epoch). The significant individuals of the bourgeois class lived and reflected their feelings not only as historical feelings, or as class feelings, but they also inseparably generalized and formulated these same feelings anthropologically as "eternal human" feelings and experiences. Hence it may be said that the modern world of feeling is peculiarly ideological. Jürgen Habermas writes that "when ideologies do not only display the socially necessary consciousness in its ultimate falsity, when they dispose of an aspect which is truth insofar as it elevates the existing above itself, even if for purposes of mere legitimation, then ideologies still exist altogether since that time. Their source would be the identity of the proprietors with men in an ultimate sense."[2] Of course, the bourgeoisie is composed of several strata even within the same period, and the emotional household and emotional preferences of these strata differ. But the ideological identification of man and bourgeois is equally characteristic of all. The bourgeois live their existence as "bourgeois" and generalize it into the human behavior and the "human" world of feeling.

To quote Habermas again: it is the bourgeois world-epoch that brought about the separated "private sphere" or, more exactly, its twofold structure. "We refer to the domain of the market as private; and the domain of the family as the nucleus of the private, the intimate."[3] The domain of the market is the world of instrumental rationality, the domain of the family is the world of emotional "inwardness." The private man unites the two worlds in himself: "Proprietors of goods and persons as well as men together with other men, bourgeois and *homme*."[4] This twofold structure of the private domain is what reproduces always anew the relationship of the bourgeois to two contradictory approaches to feelings. The first is the working out of the so-called "inwardness," the cultivation of the world of feelings; whereas the other is the rejection of emotionality as something trite, as something non-rational, in the name of the concretely given Mind which abstracts from it, and passes sentence over it. The emotional household of the bourgeois individual (as we shall see) takes place between these extremes, that is, in the attempts to reconcile these two factors.

What historical factors are generalized by the bourgeois individual depends to a large extent on what moment of the private domain does he place himself at, which does he prefer. For instance, Rousseau clearly departs from the intimate, and describes the man of the intimate domain as "the man." As a result of his opposition to the tendency of bourgeois development based on commodity production, his "bourgeois man" does away with the dichotomy of the private sphere; the intimate sphere widens into the general vehicle of human communication, and thus the family into a kind of community.[5] In Defoe's Robinson, however, the bourgeois is constituted exclusively in an activity led by instrumental activity; the intimate sphere does not exist at all. Nevertheless, it is self-evident even in the case of Defoe that "the bourgeois" and "the man" are one and the same.

While I shall examine the changes in the dominating feelings of the modern age through representative individuals, I must add that these representative individuals not only express a latent feeling of the age, but make this feeling explicit, and by being made explicit, this feeling is transformed into a fashion of feeling. "There are fashions in feeling, as in clothing," writes Charles Blondel.[6] Blondel cites numerous examples to pinpoint this "quasi" consensus of a society without community; for instance in the fashion of Freudianism. Indeed, there is no significant dominating feeling, or expression of a dominating feeling which does not become fashion for a while only to be replaced after a short period by other fashions of feeling.

As we know, no work has attempted to illustrate the historical sociology of the modern age in regard to a single feeling. Let me quote, however, from an excellent work which is a beautiful example of the fact that such a task is not impossible; I am referring to the work of Lepenies on melancholy.

In spite of the ancient interpretation of the concept, Lepenies considers the *Lebensgefühl* of melancholy to be the typical feeling of the modern age, and rightly so. He distinguishes three types of melancholy: the "nobiliary," the "bourgeois," and the "already-not-even-bourgeois." Historical consciousness is characteristic of all three and all three react equally, although in different ways, to the lack of an appropriate historical task.

> Bourgeois melancholy means a type of the 'loss of the world' that differs considerably from that of the nobility. The latter lost a world; the former gave up a world which it did not at all possess. What both types of the 'loss of the world' have in common is, however, that they are cut off from action as a kind of exerting influence in and over the world; in this form of the 'blockade of action' utopian, nobiliary, bourgeois-inward and excentric-aesthetic versions of melancholy may be found.[7]

Lepenies analyzes in a similarly sophisticated manner the duality I have described with the concepts of anthropological generalization and specific historical and class reflexes. "Melancholy may be legitimated if, while the course of anthropological reduction remains open for all, at the same time this reduction is not actually allowed for every one in an equal measure."[8]

In what follows I must abstain from the historico-sociological examination of specific feelings, for the frame of this book allows us to present only very general examples of changes in the dominating feelings of the bourgeois world-epoch. First of all, from here on I will discuss only the modern world of feeling within the modern world-epoch. And only from two aspects: one being the *valeur* or expressions of valuing feeling, and the other the relationship of the individual to the world of feeling. These two aspects have not been selected at random, but express a unified structure, as can be easily seen. For expressions of feeling obtain *valeur* precisely from the relationship of the individual to the feelings that find an explanation in the emotional concepts, and in the relationship to the world of feeling itself.

For the sake of the analysis of these two aspects I have selected two time periods. One shall be the period around the French Revolution (immediately before and immediately after), and the other the twenties of the twentieth century, from the aftermath of the First World War to the time of the world economic depression (the appearance of Nazism). Again, it is not at random that I have selected these two moments. For these are two turning points. In the first cross-section we receive a picture of the birth of the bourgeois world of feeling and bourgeois consciousness; whereas in the second we receive a picture of its crisis. We know from the above-cited work of Habermas that the first cross-section is the epoch of the formation of a bourgeois "public sphere" (*Öffentliclikeit*), one may even say that here we find its climax; whereas the second cross-section is the characteristic stage of the end of the bourgeois "public sphere." Since the task beyond the private sphere, that is, the historical task proper of the bourgeois class stems from opportunities afforded by the terrain of bourgeois "public sphere," we must assume a direct relationship between the structural change of the public sphere and the structural change of the world of feeling.

I will gather my material from those belletristic works that express most tangibly, in my opinion, the dominating bourgeois life feeling of these two periods. I do not expect to cover the subject in this respect exhaustively. In the characterization of the world of feeling of the first cross-section, I will rely on the following works: Rousseau's *La nouvelle Héloïse*, Goethe's *Werther*, Sade's *Justine*, and Jane Austen's *Emma*.

The first three among these novels are of ideological purport and are consciously historic; the fourth has no historical dimension and has a concealed ideology. But it is characteristic of each that they believe the clear, unproblematic relationship between feelings and expressions of feeling (emotional concept, behavior) not only possible, but actually even opt for it. To Rousseau and Goethe, this unproblematic relationship is precisely characteristic of the world of feeling of the plebeian-bourgeois. They portray the emotional objectivational system of the city or of the court as the "artificial" obstacle to this unproblematic self-expression. There is but one real obstacle to the spontaneous surge, expression, and formulation of feelings, to the emotional contact with the Other: the institutionally regulated conventional character of contacts. (We might as well place into parentheses the fact that in *Werther*, the world of conventions is represented by the nobility, whereas in *Héloïse* by the bourgeois of Paris.) Thus it suffices to turn away from these conventional contacts; it suffices to listen to "the world of our hearts," and there no longer can be any obstacle to the harmony between the "inner and the outer." Our heart—the source of all our virtuous pleasures and so many pains—is identical with "nature."

Werther reflects: "Auch schätzt er meinen Verstand und Talente mehr als dies Herz, das doch mein einziger Stolz ist, das ganz allein die Quelle von allem ist, aller Kraft, aller Seligkeit und alles Elends" (*Erste Fassung*). The identification of "heart" and of "nature" as opposed to convention intones the general traits of bourgeois expression of feeling; on one hand the historical bourgeois definition of feeling, on the other its being constituted as "universally human."

Feeling and expression of feeling, their internal and external correspondence, are no less unproblematic in Sade. If you like, the explication is even clearer since the basic situation is forever repeated for, while the "basic formula" of the action or of the suffering experiences contains certain degrees, nonetheless these are always but variations of the basic formation. The desire for pleasure is realized, of necessity, in pleasure, in degrading the Other to the level of being a mere instrument of our pleasure; but the sentimental heart necessarily resists being transformed into an instrument, and whatever may be done against it, nothing will spoil that heart. The relationship of Justine and her torturers will remain (no matter how many times the basic formation is repeated) without consequence to her personality. Not once does Justine make any impression on her torturers, and not once do any of her torturers affect Justine. The basic feeling always appears "pure" both in behavior and in verbalization.

As a consequence, it is not in the illustration of the basic structure of feeling that Sade differs from Rousseau or from the young Goethe, but rather in the ideological definition of the concept "nature." While with Rousseau and the young Goethe nature, heart, and morality are synonymous, or at least are reflexive definitions, Sade seizes nature in its moral antinomy. Sade does not share the pleasant illusion according to which the liberation from aristocratic conventions and prejudices will spontaneously open the road to the nature of the "beautiful heart." Although the transcendence of the world of conventions and prejudices will let "nature" free, this "nature" as I have said, has an antinomic structure in his case. Nature on one hand is identical with reduction to mere desire for pleasure and desire for possession, on the other hand with the unfolding of beautiful and moral feelings. Monsieur speaks as follows: "No, Therese, Nature does not allow us the possibility of crimes that would disturb her economy. ... The equilibrium must be maintained; it can be only maintained by means of Crime; therefore crime serves Nature. ... Can these contemptible chains, the fruit of our laws and political institutions, be anything in the eyes of Nature?" And Therese answers, in the spirit of Werther, "This indifference which you ascribe to Nature is the work of the sophism of your mind. Listen to your heart instead. ... For what is this heart to whose tribunal I refer you but the sanctuary where this Nature you violate would have us heed and respect her?"

Sade expresses the bourgeois world of feeling in both antinomic concepts of the nature of feeling. We should not be misled by the fact that the majority of the torturers happen to be aristocrats, for their behavior is not an exemplification of aristocratic libertinage. Their ideology is depicted always meaningfully and very much historically: and this, without a doubt, is the bourgeois ideology of the Enlightenment. Better said, it is the confrontation of the ideology of one wing of bourgeois enlightenment with the ideology of the other wing: Holbach with Rousseau. Two ideologies, two bourgeois worlds of feeling, in other words, two extreme possibilities of the bourgeois world of feeling. Within this limitation, however, the description of the consciousness of the bourgeois world of feeling, the structure of this description, and its description as consciously historical are completely identical in the three novels. That the contradiction of bourgeois morality is depicted as "nature's" antinomy proves beyond a doubt that the need for the anthropological generalization has not been omitted here either. The antinomic bourgeois world of feeling is represented as the antinomically structured, "universally human" world of feeling.

These works, or better said their protagonists, not only express the bourgeois world of feeling, but cultivate it as well. The feelings may not remain "unexploited" even for a moment. It is necessary to feel constantly, one must always surrender to the beauty of feeling, one must not remain without tides of feeling for a moment. There are two roads, however, for the cultivation of feelings. One is the cult of the moment: to drink up every drop of the feeling totality of the moment, and to seek all the time the objects which may elicit this enhanced state of suffering and delight. The other is the emotional construction, the cultivation of feelings in such a way as to make ourselves appropriate for a conduct of life within a human community.

It may seem paradoxical, but in this regard Werther and Justine point in the same direction. True enough—and this is morally crucial—the relations of the protagonists of Goethe and Sade to the Other are the embodiment of the two opposite poles. Nothing repels Werther more than the breaking of the Other's will; whereas the delight of the protagonists of Sade resides precisely in that. But Werther provokes the mad, self-forgetting moments of passion, much as the protagonists of Sade provoke the moments of mad, sophisticated pleasure. The protagonists of Sade undoubtedly cultivate pleasure. They are tireless when it comes to devising new methods for procuring pleasure. In this elaborate cult of sensuous delights, in the cult of their feelings of the sensuous, they approve their own superiority the superiority of their own personality. And what does Werther say but:

> Leidenschaft! Trunkenheit! Wahnsinn! ... Ich bin mehr als einmal trunken gewesen, und meine Leidenschaften waren nie weir vom Wahnsinne, und beides freut mich nicht, denn ich habe in meinem Maße begreifen lernen: Wie man alle ausserordentliche Menschen, die etwas Grosses, etwas Unmögliches würkten, von jeher für Trunkene und Wahnsinnige ausschreien musste.

Perhaps it is no accident after all that Napoleon took along with him into battle *Werther* rather than the *Nouvelle Héloïse*. In the cult of sentiments, that is the cult of superiority, the young citizen who breaks into tears at the sight of simplicity, at "the call of the heart," nevertheless is getting prepared for the bloody act. Werther turned the weapon against himself. But the heroes of Sade and Werther will meet at the "great moment" of history, the moment of blood. The two contradictory bourgeois "natures" express themselves in different terms, but equally, in the great overture the sounds of which they had intoned earlier.

The *Nouvelle Héloïse* and *Emma* are epics of the construction of the bourgeois world of feeling—one in the tone of sentimental, the other in that of naive poetry. The bourgeois world of feeling is constituted in the natural unity of the inner and the outer world. But the objectivization of feelings is here not exclusively behavior and the pertinent verbalization, nor is it verbalization and the pertinent behavior. The bourgeois world of feeling tries for something greater: for the creation of a world to its measure, for the creation of communities and systems of institutions which make possible the rich development of a world of feeling worthy of man. Although in the first half of the novel Saint-Preux seems to be the elder brother of Werther, intending to astound the world with the depth and variety of his feelings as opposed to being conventional, in fact the self-enjoyment derived from emotional inwardness is subordinated from the very beginning to the enthusiasm for Virtue. For him, feeling of itself is not yet virtue; emotions have to be transformed into dispositions to virtue: and this is a task. Thus Wertherism is but one factor in Saint-Preux's personality. Goethe's subsequent observation about his hero ("sei ein Mann und folge mir nicht nach"—"be a man and do not follow me") is an organic constituent of Saint-Preux's development. Julie too writes "How can you lower yourself to this point, cry and complain like a woman, and behave like a maniac? ... Learn to bear misfortune like a man!"

Indeed, in this case it is the task which determines the tendency of the dynamic of the world of feeling. The unfettered living of feelings becomes modified into the formation and construction of an emotional household commensurate with the task. The task shows outwards rather than inwards, although this "outwards" originates from the "inwards." If our feelings deny the conventional, alienated world of feelings, then we may turn towards the cultivation of our own nature (as did Werther, and, in a different way, the heroes of Sade), without asking about the possibility of socially generalizing the nature of our own feelings. But we may follow yet another road, the road of the task of social generalization, whereon the task reacts upon the "inner" and creates the potential for the emotional household of the individual, or what I associated with "gardening" in the first part of this book. Werther does not have a task in the world and thus does not "garden"—he does not have an emotional household; his relationship to himself is narcissistic as are, in fact, the devotees of pleasure in Sade. Saint-Preux constitutes the task, not alone, but along with Others; he is involved in something outside of himself, and thus can have an emotional household. Part of his character is the "construction of feelings." The community he and his companions create is as much utopia as later the "tower" of Wilhelm Meister and his companions, but this does not diminish the significant and exemplary nature of his experiment.

The novels of Jane Austen, perhaps *Emma* most of all, justify the exemplary nature of this experiment. Emma is the British counterpart of Wilhelm Meister; only it is not constructed philosophically, its world is narrower, it lacks the poetic, and its prose element dominates. But the literary idea is very similar: it follows the development of a disposition for human co-existence in the process of the mutual construction of moral feelings and the liquidation of feelings of rank. Here too, everyone is basically of a good nature, as in Goethe's novel; here too it is a matter of each individual developing his own nature, and of not forcing the norms of his own nature onto the personality of the Other. Even the climax is similar: the novel ends with noble-bourgeois wedding and the severity of rank feelings bends in front of the fact of natural differences (that is, in front of differences not dependent on social position), and of equality at the same time. And here, there is a significant Other (in the person of Mr. Knightley) who, at the critical moments and only at the critical moments, helps the heroine transform her feelings into dispositions of virtue.

It is precisely the prose quality, one might even say the banality, of the novel that makes *Emma* a model. For thus it is possible to illustrate the most beautiful construction of bourgeois feelings while at the same time bypassing, or even rejecting, social utopias. The harmony of the inner and the outer, the welding together of the task and of the emotional construction shines in the light of the possible. We are not on a world stage, but in a small British town. It is not the "sage" who leads us with the fatality of a tale, but an ordinarily honorable man. The task is the setting up of a farm, marriage, the raising of children, the development of human contacts with everyone according to their merits and not according to their social position. The task is modest and it is on a human scale. It is precisely the prosaic model that suggests the intention to universalize the bourgeois world of feeling: you too can do it—and you too, and you too—after all, it is possible, isn't it?

Thus the bourgeois world of feeling is well on its way, it discovers itself and its task—either on the world stage, or in the shaping of a "nice" everyday life. This is why emotional concepts in this age are so free of problems, and so numerous. Especially those that express emotional dispositions: "desire," "heart," "soul," "pain," "happiness," "suffering," "passion," "delight," "pleasure," a "bad conscience," "feeling," "sentiment" and love, again and again love! All this flows from the pen so naturally, and seems so firmly in place. So what is left incognito? The character is "open" and expresses itself, there are no "great" words, because no word is big enough to enable the soul to reveal itself through it. It is not only the beautiful soul that reveals itself, but the Evil one as well; every hero of Sade never ceases to talk of egoism and pleasure. This grand heaping of emotional expressions, this "natural" treatment of it, this "appropriateness," the complete lack of banality, the adequate "suitability" of all emotional expression, all these show that a class has identified itself with its own feelings, because it has started on its path of world conquest. Nothing has been used up as yet; it is only now that it will be exploited. The essence, provided it is unproblematic, must indeed appear.

In the characterization of the world of feeling of the second "cross-section," I will rely on the following works: Kafka's *The Trial*, the poetry of T. S. Eliot, Musil's *The Man Without Qualities*, and Thomas Mann's *The Magic Mountain*.[9] By no means should we identify the crisis of the bourgeois world of feeling with the crisis of the world of feeling of the bourgeois world-epoch, as so often happens; the world of feeling that results from the task of the transcendence of the bourgeois age pertains to the bourgeois age as well. But even if we should abstract from it, I must still assert that from the 1930s on, the bourgeois world of feeling gradually loses its representative character, and even in artistic creations it is represented only as history, as the past. The duality that was always so characteristic of the bourgeois world of feeling ceases; the positing of feelings as *par excellence* historical and bourgeois and, along with this, or rather because of this, their positing as universally human ceases as well. The anthropological generalization breaks away from what is bourgeois and class-like and, at the same time, splits into two. On one hand the "unhappy consciousness" becomes generalized into a *condition humaine*, and thus the class-like-historical identification ceases; on the other hand, the anthropological generalization is placed into a future that goes beyond the bourgeois age, into a "real history," and this becomes a regulative principle.[10]

The unity of the "class-character" and the "condition humaine" is still unbroken in the art of the 1920s; here we are still confronted, for the last time, with a bourgeois world of feelings. I do not mean to say that this is a characteristic of all artists of the 1920s, rather that there are representative artists of that period for whom this assertion still holds true. At any rate, in Robert Musil's art we can observe that change within one novel. *The Man Without Qualities*, written in the 1930s, was created under the sign of a growing abstraction from the historically-given class character.

In the novels mentioned above, no one could doubt the determination of the class character of the protagonists' world of feelings as bourgeois; this characteristic is formulated because it is so explicit and historical. The traditional bourgeois genesis has been described just as well: through the depiction of Hans Castorp's childhood, and of the ethics and *Weltanschauung* of Ulrich's father. In both cases we are dealing with the lost bourgeois, even if in a different way, and emphasis should be placed on both, lost and bourgeois. It is the same with Kafka's K. Despite the fact that the novel opens with the absurd situation straight away, the reader can have no doubt that until then the life of K was the "normal" everyday life of a "normal" bourgeois. But even in the course of the novel, the middle-class occupation of the protagonist plays a central role: its punctilious performance is of vital importance for him. The increasing deconcentration during the performance of clerical tasks (as a result of the trial) is a sign that "the game is lost." And here too there appears the bourgeois "background" in the person of the uncle. (In the projected complete version there would also have been a chapter about visiting the family.)

I had to mention all this at the beginning to underscore that in these novels the crisis of the bourgeois-world of feeling is really present. Everywhere, including in the poetry of Eliot, the adulteration of the inner and of the outer becomes explicit. The cause of this adulteration is the discrepancy between the individual and the task. In the case of Werther, for whom fate did not make room, at least there was a task commensurate with his personality in principle, if not in actuality; as I have said, the sentimental hero was preparing for the violent task. Not so in these later novels: the tasks are too petty in comparison with the individual, and therefore do not count, or too big; they are not to his measure. Where the task is too petty, it becomes grotesque, as in the relation between the personality of Ulrich and the "parallel action." Where the task is too big, it becomes absurd, as in the relationship between K and the trial. When the hero escaping from petty tasks chooses an existence without tasks, the story becomes ironic, as in the case of Hans Castorp. Hence all three protagonists are "without qualities" in

Musil's sense. The quality is an inner disposition for a manifestation commensurate with the task. In the case of Kafka, this discrepancy between the inner and the outer is expressed by the almost total cessation of emotional expression. The relationship of the hero to the world becomes purely cognitive, devoid of any self-reflection. K does not have any kind of feeling disposition. Strangely enough, he is not even disposed to anxiety. No matter how often the trial and the feeling of anxiety are mentioned in one breath, it must be conceded that K is not at all anxious. The word *Angst* appears in the novel almost exclusively as a synonym of being frightened. Yet it is not the hero who feels anxious, but the reader.

Let me cite a few feeling concepts from *The Trial*. The ones I have selected are reiterated in various contexts; and these are the only ones that are repeated. "Es wunderte K," "ich bin überrascht," "er schien getroffen zu werden," "ich wiederhole, mir hat das Ganze nur Unannehmlichkeit und vorübergehenden Ärger bereitet," "Ich scheue vor dem Wort nicht zurück," "Die Frau bemerkte sein Staunen," "Sie gefallen mir gut, besonders wenn Sie mich wie jetzt so traurig ansehen, wozu übrigens für Sie gar kein Grund ist," "Wenn Sie ungeduldig sind," "Es war natürlich kein Grund sich deshalb zu ängstigen," "fragte K erstaunt," "Die unerwartete Ansprache machte den Mann verwirrt," "sagte K freudig üiberrascht," "K war dadurch nicht sehr bestürzt," "dann fasste ihn eine derart unbezähmbare Neugierde," etc. The feeling concepts that appear most often are *being-surprised* and *wondering*.

If we analyze these expressions we arrive at the following results. Kafka applies most often those feelings concepts which have a cognitive content. Moreover, both the emotions that have a cognitive content, and those (fewer) that are not primarily cognitive refer to suddenness; even feelings that do not necessarily take a sudden course are placed into a context that refers to suddenness. These feeling occurrences that take a rapid course, as I have already mentioned, are not tied to any feeling disposition, mood, etc. Thus the split between the inner life and the outer is illustrated in such a manner that the inner life ceases; furthermore, it follows that the outer becomes reactive as well. This reduction of feelings to the outer-reactive is in organic union with the unreality of the world, the dissolution of the cause and effect relationship in the happening itself. The task (to arrive at the end of irrationality and reach the "prime mover") is too big for the hero; this is precisely why the "inner" has to cease.

The relation between the inner and the outer, in spite of the uniqueness of Kafka's literary personality, is not simply his individual solution, but rather the expression of the bourgeois world of feeling; and this should become clear if we analyze briefly Eliot's "The Waste Land" from the same point of view. First of all the relationship between unreality and suddenness is plausible: "Unreal City ... sighs, short and infrequent, were exhaled / And each man fixed his eyes before his feet." "What is that noise now? What is the wind doing? Nothing again nothing," "Hurry up please it's time." When the Self appears in the poem it never expresses feeling, but always cognitive or directly acting behavior, as in "I will show," "I end my song," "I speak," "I hear," "I was finishing," "I too awaited," "I can sometimes hear," etc. The two exceptions, "I was frightened" and "I sat down and wept ..." are likewise not expressions of feeling when taken in context.

The lyrical attitude provides the opportunity for living through and expressing every alternative in the world of feeling (even if not every poet makes use of the opportunity). Practically every experience and alternative of the bourgeois world of feeling assumes a form in the poetry of Eliot. It expresses the reflected and ironical relationship to the unproblematic world of feeling of the past in the lyrical "quotations," it expresses the pettiness of the worldly task, the world that is not commensurate with the inner life, the clinging of the feeling that finds no task, that is left to its own devices to the god of the subject; and even the formulation of the basic experience in the final reduction of the crisis of bourgeois feelings: "Between the conception / And the creation / Between the emotion / And the response / Falls the Shadow." Here too we may witness the identification with the bourgeois world of feeling, and the conscious, and consciously negative, experience of anthropological generalization:

> We are the hollow men
> We are the stuffed men
> .....
> Those who have crossed
> With direct eyes, to death's other Kingdom
> Remember us—if at all—not as lost
> Violent souls, but only
> As the hollow men
> The stuffed men.

And this is precisely the life-feeling that pervades Ulrich, Musil's protagonist. The split between the inner and the outer is formulated and experienced in a manner directly the opposite of that of Kafka. The heroes become "hollow men," "empty men" because they do not have a task. Expressions of feeling arc not only not-omitted, they are actually heaped upon the reader. There are more emotional concepts in a single sentence of Musil's novel than in all the novels of Kafka. But these bountifully flowing feelings become "pointless," one might say; they flow back into themselves, because they do not have any actual realization. Or the opportunities for realization are all so petty that they immediately kill the feeling itself, only that which does not terminate remains real. Among the many erotic relationships or attempts at a relationship in the first part of the novel, not a single one attains fulfillment. Only unfulfilled eroticism has content, whereas fulfilled eroticism is immediately emptied of its content. Becoming outer results in the destruction of feeling, and "retaining as inner" results in the destruction of personality.

We are in the fortunate position, in analyzing the world of feeling of Musil's novel, that the author himself, through the intermediary of the writings of his protagonist, formulates his own theory of feelings, and at a rather high philosophical level at that. The dramatic struggle of Ulrich to comprehend feelings is the theoretical formulation of the crisis of the bourgeois world of feeling as illustrated in the novel.

The most exciting and at the same time concluding, summarizing part of the analysis touches on the basic question regarding this illustration: the relationship of the inner and of the outer, the problem of the unity of the inner life and of feeling finding a "home" in action, in the "world." The train of thought posits this unity: "Mein Gefühl bildet sich in mir und ausser mir ... es verändert die Welt unmittelbar von innen und tut es mittelbar, das heisst durch mein Verhalten, von aussen; und es ist also ... innen und aussen zugleich ... dass die Frage, was an einem Gefühl innen und was aussen sei und was davon Ich und was Welt sei, fast allen Sinn einbüsst." The immediate next step however, is that Ulrich conceives of the Self and of the "world" as two entirely separate entities. Thus the "unity" of the inner and outer is nothing but the meeting of these two entirely separate entities in the so-called vision of the world. And in what follows he designates this "no man's land" as the source of the "basic feeling," and from here on the feelings may progress along two separate roads; one being the external evolvement ("äussere Entfaltung"), and the other the inner evolvements ("innere Entfaltung"); the former are the "determinate feelings" ("bestimmte Gefühle,") and the latter the "indeterminate feelings" ("unbestimmte Gefühle"). The world of the Self is therefore the world of the "indeterminate feelings," whereas the outer world, the stage of action, is the world of "determinate feelings." "Aber während das bestimmt entwickelte Gefühl an ein Wesen mit greifenden Händen erinnert, verändert das unbestimmte die Welt auf die gleiche wunschlose und selbstlose Weise, wie der Himmel seine Farben. ..." And after this Ulrich formulates the structure of feelings, which at the same time is the clue to the illustration of the whole work: "denn natürlich ist es vornehmlich die Entwicklung zum bestimmten Gefühl, was die Unbeständigkeit und Hinfälligkeit des seelischen Lebens nach sich zieht. Dass man niemals den Augenblick des Fühlens festhalten kann, dass die Gefühle rascher verwelken als Blumen oder dass sie sich in Papierblumen verwandeln. ..."

Still, Ulrich does not want to accept this solution without a struggle. As we know, his world of feeling is the bourgeois world of feeling, and thus he consciously wants to accept traditional bourgeois culture, as he says, the "nicht zu Übersehende Eigentümlichkeit der europäischen Kultur," the basic idea of which is "die Welt des Innern als den eigentlichen Hoheitsbereich zu ehren, und doch von ihr vorauszusetzen, dass alles, was in ihr vergeht, zuletzt die Aufgabe habe, wieder in eine ordentliche Wirkung nach aussen zu münden." The basic experience of the split between the inner and the outer, and the acceptance of the heritage of European culture cannot in this case have a common denominator. Ulrich, unable to find a solution, smilingly removes from the bookshelf one of the volumes of the *Geisterseher* of Swedenborg, and meditates on the world of the angels who "keine Vorstellung von der Zeit haben."

This analysis of the theory of feelings was written in the thirties. Its concluding accord, the turning to the "world of angels" of the mystic, already points beyond the frame of the historical cross-section the analysis of which I have undertaken. The awareness of the bourgeois world of feeling—in this case awareness of crisis—becomes anthropologically ungeneralizable.

Notes

1. As a result of the universality of commodity production this freedom takes on a "quasi"-character, because it is subordinated to a likewise "quasi"-natural necessity; I will discuss these in greater detail when I analyze the abstraction of feelings.

2. Habermas, Jürgen. *Strukturwandel der Öffentlichkeit* (Neuwied am Rhein: Luchterhand, 1968), 103.

3. Habermas, *Strukturwandel der Öffentlichkeit*, 69 (My translations throughout).

4. Habermas, *Strukturwandel der Öffentlichkeit*, 69.

5. All this was already known to Kant: Rousseau presents two solutions that are completely different, and even contradictory. His Social Contract does away with the intimate sphere from the point of view of the citizen. But even here in Rousseau, the basic structure of bourgeois ideology is maintained; it is the *citoyen* that becomes identical with the *homme*. For details see my essay on "Rousseau and the Nouvelle Héloise."

6. Blondel, Charles. *Einführung in die Kollektivpsychologie* (Bern: A. Francke, 1945), 178.

7. Lepenies, Wolf. *Melancholie and Gesellschaft* (Frankfurt am Main: Suhrkamp, 1969), 187.

8. Lepenies, *Melancholie and Gesellschaft*, 231. (Although melancholy always contains the moment of nostalgia, nostalgia is not necessarily melancholic. Nostalgia is often the ideological and feeling aspect of a new choice of values and tasks.)

9. The crisis of the bourgeois world of feeling—this being, as we learn from Habermas, the direct reaction of the crisis of bourgeois "public-sphere"—already started earlier, of course, and will continue in the future. Much as the transcendence of the bourgeois world of feeling within the bourgeois world-epoch began considerably earlier; indeed it is already reflected in the avant-garde of the beginning of the century. My "cross-section" merely seizes the culminating point of a process.

10. See, for greater detail, the essay by Ferenc Fehér, "Ideology as Demiurge in Modern Art" (San Francisco: *Praxis* 1977.2).

Chapter VII.
The Housekeeping of Feelings

The analogy expressed in the term "housekeeping of feelings" is applied, in this case, to an actual relationship. Just as the economic structure of society and within it, the place of the individual in the social division of labor, determines the limits of personal housekeeping within which the individual may operate, economize or overspend, invest or consume, so in the same way do the feeling objectivations of every society, the tasks to be solved by the individual belonging to a given class or strata and the dominating feelings developing along with these objectivations determine the "frame," or area of movement within which the individual may keep in order his "emotional household." There is saving and waste, investment and mere "consumption," in feeling housekeeping as well; here too there evolves a certain hierarchy among the feeling that need to be satisfied or that cannot be satisfied. In the long run the housekeeping of feelings is always connected with the task, whether this task is received ready made, selected, or reselected. This perennial task, therefore (again, in the long run), determines which quality feelings we waste or save, in which objects we invest our feelings and in which objects we do not, in which objects we invest more and in which less, which quality feelings are transformed into action or behavior and which are "kept to ourselves." In the last case, we are justified in using the expression "mere consumption." It is the housekeeping of feelings that decides whether our various feelings will be kept qualitatively apart or whether they are quantitatively homogenized in some alienated passion.

The autonomy of the economic sphere is an innovation of the bourgeois era: this is where "pure society" is constituted historically. The housekeeping of feelings is also an innovation of the bourgeois era—only the modern and "broad-minded" (Marx) individual has a feeling housekeeping in the real sense of the word. In the case of "narrow" individuals the "economy of feelings" means nothing but the attempt of the individual to "regulate himself" into the frame of the permanently fixed value hierarchy of feelings. The value hierarchy of feeling is "naturally given" to the individual. The "task" is already given at birth; the series, task-value objectivation-world of feeling, is unconditional and beyond appeal. The possibility of "reversal" of the series in our own image, the selectibility of values and tasks appropriate to our individual nature, this is what places feeling housekeeping in the center; the investment of feeling or saving of feeling, the object into which we want to invest or not invest, the formation of the hierarchy of feeling needs are a condition *sine qua non* of growing up and of the development of personality. At the same time, the increasing autonomy of the economic sphere and its historical tie to the rise of feeling housekeeping does not imply a necessary connection between the two "housekeepings." But it does mean that the feeling housekeeping of the bourgeois era evolves antinomically. The economic sphere that has become independent and the dissolution of "naturally given" communities creates the conditions for the housekeeping of feelings, but it also counteracts its realization in the case of the majority of individuals by subjecting the chance individual to the pseudo-natural laws of economics.

Let us take a brief look at the general structure of the housekeeping of feelings. The "narrow individual"—however great, beautiful, majestic a person he may be—has always but one task: to fill the norm he must fill according to his place. The particular tasks are always specific of this unique task. Man must be a good citizen, because the supreme good is the good of the state, said Aristotle. There is not a single classical tragedy in which the hero chooses a new value in the course of the conflict, nor is there a single one built on the conflict of tasks. In the bourgeois era he has not one task, but several. These tasks are not at all necessarily organic parts of an integral duty; they may be heterogeneous with regard to one another, or may collide with one another.

To the Anthony of Shakespeare, Rome and Cleopatra are of equal value and thus they give rise to the conflict of feelings. It is not the "desire for pleasure" that is confronting duty, the value, but rather the task of love as value, the encounter of two human beings and its conflict with another value and task. The hero Anthony acting in ancient disguise is not an ancient hero, but very much bourgeois: he is an early Don Carlos, and their fate is similar. One source of their tragedy is that they are unable to create the hierarchy of their tasks; they are unable to subordinate either one task or the other. The tragic example, however, is rather extreme in its essence. The tendency of feeling housekeeping is for the person to create a hierarchy of the various (selected or reselected) tasks and to form his hierarchy of feelings accordingly. The greatest investment of feeling is accorded the primary task (including the transfer into action and the responsibility accepted for the feelings) and those subordinated in the hierarchy receive less, or else it will be the quality, intensity, or depth of the feelings that will differ. If this does not occur, the person will feel that he has transgressed a norm and will "force" in himself the development of feelings with a quality and intensity relevant to the task. Thus, for instance, Hamlet forces in himself the feeling of revenge, both qualitatively and from the aspect of intensity. The reselection of the task, the change in the value-objects also change, of course, the proportions of the investment of feeling; I have already mentioned the beautiful example of King Lear, his late flowering of compassion for the oppressed and the humiliated. The change may also take place in inverse proportions: the "reversal" of investment of feeling may reverse the hierarchy of the tasks. If this does not happen, if the investment of feeling and the task collide with each other, then the conscience of the person is bad. If it does occur, then the world view of the individual changes (as does his ideology), as that of Raskolnikov in consequence of his love for Sonia.

I have spoken of world-view and with deliberate emphasis. For world-view is also the product of the bourgeois era, just as much as the housekeeping of feelings and the two are related; increasingly so as the bourgeois world becomes more universal.[1] As a result of the dissolution of the organized community and, along with it, of consensus, it became possible, historically, to choose the task and the value objects. The selection of tasks and values can only take place, however, on the basis of a united "picture" (although not necessarily formulated on a philosophical level), on the basis of the reflective ideological relation to the world. I must emphasize the word "ideological" as well. The world view that serves as the basis of the feeling housekeeping of the bourgeois era is ideological, in its tendency. Let me refer to what I have said in the first chapter: the individual representing the bourgeois world of feeling reflects his feelings as historical and as anthropologically general as well. This is at the source of another antinomy of the bourgeois feeling housekeeping. As housekeeping of feeling, it is commensurate with the measure of the individual's choice of values, with his own "nature of feelings," but as housekeeping of feelings that is ideologically interpreted it is intolerant as well. The ideologically interpreted emotional intolerance developed by the bourgeois individual takes effect first of all with regard to those who have selected a similar task, or should have selected a similar task according to the evaluator, yet their more intensive, greater feeling investments are placed elsewhere. With petty souls this intolerance assumes the form of narrow-minded rejection and incomprehension (the businessman feels contempt towards another businessman who contracts a *mésalliance*). In the case of great souls there is a constant attempt to raise the Other to the level of their own investment of feeling (the Posa-Carlos relationship), that is, any intolerance is directed at themselves. The famous paradox of G. B. Shaw: "Do not do unto others as you would that they should do unto you. Their taste may not be the same ..." is directed specifically at the intolerance of the bourgeois housekeeping of feeling, as is made clear by the next to last *bon mot* in the *Manual of a Revolutionary*: "Self-sacrifice enables us to sacrifice other people without blushing." Because: "The love of economy is the root of all virtue."

It may seem a paradox to refer to the bourgeois feeling housekeeping as intolerant, when the very concept of tolerance is a product of the bourgeois era. But tolerance and intolerance are reflective definitions and refer to the antinomic structure of the self-same process. To refer to medieval Christianity as intolerant is undoubtedly a bourgeois invention. Where there is no potentially free choice of values and choice of tasks, where housekeeping of feelings is not possible, it becomes equally senseless to talk of tolerance or of intolerance. Where there is no personal world-view, but collective consciousness, there is nothing towards which one may feel tolerant or intolerant. Religious intolerance is the product of the bourgeois era as well; it is connected with the pluralization of Christianity.

It is the bourgeois housekeeping of feeling that has, therefore, made possible the "emotionally open" individual. Let us recall the constituents of the individual: conscious relation to the world, capacity of self-abandon to the object, to the task, but in such a way as to he able to distance himself from it, distancing from our own particularist personality with the conscious acceptance of his own personality. "Species essence" or the idea of "humanity" as a regulative principle is also the product of the bourgeois era. The direct, emphatic relation to species character, the "Seid umschlungen, Millionen, dieser Kuss der ganzen Welt," (Be embraced, millions, this kiss for the whole world) is the emphasis stemming from the bourgeois world of feeling. Complete self-abandon to the task has always been possible; but self-abandon with the factor of distance is a product of the plurality of values. It has always been possible to distance from ourselves on the basis of values, but this, together with the cultivation of our own nature, is the opportunity provided by "pure society."

Yet—and now we reach the third antinomy of the bourgeois housekeeping of feelings—there has never existed a society that has guaranteed such "freedom of movement" to the self-indulgence of purely particularist feelings to the same extent as the bourgeois society. Not because the particularist relation to the world is some kind of "new" phenomenon, but because in the bourgeois era the particularist self-indulgence of the Self has become an ideology in itself: the ideology of egoism. The operation of raising the particularist Self above all values has become reflected instead of spontaneous, has attained "to self-consciousness." The heroes of Sade, as we have seen, made a principle out of the conversion of the Other into a mere instrument. Man, as self-objective, man, as mere instrument: both ideologies (and practice) are the constituents and sources of the housekeeping of feeling.

In analyzing the general structure of the housekeeping of feelings I started from the assumption that the task, the object of the investment of feeling, the arrangement of the hierarchy of feelings is selected or reselected; and thus I described in all its antinomical structure the possibilities opened by the bourgeois era. These possibilities, however, are only tendencies; their complete realization is therefore representative: though it may be "exemplary," it cannot be general.

Chance individual, as mentioned before, will become subjugated to the quasi-laws of economy and it is the accomplishment of work forcefully assigned to him within "natural" division of labor (a task entirely external to the abilities, the "nature" of the individual) that gets into the center of his life activity. This work is no self-chosen value that is to say goal-vocation but a mere means of subsistence. At the same time, work requires/be it chosen or not/constant and intensive feeling investment: the evolvement of orientational feelings, intensified attention, the suspension of emotions and affects hindering the accomplishment of the task. The work task that requires considerable investment of feeling is not a goal, but a means: the means to mere survival, to possession, or to the extension of possession. Analyzing the worker in the "classic period" of capitalism Marx writes that the worker feels "outside of himself" during his work and only outside of his work does he feel he is "with himself'; thus the investment of feeling into the central task becomes irrelevant from the point of view of the worker's personality, the investment does not constitute the personality. Marx attributes to this phenomenon that the worker's capacity for enjoyment finds realization in the so-called "crude" pleasures, in other words in drive reduction which, isolated from the whole world of feelings, indeed develops only the capacity for crude enjoyment. This reduction also takes place within various strata of the bourgeois class, although in a different manner. For the pleasure of possession, indeed—if we isolated it from the whole of the emotional personality—is likewise included among the "crude" pleasures; the desire for possession functions as a quasi-drive.

But once again the process outlined above is only a tendency. To what extent work may become one of the often decisive tasks that constitutes the unified housekeeping of feelings of the personality, depends on a number of heterogeneous factors. First of all it depends upon the duration of the work, that is, to what extent the feelings invested into the task exhaust the individual's energies, or whether he has anything left to tend. Furthermore, it depends upon the quality of the work activity (that is, upon whether it is at all capable of developing abilities) and to what extent this quality is adequate to the "nature" of the individual. Furthermore, it depends upon whether this task may become a value to the individual, or whether it may harmonize with other tasks occupying a higher place (or a lower place, for that matter) in the individual's hierarchy of values. To summarize: the specialization of work may be considered a negative factor from the point of view of the evaluation of the housekeeping of feelings only if the feelings invested into the work-task are not investment of personality feelings. But if they are, that is the work is more or less capable of developing the individual's capacities and represents a goal-value for the individual, or at least is also a goal-value, then the fact that we are active at a particular place within the division of labor does not undermine the housekeeping of feelings, but necessitates a special arrangement of it.

A work activity in which the person is alone or is confronted primarily with the object of his work requires a certain housekeeping of feelings; another type of housekeeping of feelings is required by work carried out in a team and yet another in the kind of work where the person enters into contact with others only occasionally. The feelings invested in work by the pediatrician or the psychologist are different from the feelings invested by a medical researcher; the feelings invested by a professor differ from those invested by a locomotive engineer—and it is one purpose that I have selected callings requiring an increased sense of responsibility. Humility in front of scientific truth must play a greater role in the case of a scientist than in the case of a businessman—but we would expect more patience with regard to human caprice from the latter than from the former. A brigade leader must try harder not to hurt others' feelings than a fireman, but we would expect more willingness to self-sacrifice in crisis situations from the latter than from the former. It is true that in meeting the special tasks provided in the division of labor there is room for "role-playing," but only if it becomes isolated from the whole of the housekeeping of feelings. The contradiction between the development of special abilities and of "Bildung" evolves in the "natural" division of labor.

As we have seen, work, as task, may be alienated, hence negative from the point of view of housekeeping of feelings, but it is not necessarily so. On the other hand, lack of work, wherever this also implies a lack of social task, is necessarily alienated. The so-called "leisure class" that has "stepped out" from the social division of labor, is a product of the bourgeois era. The ruling strata or estates, in societies organized in natural communities, could not be classified under the concept of a "leisure class." Those who were "born into" these various strata or orders are given their task from birth—and this task was always indispensable from the point of view of the functioning of society: the classical form of feudalism could not have functioned without the filling of the royal or of the priestly task, no more than it could have functioned without the filling of the serfs or peasant's task. It is true that the "do-nothing" type also appears in earlier societies, but always in a stage of dissolution, as in the case of ancient Rome. The first typical leisure class is the nobility which had lost its function with the advent of the bourgeois age; in the book I quoted above, Lepenies describes convincingly why is it that boredom (*l'ennui*) appears precisely in this stratum and at this time, as a central feeling and why does theory of feeling structure around "living together" with boredom or around the conquest of boredom.

The task filled within the division of social labor theoretically may be replaced by other tasks, including tasks which may be adequate objects for an investment of feelings. It is possible to play music with passion, to philosophize, to do carpentry, without social assignment or mission. But this may only be an exception, not the rule. To make something that is not a social assignment into a task, subjectively, to invest our feelings into it in such a way that pleasure at the attainment of a goal should go along with it, may be possible only for the aristocrats of the spirit or of morality; and even this is not enough, special capacities would be required, such as zeal, or a maximum of perseverance.

In the life of the majority without work that is socially assigned, there is no task and thus there is no longer an object for the will; there is no reason to select the means to attain a goal, to mobilize the appropriate feelings, to relegate others to the background; will degenerates into mere desire. Of the two types of joy—the fulfillment of desire and the attainment of goal—only the first remains relevant.

It may be objected that this is not so, that the creation of human relations may itself become the main or central task and that will may be directed at this goal, that here too one may speak of the pleasure of attaining the goal. This is undoubtedly true, but the truth is only partial. The building of harmonic relations, the development of feeling dispositions through mutual relations is undoubtedly an end in itself; but an end in itself that also relates to something else: the common social task. Where these common social tasks do not exist there (according to all evidence) the building of beautiful relations becomes impossible. When the cultivation of relations is dissociated from the compulsory task (I mean compulsory in the sense of living up to one's responsibilities), then the feelings lose their "frame of reference" and there no longer can be normal housekeeping of feeling (i.e., a housekeeping "according to the norms"). Let me refer once again to the *Nouvelle Héloïse* and to *Wilhelm Meister*. In both novels the creation of valid human relations is a central task, as is the cultivation of feelings and in both novels it is community action, the organization of the economy and of work which provide the framework for these relations. But the cult of feelings, if isolated from the work task assigned by society, brings about a peculiar insecurity György Lukács analyzed pertly (even if rather unjustly when applied to Rilke) the connections between "emotional refinement" (*Gefühlsverfeinerung*) and "emotional barbarism" (*Gefühlsbarberei*). A society that would abolish work would undoubtedly expose people to the barbarism of feelings. Of course, this danger does not exist in practice, but cannot even be accepted as an ideology.

From the advent of the bourgeois era to its "classical" flowering, alienated work and idleness are represented in different social classes or strata in a rigidly dichotomous manner. At the present, however, alienated work and idleness are no longer tied to specific social classes, or at least the dichotomy is in the process of disappearing. In contemporary society (at least among the great majority), both of them are characteristic of the same individual, again only as a tendency. To the alienated work that goes along with work-time is connected the "idle" use of leisure time. Therefore the feelings no longer group themselves around the so-called "crude pleasures"—the drive reductions—and their place is increasingly taken by the feeling structure typical of "idleness," the sophisticated barbarism of feeling. The gradual relegation into the background of the drive-reduction of feelings (and I include the regulating role played by the "bad infinity" of the quasi-drive of "possession"), has at the same time brought about the contrary tendency. The need of the elemental pleasure of reaching the goal—tied to other needs—negates both completely alienated work, as well as completely "idle" behavior and, by the same token, the sophisticated emotional barbarism at the primitive, or higher levels.

In the introduction to this book I mentioned that the issue around which contemporary theories of feeling center is the unity or dichotomy of feeling and thinking. I did not answer the question as to what was at the origin of this issue; which aspects of the bourgeois era it expresses or formulates. Solutions proposed by philosophy (and by psychology) may and indeed do differ widely: it may take the side of "reason" against "feeling" (as it did in Kant), or the opposite (as it did in Romanticism); it may seek, again in different ways, a "synthesis" or harmony of the two. The question arises, however, from the above-mentioned antinomical structure of the housekeeping of the bourgeois era.

The conception of "reason" and "feeling" as opposite "principles" is characteristic of the everyday thinking of the bourgeois era; what's more, it is practically a *lieu commun*. What has filtered down into everyday thinking from philosophical generalizations has also fed this *lieu commun*, as for instance, "let us listen to the word of the heart," or "let us listen to the voice of common sense." On the other hand, the ideologies which have opted for the reconciliation of reason and feeling have not become *lieux communs*, proving that while the dichotomy itself emanates from the facts of bourgeois existence, the harmony which would halt the dichotomy is a principle that is polemically directed at these facts.

The theoretical and practical confrontation of "reason" (i.e. sense, thinking) and "feeling" has nothing to do with the alleged contradiction between "spirit" and "sensuality" (body), posited as a principle by medieval Christianity. If only because in medieval Christian interpretation "spirit" is identical with morality, that is, with "soul" (the abode of morality is the soul, the spiritual), the body, as the principle of sensuality is opposed to both soul and morality, hence it is anti-moral. But the contradiction between "reason" (thinking) and "feeling" is not related to morality in an unambiguous way. At times it is reason that is considered the carrier and recipient of morality, at times the feelings (as opposed to reason, to thinking). Furthermore, even a morally noble feeling may prove unreasonable, when it fails in the recognition of a situation—usually a new situation—in knowledge of men, hence in "wisdom." A beautiful example of this is given in the *Misanthrope* of Molière. Furthermore, a morally noble spirit may also prove emotionally incompetent and will thus fail in the "simple virtues" of life, as does the protagonist of Lukács' dialogue "The Poverty of Spirit."

As we know, there is no fixed hierarchy of values in the bourgeois age, the value objects or tasks may be selected and reselected within the range offered by the given age. A person should find, or should be enabled to find the task to the measure of his personality from among the maze of ranges offered. Thus the role of knowledge (of reason) has increased tremendously in comparison with any previous age. But that is not all; others have selected other tasks and values, hence it is not enough that I should choose: I must learn to estimate the behavior, the principles and the feelings of others: in this regard, too, the role of knowledge becomes decisive. As a result of the dissolution of the hierarchy of values the task (or goal) may even become value free. The rational organization of human activity (the selection of the means necessary for a goal from the point of view of the realization of the goal) may disregard values altogether and may be reduced to the criterion of mere success. Mere goal-rationality is born (in the Weberian sense of the term), which may disregard value-rationality. Yet, in my opinion, Max Weber abstracted considerably from the specific structure of the bourgeois era when he averred that goal-rationality has replaced value-rationality. For the goal-rationality of technology and of economy has never completely penetrated all of social life; it has always remained but a tendency, which has been continually slowed down or challenged by the need to connect selected value rationality with goal-rationality.

The aforementioned innovations, the increase in the significance of knowledge and the selection of the task, as well as the development of goal-rational behavior, have together created the emphasis on "reason" and "sense." At the same time, to find a task to the measure of the personality, to choose from the "range," is an incredibly difficult task to fulfill. Especially because the "range" is only theoretically so wide, it is actually considerably limited by "solvent demand." If I have to work fourteen hours a day, if I must maintain by tooth and nail, then "solvent demand" relating to knowledge is rather limited. But it is difficult even under less limited conditions, since the individual, as an "atom" abandoned to his own devices, must orient himself solely on the basis of his own reason. Therefore the majority of persons in the bourgeois age, to quote the words of Fromm, are indeed "escaping" from freedom and since they have no community, their thinking becomes mere "subsumption," their reason is subsumed under the judgments (prejudices) of their immediate and contingent environment. At the same time, the reason choosing the task to the measure of the personality—again for lack of a community and a hierarchy of values—often becomes "morally suspect"; the "perverted" reason is a product of the bourgeois age; Shakespeare's Edmund and Iago are the first true literary representatives of this "perverted" reason.

Moreover, when and insofar as goal-rationality truly and completely separates from value-rationality and reforms the whole of human existence on the "model" of technology and economy (bourgeois economy), then reason becomes "calculating." To act sensibly becomes synonymous with calculating correctly. In the case of the important thinkers of the bourgeois era and often in everyday life as well, to appeal to the feelings, to the inner life of feelings, to the "heart" expresses a protest, even a rebellion against the "perverted" reason, against thinking as a mere act of subsumption, against the transformation of behavior into mere calculation. Everyday life has found a term for all three processes, even if these do not penetrate into the deepest layers of the phenomenon: "cynicism," "prejudice (convention)," and "calculation" itself.

We know it is bourgeois society that has created the opportunity for the housekeeping of feelings. People have the opportunity to create their own inner life and to express it, to shape their own particular structure of feelings in accordance to their own nature and to select the task to their measure. In the case of the majority of men, however, this opportunity, (as the opportunity for knowledge) is realized in an alienated form. The task may be transferred to the "building up" of the Self, itself, when the individual attempts to "isolate" himself from the world of calculation and convention; it may be transferred to the unlimited self-indulgence of the Self without regard to anybody or anything, to the theory and practice of the realization of all feelings, desires and passions. The world of feeling may become the subjective "coloring" and supplement to the eternal "prosaic" task; in such cases we may speak of kitsch-people. Everyday sense has also found the terms to designate these attitudes, although again, it does not penetrate into the deepest players of the phenomenon. It speaks of "egocentrism," of those "riddled with passions," and finally of "sentimentality." In the case of the important thinkers of the bourgeois era and often in everyday life as well, an appeal to reason, to sense, to rationality expresses protest and even rebellion against the inner life of feeling "wrapped in itself" that turns its back to the tasks of the world, to the unfettered exercise of egoist passions, against false sentimentality or sentimental convention. Both positions are right in their own way. And both positions are wrong in their own way. Yet, they presuppose one another, for they are both products of the bourgeois era.

It is in the name of reason that polemics have been undertaken against alienated feelings and in the name of feelings against the alienated reason; yet the alienation of reason and feeling are part of the same process. "Perverted reason," as well as the feeling wrapped into itself, closing itself to the world, equally abstract from morality; calculation and the exercise of the passions of the Self knowing no limits are both the realization of an egoistic principle; the "subsuming mind" and conventional sentimentality complement one another. Balzac writes about Parisian women of passion knowing no limits: "Along the line of their feelings they reach solutions which would astound even the thieves, the businessmen and the usurers" (*The Daughter of Eve*). Still, both reason and feeling (or passionateness) have their particular pathos if confronted directly with the alienated forms of the opposite principle. Instead of giving an analysis of the basic types let me give a few examples taken from works of art, which have created their own world from the "point of view" of the reason or of the feelings.

The genre typical of the world conceived from the point of view of reason is comedy. Aristotle was justified in saying that small characters are laughable, great characters are tragic. But in the bourgeois era the comic does not remain merely the description of small characters. Biron is the most substantial male figure of *Loves Labor Lost*, the comic hero of the *Misanthrope* is the play's most noble personality, as is Gregers Werle in *Wild Duck*. The comic originated with the noble and generous Don Quixote. István Mészáros appropriately defined the comic as the sudden unmasking of the irrationality masquerading as rationality. It is not evil that is unmasked, nor the petty, nor the low or base, but "the unreasonable." Which does not mean, of course, that the senseless, the blind, the one who cannot find his way around could not at the same time be bad, base, petty, narrow-minded, or pompous. But these qualities are not what make him comical, but rather that his baseness, his pomposity is at the same time unreasonable.

Plessner, following Bergson, described laughing, as opposed to crying, as "intellectual." There can be no doubt that laughter directed at something comic is an intellectual response. After all, if reason is laughing at unreason, then we are dealing with a *par excellence* "intellectual" genre. Many kinds of attitudes may be unreasonable; many things may be laughed at as comic. But for the sake of our problem, it is important to note that it makes the alienated world of feelings laughable as well, in all its manifestations. In *As You Like It*, Shakespeare describes as comic the misanthropic melancholy of Jacques (he turns away from the tasks of the world), in *Tartuffe*, Molière portrays as laughable Orgon's blind faith in his "friend" (lack of knowledge of men), in *The Miser*, he portrays as laughable Harpagon's passion for collecting wealth (for there is no rationality in giving up all pleasures for "senseless" and "presumed" possession); in *George Dandin*, he ridicules extreme ambition (there is no rationality in it, since one always falls short); in *L'école des maris*, he ridicules jealousy (there is no rationality in it, since the more jealous one is, the more one gets cheated). Although Lessing does it with considerable tenderness, he nevertheless ridicules

Tellheim's pride, because it is silly to be proud with the person who loves us and whom we love.

As the faith in reason becomes problematic—and here Romanticism has already tolled its knell!—pure comedy is increasingly directed at ridiculing conventional feelings (the kitsch souls). At the time of Molière conventional feelings were not at all ridiculous as yet. Shaw is the great "ridiculer" of conventions of feelings. The opening sentimental love scene in *Getting Married* is followed by this exchange in the second act: "Do you love money?" "Very much," comes the snappy reply and the "great feeling" is revealed as the "inner life" of petty interest. The "tender women" prove to be giant snakes chasing men and the gentle, angelic poets prove to be very average persons who know just what they want.

Whenever "common sense" appears as an actor in a comedy and takes the side of or incarnates "sensible" feelings of a high order or those led by reason as opposed to "senseless" feelings, this principle is almost always represented by a woman: thus from the *Merry Wives of Windsor* through Molière and Lessing's *Minna von Barnhelm* all the way to Shaw's *Candida*. And nothing could be more natural. The contradiction between rational thinking and the inner life of feelings in the bourgeois era also appears in the form of division of labor between the sexes. It is true that the tasks of men and women have always differed, hence the feeling norms and expectations for men and women differ. But the fact of life, also recorded as a *lieu commun*, according to which it is man who incarnates "thinking" while woman embodies "feeling" is unquestionably the product of the bourgeois era. And the fact of life to which this *lieu commun* owes its origin is the formation of the bourgeois family. This family, at least in its tendency and principle, is characterized by inwardness: "my house is my castle." The creation of the inwardness is primarily the task of the woman, it is she who has to shape and tend within herself and in her environment the appropriate feelings: love, tenderness, tact. On the other hand, it is the husband who lives in the "world"; it is he who must recognize the tasks, it is he who must calculate, it is he who must plan goal-rationally, it is he who must be "clever," have insight, be familiar with the field of action rendered by a particular situation. All this does not signify, of course, that there are no representative men of "feeling" to be found in bourgeois society. They, however, are always at odds with reason deemed alienated. But if sense is represented by a woman, whether as "common sense" or from the point of view of "moral reason" of a higher order—then she does not surrender but preserves the inward and "emotional" character worked out in the bourgeois world, or at least takes the side of feeling against mere calculation just as much as she sides against the male passions judged morally negative. Hence the peculiar role of women in comedies ridiculing alienated feelings.

If, however, we want to analyze pure emotional inwardness turning away from the task, i.e., the "working out" of feelings as an end in itself, then a male figure must be selected, for the same reasons as discussed above, because it is only in the case of men that such behavior is polemically representative. I have already discussed Werther; the conscious cultivation of feelings opposed to the "calculating" world is indeed characteristic of him, as is the cult of subjectivity in contrast with the "wisdom of common sense" evaluating various paths of life. But for the sentimental heroes of the 18th century there still exists in principle a task, moreover, this task stands in front of them and, even if they cannot reach it, they are quite capable of formulating it. Albert, representing "common sense" speaks thus: "denn freilich ist es leichter zu sterben als ein qualvolles Leben standhaft zu ertragen." Werther's reply provides a glimpse of the secret of the sentimental hero: "Du nennst das Schwäche! [...] Ein Volk, das unter dem unerträglichen Joch eines Tyrannen seufzt, darfst du das schwach heissen, wenn es endlich aufgährt und seine Ketten zerreisst."

Thus Werther is extreme, but not eccentric. The task for which bourgeois inwardness had prepared itself could be carried out already in the French Revolution. The "great feelings" have increasingly less for which to prepare themselves; hence beginning in the 19th century (already during the Romantic period) these are not merely extreme; they do become eccentric. The strict turning inwards and the exclusivity of the construction of feelings is most brilliantly embodied in the poetry of Baudelaire. There is no longer an outside task, so the requirement of a housekeeping of feelings is all the stronger. In the housekeeping of feelings isolated from the world, the Ego itself becomes the world. There is no object outside the subject. The exclusive object of analysis is the subject; all analysis is self-analysis. Objects only gain value by eliciting feelings in the subject—the value is the feeling and not the object. It is my feeling that gives light and color to the world, my feeling is what makes it all "object-like." But if there is no object value and no action-value, only feeling-value, then the clarity of the meaning of feelings becomes lost altogether. Every feeling becomes polyvalent and has to be analyzed constantly. The fact that all analysis is self-analysis also means that the self-analysis is itself "open"; I have to analyze "my psyche" again and again. The "valeur" of the mood, of the instant impression is incredibly swollen—every trembling of the soul assumes exceptional significance—the whole of the world of feelings is made up of the "valeurs" of tremblings of the soul.

The feeling concepts become heaped together, one is in touch with the other; these constitute the lyrical forms. All feeling-concepts are constitutive: those that express feelings of sense perception, those that express moods, those that express affects, those that express emotions. Colors, sounds, smells, pleasures, desires, emotions, passions homogenize the lyrical form; but there is no will. The subject inhales himself and exhales himself: hence the stale atmosphere of poetry. Everything is full of *mon coeur* and *mon âme*—and both may be *plein* or *vide*; all is *désire, tristesse, spleen, souffrance, volupté, espérance, joie, passion, langueur, remord, douleur, colère, mélancholie, solitude, enchantement, malheureux, désespoir*—and it's all so *profond*. The dark (because without colors), infinite (because without object) world is "nothing" itself; delight and pain, pleasure and desire, wealth and color—all this is *heart*. This is a tragic contradiction; one that cannot be resolved in life: "O Mort, vieux capitaine, il est temps! levons l'ancre! / Ce pays nous ennuie, o Mort! Appareil-lons! / Si le ciel et la mer sont noirs comme de l'encre, / Nos coeurs que tu con-nais sont remplis de rayons!"

Sartre writes about Baudelaire: "Tout est truqué parce que tout est inspecté, la moindre humeur, le plus faible désir regardés, déchiffrés. Et, pour peu qu'on se rappelle le sens que Hegel donnait au mot d'immédiat, on comprendra que la singularité profonde de Baudelaire est qu'il est l'homme sans immédiateté."[2] Why does immediacy, the spontaneity of the world of feeling get lost? Sartre indicated the root of the evil: it is not the fault of poetry, but of man; it is the problem of the bad infinity of self-analysis, of self-reflection.

But I have described self-analysis and self-reflection, or "gardening," as an indispensable aspect of the housekeeping of feelings, and moreover, of the con-scious, individual housekeeping of feelings. Indeed, it is indispensable; no "normal" housekeeping of feelings can exist without it. But self-analysis and self-reflection are still but one aspect of normal housekeeping of feelings (of the housekeeping given to us as a norm). If the individual selects values and tasks that he must meet, he must always return to the self and examine whether he is indeed feeling in accordance to his values, whether indeed he has met his task emotionally. But from the point of view of the tasks, of the values, he gardens, or he selects values and tasks in accordance with the nature of his feelings; his eyes look primarily outwards; one part of his feelings become act and behavior and it is these acts and behavior that judge over his feelings; reflections reflect the act itself; hence they also reflect the world of feeling from the angle of the Other. Thus the supervision of the authenticity of feelings, of their hierarchy, is not a continuous process; it takes place at junctions, in conflict situations. If our behavior and our actions live up to the image we have constituted of our own world of feelings, why would we turn our eyes inwards, why would we make our own "soul" into an object? Being directed at the world, the task, the action and the expression of behavior themselves create a hierarchy among our feel-ings—the *valeur* difference between the decisive feeling disposition, the emo-tion and the ephemeral mood, may be explicated in action. The reciprocal influ-ence of the task and of the world of feeling "regulates" the housekeeping of feeling; we "waste" our feelings on those that are significant to us (from the point of view of our chosen values, our tasks, the important Other we have cho-sen as models, or from the point of view of our nature) and we "save" them from those that are not significant to us. If the inwardness of the world of feelings is the only object of our reflection, then our psyche and behavior assume narcissis-tic forms. And the world of feeling always becomes narcissistic, if we confront it polemically with cognition and action directed at the alienated world.

In principle, I started from the argument that the dichotomy of thinking and feeling is philosophically incorrect; since in every cognitive process, as in every directly acting behavior, feeling is necessarily present (even if only as back-ground feeling). At the same time, thinking may be reintegrated into every one of our feelings, even into our most subjective feeling dispositions, no matter how much its emotional character may be in the forefront. We are always involved in something. This philosophical observation does not in the least respond to the questions prompted by certain facts of life. Is it possible to realize in actuality, in conjunction and simultaneously, the behavior aimed at knowing and acting in the world and the emotions and the behavior aimed at the cultivation of emotional dispositions? We have seen that alienated emotional behavior and alienated "rational" behavior have always existed side by side peacefully. The priority of one behavior or the other (rational or emotional) has been asserted by those who stood in a polemical relationship with the alienated world of feelings (that is with the totality of the facts of life of the bourgeois era). Is it possible, however, to have a harmony of these two polemical behaviors in actual life? Can the philosophical principle, which I myself have advocated, become a constitutive practical idea rather than a regulative one?

Notes

1. Where the choice of world-view and. along with it, the houskeeping of feeling has appeared within societies led by consensus, as in classical Athens, it has also been a consequence of the commodity production.
2. Sartre, Jean-Paul. *Baudelaire: Let fleurs du mal, preface* (Paris: Gallimard, 1961).

Chapter VIII.
The Abstraction of Feelings and Beyond

There is a central, anthropological consequence of alienation in the bourgeois era that I have not mentioned as yet; the split of the human being into bourgeois and *citoyen*. This split does not take place between the two levels of public and private life; the citizen active in public life, the nobleman who becomes a bourgeois, the socialist politician who steps on the stage of bourgeois public life—all act as bourgeois, more than anything else. It will suffice to refer to the ministers in the novels of Balzac or of Anatole France, or the analysis of Millerand and his companions by Rosa Luxemburg. It is not political activity in itself that constitutes the citizen, but rather the *relationship* of the individual to this political activity. For the *citoyen*, political activity (and not only that activity) is deduced from principles; it is the application of principles to life; whereas in the case of the bourgeois, it is the "prolongation" or extension of individual interests.

The bourgeois-*citoyen* schism is latent throughout the whole bourgeois era, but it only becomes explicit at times of deep crisis. And at these times it becomes obvious that *citoyen* behavior and bourgeois behavior are not only both the products of the bourgeois era, but are also requirements of that era. The bourgeois era is not only the culture of the independent power of economics, of the universalization of commodity production, of "prosaic" industry and commerce, but it is also the only culture which requires, in order to come into being and reorganize at a higher level, a purely political revolution. Although the *citoyen* is not needed to carry out the "industrial revolution," he is very much needed to carry out the purely political revolution. For the execution of a purely political revolution, the *theatrum mundi* needs people who constitute their activity from principles, who are disposed to the greatest sacrifices, who are capable of suspending their particularist interests. In order for the bourgeois world to install itself, it is necessary to undertake the self-sacrificing struggle for "liberty" or "against tyranny."

Yet the bourgeois era is also the era of the formation of nations—the nation being the "ideal community" of bourgeois society. The creation and defence of this ideal community (in wars of liberation and national wars) requires the *citoyen* pathos and the *citoyen* attitude just as much as the political revolutions. Unselfish people are required to realize national selfishness.

The housekeeping of feeling of the bourgeois and of the *citoyen* differ radically. They have one trait in common—and this trait explains how it is possible to shift, as an absolute "matter of course" from one to the other—and this is the abstraction of the world of feelings. The bourgeois attitude is constituted or rises out of the "prose" of everyday existence. It is the war of everybody against everybody for the mere preservation of life, for possession, for having more. The "contingent" individual without a community knows himself to be a free atom facing "necessity" as such. To recognize this necessity and to act accordingly means to succeed, whereas to come into conflict with "necessity" means to perish.

How does this basic attitude constitute the housekeeping of feelings? First of all, the value orientational pair of categories that are primarily in charge of guiding feelings becomes the category of useful-harmful. The Good-Evil pair becomes synonymous with the useful-harmful, at least as tendency. The person who does not adopt the value of utility (the banker who failed, the businessman who suffered bankruptcy, the one who is incapable of being astute, the one who has made a bad love match) is surrounded by the aura of moral contempt. The useful is preferred both in case of cognitive background feelings as in case of the emotions and emotional dispositions. (At the same time, the value orientational category of Good-Evil receives a secondary role, within the notion of "utility": feelings that are equally useful are not considered equally valuable morally.)

The guidance of the value orientational pair of Good and Evil in the world of feelings may lead, as we know, to the complete blocking of the particularist world of feeling (primarily the particularist traits and desires), or their repression; yet, the more heterogeneous and the less concretely given the values, the pair of Good and Evil may also lead in the individual development of one's own nature, in the development of a variegated world of feelings, of a wealth of feelings. The guidance of useful-harmful may also block or repress particularist traits and desires which do not prove "useful," without providing a measure, a system of values for the development of a variegated world of feelings, of a wealth of feelings. Indeed, it would be incapable of providing such a measure, because utility, as long as it is not subordinated to the Good as a qualitative category, is always quantitative.

The needs of the bourgeois oriented at utility are quantifiable: the needs are directed at such objects, or the enjoyment of such objects, which may be "increased" indefinitely, which are theoretically boundless. These compose the world of feeling of the bourgeois. And Kant appropriately characterized this world of feeling with the term "Sucht." Three "*Süchte*" dominate the bourgeois housekeeping of feelings: *Habsucht, Ehrsucht, Herrschsucht* (or desire for possession, desire for glory and desire for power). All three desires are boundless. One may never own enough not to want more; one may not have enough power not to desire more power; one may not have enough glory not to desire more glory. Kant differentiated between desire for glory and love of glory (*Ehrliebe*), the latter being neither quantifiable nor boundless. In the same way, one might differentiate between desire for power and love of power, or desire for possession from love of possession, since these too may be qualitative yet are far from being necessarily boundless. (Of course, this still says nothing about their evaluation). But bourgeois culture produces the *Sucht* manifestation—"expanded reproduction" is also valid for the objects of the world of feelings. If you have not produced "expansively," you "lose." Shakespeare's Richard the Third is led not by love of power, but by desire for power (*Sucht*)—he feels that power is never sufficient, he is never king enough.

In the bourgeois world of feelings it is undoubtedly the desire for possession that plays a decisive role among the "*Süchte*." Money is "pure" quantity, if you have money, you have everything, even glory and power. Marx writes: "Alle Leidenschaften und alle Tätigkeiten müssen also untergehen in der Habsucht."[1]

This desire (*Sucht*) is passion. I have called passion the emotional disposition which subordinates every feeling to itself and which annihilates every feeling that opposes it or differs from it. We know: there may be qualitative passions which may cease to be passions—but not feelings!—as soon as there is no obstacle to their realization, as soon as their goal can be attained. The quantitative passions, as we know, are not like this. They can never realize themselves, for they are characterized by bad infinity. All heterogeneous feelings are subordinated to them; they impede all those that oppose them without giving them, the opportunity to come back ever again. The desires (*Süchte*) destroy within man the variegated value qualities and they homogenize the "soul" in a single passion. I must add, however, that adopting a single passion is far from being necessarily passionate. The desires (*Süchte*) as passions may be cold and calculating; because of this, it is not possible to speak of "engagement" in the case of desires (*Süchte*). Engagement—or passion in the positive sense of the term—is always directed at specific, qualitative objects of value. But the passion of the *Süchte* is only exceptionally like this; it is mostly quite prosaic.

Hegel wittily referred to bourgeois culture as the spiritual animal kingdom. The expression is appropriate because the *Süchte* function as quasi-drives. The psyche homogenized in the desire to have follows its desire as unconditionally as the famished person follows his hunger. What more: this kind of hunger can never be satisfied completely, the desire to have is never sated, can never be reduced. In accordance with the quasi-natural laws of nature of bourgeois world the bourgeois Ego evolves its own quasi-natural laws. Yet this "animal kingdom" spiritual because the realization of the quasi-drive is a goal-rational (calculating) act.

The expansion of the Self is always part of the homoeostatic functioning of feelings. But in the case of the desire to have the expansion of the Self cannot be equated with the expansion of the Self's capacity to enjoy or capacity to feel. We are not involved in ever new qualities, in heterogeneous objects, values and Others, but always in the selfsame one always in the increase of the same one. To borrow from Goethe: the worth of man is not what he is, but what he has. The Self remains "poor," while the person becomes rich; his luster is a borrowed luster, not his own. As a result of the reduction to the only passion, a quantitative passion or quasi-drive, a Self is constituted which is homogeneous in feeling (homogenized by the *Sucht*), hence it is also personality; the unity of the

personality is guaranteed by possession. This unified personality is at the same
time abstract, because it became abstracted from the specific feeling qualities.

Marx confronted the abstract *citoyen* with the "concrete bourgeois." Insofar
as we take the structure of feeling of the bourgeois into consideration then the
distinction, in this context, does not hold valid under close examination. The
world of feeling of the bourgeois is led, although in a different manner, by abstraction, as is the world of feeling of the *citoyen*. The Selves of the quantified
Süchte are homogeneous, but also abstract. The bourgeois world of feeling
sketched above has prevailed only in tendency, of course, that is by no means in
everybody; nor has it prevailed to the same extent in every bourgeois stratum or
individual. To quote Polanyi, even the self-regulating market has been but the
utopia of bourgeois society and the socially generalized bourgeois world of feeling has likewise been "merely utopia." Value rationality has never entirely dis-
appeared; the tendency of "abstraction" of feelings has again and again elicited
contrary tendencies.

The representatives of the ideology of superman posit the negative utopia of
the modern world of feeling as the only reality. While they consider the Self
reduced to *Süchte* as the potential individuality of bourgeois society, they despise and even abhor this society and all those who subject themselves to its
laws. But it is not the *Süchte* themselves they abhor, but rather the inconsisten-
cies in the realization of the passion for possession, its prosaic characteristics.
They are convinced that they, unlike the prosaic bourgeoisie, indeed see through
the moving springs of bourgeois society and by the same token the moving
springs of the members of that society, without any rationalization whatever. At
the same time they anthropologically generalize the bourgeois: here is man!
They are of higher order, they deem, because they are able to see through and
they bear contempt. The attitude of seeing through and contempt, they deem,
make them appropriate to stylize prosaic egoism as "poetical," and wrestle the
"prosaic" souls to the floor. The "truly strong," the "truly brave" smash all tablets of laws, since these are no longer valid anyway. Balzac has represented this
"superman" in two gigantic figures, Vautrin and Gobseck.

Vautrin is the bourgeois become demonic. He is demonic, because it is not
only on the practical level that he places himself beyond morals, but makes a
principle out of it and owes his power of attraction to this consistently applied
principle. The demon of egoism, however, only attracts those who themselves
live within the magic circle of egoism, although "inconsistently," because they
have some "weaknesses:" for instance, their pure feelings. It has no power over
the *citoyens*. "Virtue, my dear sir student, cannot be split; either it is there, or it
isn't," Vautrin tells Rastignac. If someone should begin to divide up virtue he
comes into Vautrin's domain. He is the only one for whom it is worthwhile to
raise the level of the incognito (for the demonic bourgeois, like all other demons, goes "incognito").

> You will never get anywhere with respectability. ... I do not mean the sad helots
> who are toiling incessantly and never gain the reward of their toil. [...] There

you do have virtue, indeed you do, in the full flower of its stupidity; but misery is there as well.... Man is an imperfect being.... I do not accuse the rich for the sake of the poor: man is identical above, below, or in the middle. Among these animals of a higher order for every million you have ten tough guys who place themselves above everything, even above the laws: I belong among them. If you are a man of a higher order, go forwards with a proud bearing.

Gobseck is also a bourgeois become demonic; he too lives in "incognito." He never reveals his incognito in front of those who live within the magic circle of the desire for possession; he goes among them concealing his rank, as an ordinary usurer. He saves self-revelation for the honest man, for the attorney Derville. This somber and uncrowned king of the world of finances does not place himself outside morality: he intentionally strikes those who live in the world of *Süchte*; he considers himself a "punishing power:" "You must pay for luxury, pay for your name, pay for your happiness, pay for the privileges you enjoy!" He has but one weapon: money, gold. "There is but one worldly value which deserves attention. And that is gold." One may punish only with what is everybody's supreme good, goal, the content of his life—namely with money. He does not place himself outside society, but rather takes advantage, realizes its basic tendency to an extreme: the pure *Süchte* that have annihilated all other feelings. "I am rich enough to buy the conscience of those who control the ministers: is that not Power? The most beautiful women can be mine, their most tender caresses: is this not what Pleasure is all about? And is it not Power and Pleasure that together symbolize your social system?" The *Süchte* not only guide Gobseck in practice and do not guide him across conflicts. They will not encounter heterogeneous feelings opposing them, for these feelings have ceased to exist.

In his great mythology, Balzac mercilessly designates the place of "supermen." The bourgeois demons of the bourgeois world belong to the same prose as its petty bureaucrats. The fate of Gobseck is to become empty, to become poor. He is the most solitary demon. His legacy is the materials that are perishing, as a symbol of wealth becoming bleak and useless. The great Vautrin enters into the service of the police as the culmination of his career. The demoniac bourgeois proves to be an ordinary bourgeois and the "superman of a higher order" covers the path of the man of the lowest order. The "superman" in the 19th century, that is the pompous bourgeois who places himself above the law and above the Other, lives in the spell of Napoléon's personality. Napoléon, the universal bourgeois ideal, becomes in their case the *par excellence* bourgeois ideal, who both embodies bourgeois society and is contemptuous of it. The same applies to Raskolnikov, who unites in himself the principles of Vautrin and Gobseck. "Following Napoleon," he raises himself above law and morality, as does Vautrin, and punishes privately, as does Gobseck. Goodness redeems him by liberating the feelings subordinated to the *Süchte*: compassion, empathy, love.

The bourgeois, as we have seen, may be not merely bourgeois, but also citizen. The world of feeling of the *citoyen*, partly in reality, partly only in appearance, is the direct opposite of the bourgeois world of feeling. Virtue cannot be split, said Vautrin. Well, the *citoyen* does not split Virtue. He is the champion of Virtue. Even the champion of Virtue subordinates the whole of his world of feeling to something. This something, however, is not desire for possession, not egoism, but the Cause. He picks a *Cause* for himself and this Cause constitutes his whole housekeeping of feeling. Every feeling receives light from the Cause, every emotion refers to the Cause. From now on, I will refer to the feeling elicited by the Cause, or referring to the Cause—in the wake of Kant—as enthusiasm.

The enthusiasm of the *citoyen* is passion to the same extent as the pure desire for possession. It too homogenizes the Self, it too subordinates all emotions to a single one: worship of the Cause. Any feeling that weakens this enthusiasm, by "dividing" the Self, involvement with every object or person that is not related to the Cause becomes secondary, and is taken as a sign of weakness. All our feelings belong to the Cause, there is no "waste" involved, yet we must be economical with feelings towards any other object so that the enthusiasm for the cause should not have to share with something else. The champion of the Cause deals all wavering of feeling as particularist which stems from "private" roots.

I mentioned that Napoleon is the cause of the bourgeois and I have presented the bourgeois' Napoleon image. But the *citoyen*, too, has a Napoleon image. This Napoleon image is the ideal of his enthusiasm. Heine writes in the Die zwei *Grenadiere*: "Was schert mich Weib, was schert mich Kind [...] mein Kaiser, main Kaiser gefangen." Woman and child, that is every personal emotional tie, every emotional disposition becomes as if naught in front of the Cause, which alone deserves feeling and enthusiasm.

Thus the enthusiasm of the *citoyen* abstracts man's world of feeling as much as the "desires" of the bourgeois. If not in the same manner, but to the same extent, because the wealth of specific feelings is constituted out of the wealth of specific relations, of heterogeneous qualitative involvements. If the object of a single passion pumps up into itself all the feeling potentials of a person and in such a way that this psychic structure becomes a predisposition and a priori eliminates all objects that diverge from this as the potential objects of deep feelings, then the housekeeping of feelings necessarily becomes abstract, no matter what the object of the passions. Whether it is a Cause or a system of Causes, this will not alter the fact of the abstraction of the world of feeling. Therefore, I will talk of abstract enthusiasm when dealing with the enthusiasm of the *citoyen*. This abstraction, however, as I have mentioned, does not happen in the same way as in the case of the *Süchte*. The *Süchte* function as quasi-drives and therefore they abstract from the world of feeling spontaneously, practically "by themselves," whether the individual knows about it or not. In the case of the enthusiastic *citoyen*, however, the abstraction of feelings is intended. The abstract enthusiast willfully impoverishes his own world of feelings. He indeed "gardens" on the soil of his own "nature," but in such a way as to weed out every flower and condemn every productive seed to destruction, in order for a single tree to grow tall.

This "abstracting" structure of the *citoyen*'s enthusiasm is, of course, not independent of those ideas to which it is directed, that is of the status of these causes in the bourgeois era. Ideas are always abstract, theoretically speaking. Yet from a pragmatic point of view we may differentiate between abstract and concrete ideas. For the idea is never merely one idea, but always belongs to a system of ideas. This system of ideas may abstract from the specific needs of extant specific persons, from their needs and desires lived and formulated in everyday life or, on the contrary, may grow from the possibilities of concrete and variegated needs. Last but not least it may become identical with the system of needs of everyday life. The system of ideas connected with this last variant does not at all require enthusiasm (such is the liberal system of ideas), hence I am justified in placing it into parentheses in this analysis. But enthusiasm is connected with the first two variants mentioned. I refer to as abstract idea the system of ideas which confronts life with the idea by abstracting from the existing needs of the existing persons; whereas I refer to as concrete idea that system of ideas which derives from the possibilities of actual human needs. The ideas of abstract or *citoyen* enthusiasm are abstract ideas in the above sense of the term.

Thus the abstract enthusiast always places himself as the "incarnation" of the idea in face of the stubborn world, the uncomprehending people. His basic attitude may be of two types, depending on the status of his idea—yet these two attitudes are identical in final analysis. He either confronts the world with the relation of absolute denial (he confronts the idea with actuality) and then everyone who does not stand in the same absolute sense outside the world without an idea is condemned and deemed superficial, or he relates to the world in the sense of the absolute affirmation (when it is governed by the "incarnations" of the idea, that is Virtue) and then everyone who does not identify to the same absolute extent with the world constituted by the idea is judged or deemed superficial.

However democratic the ideology of the abstract enthusiast may be (and it usually is), his attitudes, his housekeeping of feeling is always aristocratic. Not everyone can become enthusiastic, just like not everyone can become a "superman." Yet the enthusiasm of the *citoyen* is connected with emergency situations; it cannot penetrate everyday life, for the idea has not "developed" from there. Since it is par excellence a political passion, in any case it would become pointless in everyday life.

We cannot deny grandeur from the enthusiasm of the *citoyen*. First of all, its very existence and continuous rebirth shows—although not only that—that feelings have always revolted against the dictatorship of *Habsucht*, that a world of feeling not centered on egoism and greed always does exist, that the involvement that is not particularist cannot be totally exterminated, that the useful-harmful orientation can never entirely replace the orientation of Good-Evil Jacobinism, among other things, demonstrated these facts to the contemporary Kant.

But criticism need not become mute in face of the self-sacrifice contemptuous of death exhibited by the *citoyen* enthusiast. Especially not today, when concrete enthusiasm has already appeared on the stage of history. The emotional structure built on abstract enthusiasm has two "danger zones," which cannot be neglected. Speaking about the *citoyen* enthusiast, I mentioned rising above particularity; but this is true in part only or, better said: it does not apply to every type of enthusiast. As we have seen: the abstract enthusiast is not "engagé," in his case the feeling bearing on the cause-object is clearly a passion. He cannot distance himself from the object of his feeling and surrender to the object also means an uncritical identification. This becomes all the easier, since we are dealing with an abstract idea. Even if all the facts contradict the abstract idea, the answer can only be "too bad for the facts." Hence the abstract enthusiast is most of the time a fanatic.

I argued that the abstract enthusiast consciously abstracts his own world of feeling. He lacks the joy of life. He is a foe of sensuality, since the abstract idea requires asceticism. The *citoyen* enthusiast not only represses his affects, but also his emotions. But the repressed "nature" of the Self usually avenges itself. The repressed particularist inclinations—not developed into virtuous dispositions—find a path for themselves through the ideology of the realization of the idea, without the enthusiast of the idea even knowing about them. The fanaticism of the abstract cause even befogs self-knowledge. The most beautifully formulated representative of this *citoyen* enthusiast is the Gamelin of Anatole France. This fanatical and truly self-sacrificing enthusiast of the cause does not even notice that when he strikes the "Enemy of the Idea" with the "axe of the Cause," he has rationalized and carried out one of his most particularist feelings, his jealousy.

The housekeeping of feeling of the enthusiast, therefore, is one-sided and troublesome in its own medium, in borderline situations. He is the "albatross" of borderline situations and then he is soaring; but in everyday life he is only able to limp along at best. Yet the most attractive types of enthusiasts are precisely the ones who limp in everyday life. They carry the stamp of unreason and in this they appear comical. But they incarnate the grandeur of the idea and of Virtue even in the prosaic world—and in so doing they are tragic. With his "ideal demands" Werle Gregers is such a tragi-comic enthusiast, such a limping albatross.

The abstracting, impoverished structure of the housekeeping of feelings of the enthusiast does not become explicit in the after all noble examples of the limping albatross; rather, it becomes explicit when seeing its partial realization, the *citoyen* gives up the abstract idea, or simply resigns, because he considers the idea unrealizable. The moment the enthusiast loses "his cause" one way or another, he also loses the only orientation of his housekeeping of feeling. The affects that had been repressed while an interest in the cause was maintained "break out" all of a sudden and the world of feeling that is not individually formed, not constructed, swirls in chaotic anarchy. The psyche of the former enthusiast either dissolves in this anarchy, or seeks a new "principle of order," a new idea, whatever it may be; the enthusiast who falls back into everyday life is the typical convert. Or and this is the most frequent case, he is seized by the "law" of bourgeois life, the palace of the ideas is taken over by the quasi-drives, the *citoyen* is transformed into a bourgeois with incredible speed. For enthusiasm does question the drive characteristic of the *Süchte* but, since it is incapable of forming the world of feeling concretely and individually, exposes people to these same drives. Thus ultimately egoism and altruism, desire for possession and enthusiasm for the idea belong together. Bourgeois enthusiasm may in principle transcend the bourgeois era, but it can never transcend it in its personality structure, in its world of feeling.

Let me emphasize once again: the housekeeping of feeling of the enthusiast as described and questioned above is but a tendency. Just as in the bourgeois everyday life led by the *Süchte* there are contrary tendencies, counter-tendencies appear again and again in enthusiasm as well. Just as in the case of the man of interest the man may rebel against interest, so in the man of the idea often rebels against the idea. The opportunity of free choice of values and tasks does not become totally alienated either in free competition, or in tyranny of freedom. The abstraction of concrete human beings can never be complete.

While analyzing the *Süchte* I mentioned the demonic bourgeois. My question now is: is it possible to have a demonic citizen? There is demonic egoism; is demonic enthusiasm also possible? The demon of the *Süchte* is as old as bourgeois society. We meet with them from Richard the Third through Vautrin. But the demonic bourgeois begins to die out from literature beginning the middle of last century. Dostoevsky created its last great representatives.

Bourgeois life oriented toward the *Habsucht* becomes bureaucratized: the person who wants to own always more, "may not step out of line." But demonic enthusiasm appears in literature precisely at the time the demonic *Habsucht* disappears: in the era of the crisis of the bourgeois world of feeling, the twenties of the twentieth century. At the time of the birth and flowering of the bourgeois world of feeling enthusiasm could not have been demonic, because it never placed itself outside morality. What more, as we have seen, the *citoyen* considered the realization of the idea the realization of Virtue by the same token. Liberty, Fraternity, Equality, the Revolution, the Fatherland, Progress, all of these are reflected at the same time as virtue, as the source of "pure morality." In order for enthusiasm to become demonic bourgeois principle had to become without an object; demonic enthusiasm opposes bourgeois *Süchte*, the "prosaic reality," by opposing bourgeois principles as well. But does it actually oppose the basic structure of the bourgeois world, its housekeeping of feelings in general?

It is customary to describe Settembrini and Naphta in Thomas Mann's *The Magic Mountain* as two opposite types. I will not deny the opposition, but let me emphasize their common trait: both are enthusiasts. Settembrini is the traditional enthusiast, in as much as his values are traditional: reason, progress, liberty, fatherland, etc. Hence he is not demonic. Naphta's enthusiasm, however, is not nurtured by bourgeois values; his world of values is a peculiar mixture of principles which have preceded and supposedly transcended bourgeois principles. By placing himself outside the *par excellence* bourgeois principles, he likewise places himself outside Virtue—hence his enthusiasm is demonic. But no matter how opposite their principles, the housekeeping of feeling stemming from the enthusiasm of Naphta and Settembrini are structurally completely identical. Both "disapprove" everything in the world of feeling of Hans Castorp that contradicts his own principles. Sensuality and love are "suspect" in the eyes of Settembrini, the search for personality by detours is a sign of "weakness," whereas Naphta resents every feeling led by enlightened reason and the desire for knowledge. Both abstract, although not in the same measure, from the specific desire, the specific needs of the concrete man. The demonic enthusiasm that appears in the crisis period of the bourgeois world of feeling does not go beyond the structure of the *citoyen*'s world of feeling. This demon is also the demon of the bourgeois world.

Those who mean to consistently transcend bourgeois society, also intend to transcend both structures of feeling, both forms of "abstraction," that of the *Süchte* and of enthusiasm. I want to quote Marx, who formulated this problem at a time when the aforementioned opposite tendencies could not have been expressed in articulate needs. Marx confronted the reduced, abstracted, impoverished life of feeling in an alienated society with the qualitative wealth of feelings of man active in many directions and involved in many directions: "Die Genüsse aller bisherigen Stände und Klassen mussten überhaupt entweder kindisch, ermüdend oder brutal sein, weil sie immer von der gesamten Lebenstätigkeit, dem eigentlichen Inhalt des Lebens der Individuen getrennt waren."[2] On the other hand: "Der reiche Mensch ist zugleich der einer Totalität der menschlichen Lebensäusserung bedürftige Mensch."[3] Naturally every person also has fixed desires (*fixe Begierde*); these are connected with those feelings that also serve the preservation of our natural homoeostasis (what I had designated as drives). The desires that stem from the feelings of not natural homoeostasis may only become fixed if human need and activity are reduced, or if our needs cannot be satisfied. Undoubtedly Marx regarded the desire for possession as one of these *fixe Begierde*. Desire for possession becomes a fixed desire (a passion), because human need is reduced to ownership and because this need is quantitative—theoretically unsatisfiable and self-reproducing.

Marx, however, rejected enthusiasm at least as much as he rejected the *Süchte*. In the vehemence of his rejection he occasionally even forgot about his own historical methodology. I am referring to the confrontation of Shakespearean drama with Schillerian drama. Shakespearean drama is superior to that of Schiller, because in Shakespeare the principles of the individuals emanate from life situation, from the totality of the character, whereas in the case of Schiller the heroes are merely spokesmen for ideas. I do not mean to debate the hierarchy, for Marx is definitely correct about it. I only mean to question the expectation that on the foundation of an already developed bourgeois world of feeling (and not extant *in statu nascendi*) it should be possible to depict anything at all in the manner of Shakespeare. Schiller's heroes are spokesmen for ideas not because the poet opted for a poor device, but because the enthusiasts who appeared on the world stage at the time of the French Revolution were indeed spokesmen for ideas; because their principles truly do not "stem" from concrete bourgeois life, but are placed precisely in opposition to that concrete life. Marx rejects Schiller because he rejects bourgeois enthusiasm.

I have analyzed the crisis of the world of bourgeois feeling in the twenties of the 20th century; this was when the crisis became explicit, this was when it was expressed for the last time in great art. From this time on it is not the bourgeois world of feeling that stands at the focus of the great art of the bourgeois era. In spite of all their contradictions what the *Joseph* novels of Thomas Mann, the novels of Heinrich Böll, the plays of Brecht, the farces of Beckett have in common is that they have not been formed from the point of view of the bourgeois world of feeling. All this, of course, does not signify that the typical bourgeois feeling structure has "died out" from one day to the next; but rather that art reacts to new tendencies rather fast and to diverse tendencies at that. Even today, we cannot speak of the complete disappearance of the bourgeois feeling structure—but its retreat has become obvious, especially during and after the Second World War. The new structures of feeling that appear in its wake—judged by my own anthropological standards—cannot be unequivocally described as either of a "higher" or "lower" order, since they contain both "tendencies." But no matter how we evaluate them, no matter how heterogeneous or even contradictory the values (or non-values) they elicit (again, from my point of view), the formation of the structure of feeling has one common trait and this is concretization: the abstract quality of the *Süchte* and of enthusiasm is increasingly vanishing.

Let me make a preliminary observation important from my point of view. The reign of terror and disgrace of Hitler killed the myth of the superman. This myth may not resurrect again, because its consequences have made its demonic nature explicit. Hitler's personality has become negatively representative, because it had been the demon of enthusiasm, but it was also the last demon of the *Süchte*. The fact that Hitler killed the myth of the superman does not imply, of course, that he tolled the death knell over the charismatic leader. The category of charismatic leader is much broader than that of "superman." The latter is the demon of the bourgeois world of feeling; the former may be the representative and mobilizer of the most varied feeling structures.

Let us take a look at the process of "concretization" of the structure of feelings that is taking place before our eyes, first from the point of view of the *Süchte*, then from that of enthusiasm. In the analysis of the concretization of the Self homogenized from abstract "*Süchte*," I will take my materials from American sociology. There the tendency is the most clear-cut and it was there that the tendency was first recognized. Sociology dealing with the critique of society has noted the phenomenon of the transformation of the structure of the personality beginning in the fifties: thus C. Wright Mills in his work on white-collar workers, Whyte in his *The Organization Man*. Riesmann's typology is widely known; he calls the classical bourgeois personality "inner-directed" as opposed to the contemporary "other-directed" type of personality.

The correct-incorrect, successful-unsuccessful orientation that moves in is gradually and increasingly replacing the useful-harmful orientation. While at the time of the useful-harmful orientation there was but a single value: having (always more) and there was no "success" other than having more, in the case of the correct-incorrect orientation the leading value is that of adjustment. It is not just a matter of adjusting to society, but every specific task, every place in the social division of labor requires total adjustment. Yet the adjustment orientation does not in the least prevent the *Süchte*; these function within the adjustment, in relation to it.

If the leading task is a single one: to have, then the Self is abstracted, is aimed at a single quantifiable goal, yet it is homogeneous. The bad infinity of the orientation to have is capable of making the personality integral. But if the supreme task is adjustment to the permanent specific system of expectations, if this be the exclusive (or at least, main) object of our involvement, then the world of feeling is characterized by the formation of concrete feelings to the measure of the system of expectations. We know that work always provides special tasks for the housekeeping of feelings; this becomes positive and constitutive in the housekeeping of feelings only if this work allows for the realization of personality, if our involvement in the work is also connected with other tasks (general social tasks, or with the development of our disposition to feel through harmonic human contacts). But if this is not the case, if our world of feeling is regulated only by the place we occupy in the social division of labor, what more, as a result of mere "adjustment," then the specific feeling structure determined by work dissociates from the whole of personality. What more: man is faced by alternating tasks; the feeling capacities developed in one become pointless in the other. The concrete structure of feelings alternates, hence, theoretically it cannot be deep. Moreover: man must adjust to not one, but several tasks. These tasks require completely heterogeneous investments of feeling—the more tasks we "adjust to" the more equally superficial surfaces of feeling evolve. Thus our feelings become roles; every role is specific, but the roles are not "tied together," but remain independent of one another. The personality does not have a principle of organization; hence it does not have a housekeeping of feeling. The emotionally abstract Self did have a housekeeping of feeling, no matter how we evaluate it. The Self adjusting to specific roles, however, merely imitates, for want of a housekeeping of feelings; the place of the housekeeping of feelings is occupied by the imitation of patterns of feeling—and these patterns are mass-produced by the film, by the media.

The "ordering function" of specific moral values in the world of feelings thus vanishes even more than in the case of the man of *Süchte*. Although the man of *Süchte* subordinated morality to utility (or rationalized the useful into the Good), in order to homogenize the personality, in order that "harmful" particularist feelings or even emotions be subordinated to the ever given goal rationality, it nevertheless needed the functioning norms abstracted morally from specific situations. Authoritative education made man tough and cruel, but gave him will-power and developed the consciousness of responsibility for the fate of the personality. In its ideology, the permissive education that pertains to the adjustment orientation is directed at the development of personality, but in practice it is wholly inappropriate for the purpose. A child's own nature may never develop if at least at the junction points it is not confronted with feeling objectivations functioning as norms, with moral requirements. Permissive education does not provide points of crystallization for the personality, or exposes the possible development of personality to chance. Without the points of crystallization given to or required of the child an authentic personality can never grow up. Although the particularist feelings are not repressed, they are not regulated either, hence the hierarchy of the Self cannot be formed, cannot be structured. Permissive education—in spite of all attempts at ideological legitimation—belongs, I repeat, to the adjustment orientation. The Self that is not hierarchic and not structured becomes particularly apt at adjustment to any role; where there is no depth, the superficial imitation of feelings is given free reins.

The relationship of permissive education and of "adjustment" is also indicated by their common ideology. And this ideology is psychological determinism. The permissive parent believes that he must not place requirements in front of his child, or else the child may acquire "complexes," he may become "frustrated." The ideology of adjustment argues: if one cannot adjust totally one's psyche is disturbed; one is "not normal." Society cannot function unperturbed because some of its members have developed various "complexes" in their childhood. As Bertalanffy drolly observes: "After all, when a child is asocial or fails in school, when a juvenile commits a rape, or a criminal poor chap that he is—becomes a murderer, it's all the fault of wrong upbringing, sibling rivalry and the like."[4] The detective story—as a good seismograph—was quick in accepting this ideology.

Archer, Ross McDonald's nonchalant private detective, deeply sympathizes with the "poor" little girl who sent a blackmail letter to her mother and pushed her grandmother into the water, because she was in love with her father (who, as it turned out, of course, was not her real father); another young lady sends four men into the other world, but that is quite understandable, because her foster father had always criticized her for being an illegitimate child. In other words, how could an indigent single woman *not* raise her daughter to become the murderer of four men?

The psychologizing ideology of adjustment, however, conceals far greater dangers. For it declares as sick all those psyches which cannot, or are unwilling to adjust totally, whatever may be the sign or the form of non-adjustment. The feeling concretized or incarnated in role-playing, as we have seen, makes all morality impossible. The honorable man is the person who adjusts successfully. Not only all those ethical norms that impede adjustment, but any feeling of morality, however vague it may be, that rebels against adjustment is a sign of psychic disturbance, of illness. This tendency of everyday thinking penetrates even science, in order to stream back into everyday thinking. A frightening example of this is the work of Grinker and Spiegel, *Men under Stress*. It contains case studies of pilots who have experienced stress and have been cured of it. One example: A twenty-five-year-old captain loses his friend in combat. He had not given his friend adequate information before the battle, hence he has a tortured conscience; he feels responsible for the death and is frequently depressed. "He should have stayed in formation. He didn't stay where he was supposed to. Maybe I should have given a talk before we went about staying in formation. Why didn't I do that?"[5]

For every morally normal person this would be a fair question and the bad conscience seems appropriate as well. But not for the psychologists! They meant to cure the captain of the "disease" of bad conscience and they actually did it. They "analyze out" that the captain had "projected" his childhood sibling rivalry on his friend and this is the origin of his false bad conscience. The curing of the pilot is illustrated by the following statement: "It is silly for intelligent people to let things bother them the way I did."[6]

Another case. During a drill, a twenty-seven year-old captain shoots out his friend's eye and he consequently feels guilty. The psychologists again undertake therapy and the man indeed is cured: "he began to joke and laugh."[7] There is no need to feel surprised, under the conditions, that bomber pilot Eatherly was declared "abnormal" because he acquired a bad conscience; and that happened to him because the atomic bomb dropped on Hiroshima at his command extinguished the life of over 200,000 persons.

The abstraction from the moral content of feelings is particularly inadequate when the individual whose problems we wish to help solve has moral feelings. Guilt and bad conscience are negative moral feelings—we are involved negatively in our act, our behavior—and their very existence demonstrates that the individual is also guided in his feelings by moral values. In this case it is not possible to substitute the confession booth of the priest by the couch of the determinist psychologist. Of course, everybody would like to get rid of feelings of guilt, or of bad conscience in some manner. If the latter become permanent, self-assertion is blocked; and that is a need for everybody, to a greater or lesser extent. The confessor absolves, but condemns at the same time. The psychologist, however, treats my sin as an "illness"; he deprives me of the feeling of responsibility insofar as he seeks and "finds" the cause of my guilt feelings in forces or circumstances outside my control. Thus he absolves me, but does not condemn me. The man who is capable of moral feeling, however, needs to have his act judged, just as much as he needs to have his personality approved. If this judgment is omitted, then often real psychic disturbances take place, because the personality cannot bear the omission of judgment. Eatherly demanded that he be placed in front of the Nurnberg court as a war criminal: he desired the judgment as true absolution.

This practical significance of moral judgment has been recognized and formulated by a number of American psychologists. Let me refer to Angyal, who saw one factor of recovery in the eliciting of "realistic guilt feelings," or to Mowrer, or to the "third way" I have already referred to a number of times. The representatives of the "third way" raise the question even more broadly and deeply. They do not analyze the psychical disturbances caused primarily by divergence from adjustment, but rather those disturbances which stem from successful adjustment itself. Hence the criterion of "normality" differs from that of determinist psychology. For them "normal" is a value category; they considered the many-sided person "normal," the person who has a strong Self and who is able to order and establish a hierarchy in his world of feeling. Maslow has formulated it thus: "what we call 'normal' in psychology is really the psychopathology of the average."[8] As for Rollo May, he writes: "An adjustment is exactly what neurosis is; and that is just its trouble."[9]

It is the behaviorist utopia of Skinner's *Walden Two* that is being questioned. In Skinner, the representatives of successful adjustment are satisfied, gleeful, and happy. The third trend, however, avers: successful adjustment is the source not of "happiness," but of permanent anxiety. Before turning to the analysis of the contradiction, let us stop a moment at what may be in common between these ideological adversaries. This would be undoubtedly giving priority to the state of happiness. This is where it becomes obvious that both the adepts of adjustment and its adversaries, do not base themselves on the bourgeois world of feeling. For in the bourgeois world of feeling—unlike in antiquity—happiness received a low rating. Happiness, as an end of life, has remained, of course, even in the bourgeois world as a *lieu commun* of everyday life, but complete surrender to the pleasure of the moment, the harmonious settling into an achieved state, are de facto alien from the bourgeois world of feeling. The person of the bourgeois world of feeling (whether the man of the *Süchte* or the enthusiast) is removed by the devil, like Faust, if he ever should say to the moment, that it is beautiful and should remain ("verweile doch, du bist so schön"). But with the concretization of the world of feeling the happiness value strives again for something higher and in the case of "successful adjustment" we may say: enough! We are respected officials, or heads of a large family, hence we are happy. But the opponents of "adjustment" give priority to happiness from a completely different point of view. On the one hand, to them the personality who has arrived at enjoying himself (or who enjoys his Self) is happy, since he has become a complete personality, there no longer remains anything to transcend. On the other hand, the moments of happiness are given back their rights, in the self-indulgent and total peak experience.

For the time being, I wish to add nothing to the priority given to happiness value in the second sense. But I do want to add a great deal to the first. The fact that the "third way" has identified the personality enjoying the self with the "happy man," is related to the naturalism of the personality theory that places conflicts and tasks into parentheses. Even nowadays the person involved in the solution of great social tasks (no matter how developed the personality) cannot be identical with "the happy person." The feelings of the person who is happy in this world of ours because he may approve of his own personality are not adequate for the task. The person who has done his duty has the right not to have a bad conscience; has the right to live in peace with himself. But negative moral feeling is not the only painful feeling. And the anxiety of the disintegrated person is not the only form of fear. The fate of others may also be painful and we may feel fear on behalf of others as well. And the fate of others, the fate of the world, creates so many problems, that we may consider it practically infinite.[10]

But let us return to Skinner and the confrontation with the "third way." Skinner's *Walden Two* is undoubtedly utopian which, unfortunately, does not signify that it cannot be realized in theory, though it certainly means that it cannot be extrapolated from the present. The experiences of the present seem to confirm the assumptions of the "third way." Adjustment does not stop neurosis but, on the contrary, increases it. Indeed the role-like and adjusting concretization of the world of feeling leads to continuous anxiety. The weakened Self deprived of its control center can only change, but cannot grow; the feelings do not select from the Self-center; they receive the selection ready-made and accept it. The Self cannot expand; its own world is not structured. The ready-made or imitated emotions function as mere orientation feelings, since contact with other human beings becomes a "skill" in itself; thus one of the most characteristic particularities of the emotions and of the emotional dispositions goes lost: their "binding" character. If the world of feeling of the man of the *Süchte* is ordered around quasi-drives, then the modern role-like concretized world of feeling is ordered around the quasi-orientational feelings. About the orientational feelings strictly speaking we know that their measure is first of all the value orientational category pair of successful-unsuccessful. Except for the one feeling of morality (which refers to the moral common sense) they do not have a moral value reference. Generally orientational feelings are not feelings constituting the personality, or only indirectly.

The objects of our fear, as we know, are determined either by personal experience, or by social knowledge communicated to the person ("what is dangerous"). The stronger the personality the more these two coincide. To borrow from Aristotle again: the brave man is afraid of what he has to be afraid of, no more or less. But in the case of the weak personality, of the personality without an Ego core, this coincidence never takes place: every experience conceals a trap; everything becomes frightening. Only the person who has strength can "find strength in himself." The man at the mercy of his roles is characterized, precisely because of this, by permanent neurotic anxiety. The series: task-emotional value objectivation (as a norm)-feeling, as we have seen, is modified in many ways during the bourgeois era, but this threefold division has persisted in some form enduringly. But in the case of the modern feeling concretization a relatively new sequence evolves; one of the links in the series falls out. There remains the direct interrelationship of the task and the feeling, but in such a way that clearly the task takes the lead. There is no longer mediation of value; there are no longer guiding feeling objectivations, moral norms that function independently and shape the feelings in general.

Of course, here again we are dealing only with a tendency. A tendency which, as always, sets into motion a counter-tendency. Naturally this counter-tendency has something to build upon. It builds not only on the rebellion of the feelings against the role-like concretization, but also on the fact that the role-like concretization has not been completed, not even nearly. The communication of value objectivations has weakened, but it has never entirely ceased. We might say, then, that the neurosis itself is a form of rebellion. The neurosis is the unconscious protest of the organism, of the nervous system against the depravation of the personality. The feeling cannot fill the expanding function of the homoeostasis. In the case of the bourgeois dealing with *Süchte* the feelings undoubtedly fulfil their function of expansion of the homoeostasis: the bad infinity of possessing ever more has "expanded" the Self, even if only in the direction of quantity. But with the role-like concretization of feeling the blocking of the expansion of feelings becomes general and as a result wider and wider strata of society, that is the individuals filling the most varied positions in the division of labor begin to "feel bad" in their alienation. The reaction of neurosis, however, is not typical of every sort of alienation; it appears as a general social manifestation where alienated work and idle behavior are characteristic of one and the same individual. And this is characteristic, as a tendency, of the typical person in the contemporary world.

But the rebellion against role-like feeling concretization also assumes conscious forms. One of the leaders of the "sit-in" at the University of California at Berkeley, Mario Salvio, has formulated it thus: "There is a time when the operation of machine becomes so odious, makes you so sick at heart, that you can't take part [...] you've got to put your bodies upon the gears and upon the wheels, upon the levers, upon all the apparatus and you've got to make it stop."[11] Both the expression "sick at heart," and "you can't take part," as well as the putting of "your own body against the machinery" convey well the life feeling which is at the origin of the rebellion. "You can't take part" is the cry of despair of the person losing himself in deprivation. Throwing the body against the machinery is no less the gesture of despair. But "you can't take part" means, by the same token: we do not want to take part and the body placed in opposition to the machine, as symbol of the organism, of the indissolubly and perpetually individual organism, also incarnates an obligation: the obligation to halt the machine.

The rebellion against the role-like concretization of feeling is revealed in the first part of the sentence quoted, and not by accident. The exodus from roles, the modern exodus, has become massive and this remains true whether the masses become larger or smaller and even if some of those who left always return to the flesh-pots of Egypt. The object of the exodus: the conquest or reconquest of the "core" of the personality (of one's "identity") in communities of free people. Those who "walk out" of the roles in the division of labor have created their own value hierarchy of feeling. The apex of the hierarchy of feelings is occupied by the emotional dispositions: love and friendship.

To feel is to be involved in something; the feeling is foreground or background feeling, depending on whether the emphasis is on the involvement, or on the object of the involvement. Feeling dispositions, as we know, are always foreground feelings, it is their "figure" character that makes them emotions. In order for our foreground and background feelings to develop harmonically and proportionately, we need tasks (first of all work), which are primarily cognitive or manipulative processes and in which feeling—disregarding borderline situations—plays a background role. If the cultivation of emotional dispositions becomes exclusive within the Self, then a "normal" housekeeping of feelings is likewise impossible; the pleasure of the satisfaction of desire completely takes over the role of the pleasure of reaching the goal and the world of feeling is composed of series of sensations.

The maximum of the sensations of emotional dispositions is undoubtedly the peak experience, in which the dichotomy of subject and object ceases: subject and object become one in the "great moment." A similar peak experience may be felt in erotic activity, in the reception of the work of art, in community celebrations. The peak experience is part of the housekeeping of feelings, but on the other hand, it is also necessary that the world of feeling should not become centered on the peak experience.

Undoubtedly the role-like concretization of feeling prevents authentic feelings, the possibility of feeling dispositions, hence the peak experience. As the continuous self-reflection (narcissistic behavior) has also prevented the possibility of directness, directness is blocked by the imitation of feeling; the reduction of feeling to "skills," for the directness of feeling is pure Ego expression. Thus it is no wonder that in the case of those who "walk out" on the world of roles, the counter-tendency develops radically: pure directness, the cultivation of the spontaneous self-expression. The expression of direct sensation is not necessarily peak experience, but every peak experience is also directness. The cult of directness is also the cult of peak experience.

The counter-culture aims to re-conquer the alienated personality. It has chosen as one of its forms the development of the direct capacity to enjoy. The supreme values are the emotional dispositions; the direct capacity to enjoy in the case of emotional dispositions reaches its full development in the peak experience. It is for this reason that the counter-culture forces the peak experience—first of all in the form of direct identification with the Other. Hence the cult of eroticism and hence the cult of drugs. Of course, the cult of sexuality also characterizes the role-like concretization of feeling. Only it has another function there—one might say a hygienic function. "Sexual hygiene," the sexual life without complexes, insures successful adjustment. But in the counter-culture, it is not sexuality but eroticism that is being cultivated and the objective is the peak experience, the rediscovered directness, the identification of subject and object. That the peak experience must be forced with drugs is not surprising. For the peak experience pertains to the "normal" homoeostasis of man, but it is far from being an everyday occurrence. If we want to render it an everyday experience, then we must "concentrate" our organism for this purpose. This process, however, would lead to the disintegration of the housekeeping of feelings. Even if we disregard the fact that some drugs cause biochemical damage to the organism, the forced peak experience itself upsets the psychic balance. Since our energies are not infinite the forced peak experience in the last resort diminishes the capacity to feel.

I will call the behavior aimed at directness, at the peak experience, the radicalism of mood. This radicalism reduces the world to the direct relationship between the I and the You. It cannot be averred that this radicalism builds the world on that relationship for no sort of world or society could be built upon mere directness. At the same time: it is radicalism, because it denies radically, because it turns its back radically not only on contemporary American society, but on the bourgeois era in general.

Thus we have reached the antagonism of the contemporary world of feeling—an antagonism that may be transcended, but only if the limits of the antagonism is transcended en masse. On one hand we have participation in the social division of labor; this participation, however, leads, in its tendency, to the role-like concretization of feelings and the loss of personality. On the other hand, we have the exodus from the social division of labor, but this leads to the radicalism of mood. The radicalism of mood, as a way of life, is again inappropriate for the development of the many-sided individual rich in feelings. Because without work goal the personality loses one of its key "ordering principles." Not to speak of the fact that the only type of housekeeping of feeling that really provides a standard is the one that can be in theory generalized. Walking out on the division of labor makes the "radicalism of mood" a priori ungeneralizable.

How to transcend this antagonism? Undoubtedly this might happen if the radicalism of mood should meet with enthusiasm. But not with the bourgeois enthusiasm of abstract ideas, but with a new kind of enthusiasm, which would "invest" its feelings in the realization of the specific tasks of a new society, with an enthusiasm the tasks of which are to the measure of concrete man. But the meeting has to be an actual meeting. Because enthusiasm, no matter how concrete, needs the radicalism of mood; the feeling composed of ideas needs the sensual capacity. I do not intend to discuss here the history of enthusiasm in our century. I will discuss neither the last great flickers of the flame of abstract enthusiasm, nor the repeated disillusionment with that enthusiasm, always accompanied by the contemptuous rejection of "great words." I will limit my task to the analysis of the appearance of concrete enthusiasm. And the materials on which I will rely are the last letters of antifascists condemned to death.

We are dealing with a borderline situation, the final borderline; every letter-writer stands immediately before execution. The borderline situation, as we know, is the fertile ground of abstract enthusiasm. These particular sworn adherents of the Idea, the majority of whom see the realization of their lives in their own deaths—people who have not only suffered, but who have actually chosen their fate—among them, how low a rating do the so-called great words have! Precisely for this reason, in such a final borderline situation, it is astounding that the rejection of "great words" never implies the denial of a life centered on idea. On the contrary: precisely because they have accepted that life, they reject or omit the "great words." Their ideas are worldly ideas which cannot be designated by the abstract word: they have to rely on description, on explanations, on concretization. Their ideas are derived from the needs of real people (and they are referred back to it). Pathos shines in every sentence; but it is a subdued pathos, it does not appear directly, but through very factual formulations.

I do not mean to pretend that in these letters one never meets with abstract enthusiasm in the old sense. There is quite a bit of that. But I think this is only to be expected. What is unexpected, what does require analysis, is the opposite tendency. The characteristics of this concrete tendency: how were they expressed in the important letters of *adieu*?

First of all, what strikes us is the rejection of the glorification of heroism of martyrdom. These wonderful people do not consider themselves "heroes," nor do they expect heroism from others: "Ich bin nur ein Vorläufer gewesen in meinem teilweise noch unklaren Denken und Wollen"; "Ich gebe mein Leben wie tausend und abertausend andere jungen Menschen"; "Ich bin auch kein Held oder Märtyrer, sondern ganz einfach, was ich immer war, ein einfacher, ganz einfacher Mensch"; "Du sollst kein Märtyrer sein."[12] Heroism, the idea of martyrdom for an idea, pertains to abstract enthusiasm. This heroism demands the total subordination of the world of feeling to the idea and only "special" people, those who rise above the potentials of the average, are capable of it. But if the death selected is the "death of simple people" then the emphasis will fall on the life of simple people, something everybody may select, some-thing everybody may pursue. Chosen death is the completion of a chosen life: "Dieser Tod passt zu mir. ... Es ist sozusagen mein eigener Tod, wie es einmal bei Rilke heißt."[13] The goodbye letters do not point to the deaths of martyrs, but to lives that everybody may pursue.

What kind of life reaches its completion in this death? Why do these people die? One recurring motive is that of carrying out duty; the other is related to this motive: to save others. "I have done my duty to the best of my ability." "I could have saved my head in various ways. But I prefer execution to treason, so I die in decency." "I have a calm conscience." "I also have a great consolation: no friend will have to follow me in prison." "In this ride between death and the devil, death is the noble companion." "Think about the fact that thirty Russian girls will get to keep their fiancé; ten English women their husbands and thirty American children their father and so on, instead of you keeping me." What is the norm of life behind these messages? That of carrying out one's duty, which is always expressed in involvement in specific people, in the life of fate of Others. Here we have a life that is to the measure of everyday man. Here we have duty that is accompanied by love, not with the love for an idea, but with love for human beings and at the same time love for life, of every little pleasure and beauty of it: "I love life and people infinitely and that is why I leave life without a regret, or without hatred." "Love life, love each other, learn love, share love, stand up for love."

These men consider their own life and death as the guarantee of a more humane future and rightly so. Not because they consider themselves exceptional, but precisely because they know that they want and incarnate the possible for everyone, they believe their life can become an example and thus will form part and parcel of a future in which their attitude will become generalized: "I consider myself a little like the leaf that falls from the tree to become manure. The quality of the manure depends, however, on the quality of the leaf." The accomplishment of duty paired with love is the simple love of life, the significance of the life of Others for us; all this outlines the concrete idea from which these people have gained their pathos. No one doubts the realization of the idea, for it is "close to man." Yet at times they question the human closeness of the concrete idea, they question it all the time. One of them has formulated it beautifully: "Perhaps I seem a little selfish to you, when I speak ... of my ideals, which I guarantee with my life." The man on death row speaking of his ideal sees selfishness even in the pathos of the concrete idea, the egoism of the anti-life self-sacrifice that pertains to the abstract idea.

Concrete enthusiasm always attempts to formulate the future in which its life attitude becomes generalized; a future that offers rich opportunities of life to everyone, a future contrasted with the present and at the same time projected from specific necessities. It is precisely this concrete future that "guides" its enthusiasm.

> The truth is that after pain profundity comes and after profundity comes the fruit ... but consider and all should consider it not to dream about the return of pre-wartimes; instead, dream you all, young and old, about creating a not one-sided but purely humane country for all of us. This is the great donation for which our country feels thirst, something what all young peasant lads can know and feel with joy, in which they can participate.

Or: "I wish a free France and happy Frenchmen, not a proud France, first nation of the world, but a laboring France, laboring and decent" Or: "Such is the fate of all those who do not acknowledge the world of today and tomorrow as the fundament but who think under all circumstances of a future in which norms based on different values will regulate the contact of man to man."

In the appeal to the future we often find chiliastic aspects. After all, the belief that the terrible ordeals of the world will lead to the catharsis of all of Europe remains alive in many; the myth of the dawn, of the sunrise, of resurrection can be found in the letters from the condemned to death of the most varied ideologies: "we await the dawn in which the golden sun breaks through the jet-black sky!" "Great times are coming. A new historical era is about to come over Europe. Socialism will come in the aftermath of the war."

But just as often we find the questioning of chiliasm; the majority of concrete enthusiasts see duty even in the sunrise of the future. Let me quote again: "Such is the fate of all those who do not acknowledge the world of today and of tomorrow as the foundation." Or: "Our work begins precisely after the war." Or as a twenty-four-year-old Belgian partisan girl formulated it with poetic conciseness, expressing both attitudes in one: "Today it is beautiful and warm and that for me is a symbol of the dawn, which I see breaking. Use it well!" Indeed the attitude of the individual in this new enthusiasm becomes attainably significant. The man of bourgeois everyday life may have admired the enthusiast, but had no use for him. But the enthusiast of concrete ideas is not an Albatross. He can fly not only in the stratosphere, in the ratified air of borderline situations; his feet are well planted on the earth. He loves life, the pleasures of life, men. He is not an ascetic; he does not despise the capacity to enjoy. The enthusiasm for the idea does not repress the totality of his feelings, nor does he expect this from others. But at all times he points to the task. He is the significant individual of the modern age; the one Brecht, in his *Lied über die guten Leute*, simply called the "good man," hitting at the core of the matter:

> Die guten Leute erkennt man daran
> Dass sie besser werden
> Wenn man sie erkennt. Die guten Leute
> Laden ein, sie zu verbessern, denn
> Wovon wird ein kluger? Indem er zuhört
> Und indem man ihm etwas sagt.
> ...
> Für ihre Geschenke wissen sie Gründe anzugeben
> Sie weggeworfen wiederfindend, lachen sie.
> Aber auch darin sind sie verlässlich, dass wir
> Uns selber verlässend auch
> Sie verlassen.
> Wenn sie Fehler machen, lachen wir:
> Denn wenn sie einen Stein an die falsche Stelle legen
> Sehen wir, sie betrachtend
> Die richtige Stelle.
> Sie verdienen jeden Tag unser Interesse wie sie sich
> Ihr Brot verdienen jeden Tag.
> Sie sind in etwas interessiert
> Was ausser ihnen liegt.

It cannot be denied that there are concrete enthusiasts, that there are "good people." It is practically undebatable that with their example, by not being involved in themselves (and this is precisely why they invite us to improve them), they incarnate a type of person to be imitated and who can be imitated. But that this type person can, in general, be imitated, *hic et nunc*, is very debatable indeed.

The psychic structure of the "good man" is not aristocratic, as is that of the bourgeois enthusiast, but this same "good man" at present and in practice, is nevertheless aristocratic. For there is a wide gap between the concrete life and the concrete idea; life arranged around the cause is continuously elitist. The "elite" of concrete enthusiasm, unlike the social, or even the intellectual elite, is the only promising, future-bearing elite. Yet it does not cease to be an elite as long as the concrete idea does not meet with concrete life, as long as the future does not become the present. In that future, to quote once again a letter from death row: "Norms based on different values will regulate the contact of man to man." Concrete enthusiasm must meet with the radicalism of mood; the idea must meet with needs, not in order for such a world to come about, but merely to begin the work that would make its creation possible.

Notes

1. Marx-Engels *Werke* (Ergänzungsband), 550.
2. Marx. *Deutsche Ideologie* (MEW III), 404.
3. Marx. *Ökonomisch-Philosophische Manuskripte* (Ergänzungsband), 544.
4. von Bertalanffy, Ludwig. *Robots, Men and Mind* (New York: Braziller, 1967), 8.
5. Grinker, Roy R. and John P. Spiegel. *Men Under Stress* (London: Blakiston, 1945), 283.
6. *Men Under Stress*, 288.
7. *Men Under Stress*, 298.
8. *Existential Psychology*, ed. Rollo May (New York: Random House, 1961), 60.
9. *Existential Psychology*, 77.
10. For a more detailed analysis of the problem of happiness see my *Everyday Life* (London, New York: Routledge & Kegan Paul, 1984).
11. As quoted by Rollo May in *Psychology and the Human Dilemma* (Princeton: Van Nostrand, 1967), 27.
12. "I have been but a precursor in my partly still unclear thoughts and desires." "I gave my life as have thousands and thousands of other young men." "I am also no hero or martyr, but very simply what I have always been, a simple, very simple person." "You should not become a martyr."
13. "This death is to my measure. In some sense it is my own death as it was once put by Rilke."

Epilogue
On Human Suffering

We must differentiate between pain and suffering. Pain (by which I mean mental pain) characterizes human relationships in all of their forms. Pain signifies that something is not in order in a relationship. At the same time, this pain signifies: "help yourself" and "help others."

Pain is a negative feeling. This negativity may be reflective, inasmuch as it reflects on something that has already happened. I made a mistake, I hurt someone, I made a false move, I made the wrong decision—so "help yourself," "help others." The negativity may have the character of omission; I have not satisfied my needs—I have not satisfied others' needs: so "help yourself," "help others." The opportunity for help is always entailed in the significance of mental pain.

But pain develops precisely when action or refraining from action has been tied together with intention from the beginning; tied to conscious or unconscious decisions; tied together to our selection. It is the individual who brings pain into his own world and into the world of Others, hence pain is not outside of him. It emanates from him, it is his fate: "Du stolzes Herz, Du hast es ja gewollt." It is his fate even though it is the cause of the pain of the Other. After all, it was he who had selected the Other in human relations. If my friend betrays me, my knowledge of human character is at stake. Even when a person's tasks prove to be worthless, it is a matter of his fate, for it is he who chose the tasks. Here too: "Du stolzes Herz, Du hast es ja gewollt."

Pain is an unavoidable aspect of human life. There can be no normal housekeeping of feeling without pain. The many-sided capacity to feel includes the capacity to feel pain: the face of poverty within wealth.

Suffering, on the other hand, is a kind of pain that falls on us completely from the outside. It does not depend, not even relatively, on our intentions, our decisions, our choices. It is not active, but passive (it suffers action). Suffering does not signal "help yourself, help others," because suffering is a kind of pain that cannot be helped. Suffering can at most be suffered.

As natural beings, we are unavoidably exposed to suffering, for we are exposed to death. We can convert our own death into pain only—and very exceptionally—if it is not natural, if we have chosen it; but natural death always comes from the outside: we have nothing to do with it, whereas we experience the death of Others, of our loved ones, as suffering. Nature is alien from us. We can only learn how to endure suffering.

As social beings we are not unavoidably subjected to suffering. And yet we are subjected to suffering as social beings. We are subjected to famine, to wars and to oppression. The majority of mankind thus suffers. The human being should become an individual, rich in many-sided, qualitative feelings. Yet the majority of humankind suffers. Can we tell the person struggling with famine, those subjected to oppression and wars, those who will never have the chance to decide, those for whom it is always others who decide, can we tell the sufferers: become individuals, become rich in many-sided, qualitative feelings?

In the bourgeois world of feeling, *humanity* is a regulative idea in general; it only becomes constitutive in morality. It follows from the idea of humanity that we must respect in ourselves, and in the Other, the human being, human dignity, human freedom. This has to be so even today. But today this is not enough. Humanity is no longer an abstract idea, but a problem; hence it must become a constitutive principle. To become an individual, to become rich in many-sided, qualitative feelings, depends on whether humankind can become a constitutive idea, a problem for the individual.

In other words, the suffering of humankind must change into pain, in the case of those who themselves suffer, as well as in the case of those who know that others suffer. Only thus can we say "help yourself" and "help others."

As we know, we must learn to feel. But in order to learn to feel, suffering has to be converted into our pain. So suffering must be made to cease. For as social beings we are not unavoidably subjected to suffering.

To make suffering cease is the primary task for contemporary people, for us. And never has a task been so difficult, because never has the danger been so great. The nuclear bomb and methods of current conflicts threatens human beings with extermination. While we know beyond a doubt that in the period following birth, undernourishment—primarily the undernourishment in proteins—causes irreversible damage to the development of the brain. Yet seven out of ten children in the world are undernourished.

To feel means to be involved in something.

Suffering must be converted into pain in order for us to become involved in the cause of humankind. *Help yourself* and *help others*.

Made in the USA
Coppell, TX
23 November 2020